HOW THE BOND MARKET WORKS

THIRD EDITION

ROBERT ZIPF

NEW YORK INSTITUTE OF FINANCE

NEW YORK • TORONTO • SYDNEY • TOKYO • SINGAPORE

Library of Congress Cataloging-in-Publication Data

Zipf, Robert
   How the bond market works / Robert Zipf.—3rd ed.
   p. cm.
   ISBN 0-7352-0266-4
   1. Bonds. 2. Government securities. 3. Bond market. I. Title.

HG4651 .H68 2002
332.63'123—dc21   2001060355

Printed in the United States of America

10   9   8   7   6   5   4   3   2   1

This publication is designed to provide accurate and authorative information in regard to the subject matter covered. It is sold with the understanding that the publisher is not engaged in rendering legal, account, or other professional service. If legal advice or other expert assistance is required, the services of a competent professional person should be sought.
—*From the Declaration of Principles jointly adopted by a Committee of the American Bar Association and a Committee of Publishers and Associations.*

ISBN 0-7352-0266-4

ATTENTION: CORPORATIONS AND SCHOOLS

NYIF books are available at quantity discounts with bulk purchase for educational, business or sales promotional use. For information, please write to: Prentice Hall Direct, Special Sales, 240 Frisch Court, Paramus, NJ 07652. Please supply: title of book, ISBN, quantity, how the book will be used, date needed.

 NEW YORK INSTITUTE OF FINANCE
An Imprint of Prentice Hall Press
Paramus, NJ 07652

http://www.phpress.com

NYIF and NEW YORK INSTITUTE OF FINANCE are trademarks of Executive Tax Reports, Inc. used under license by Prentice Hall Direct, Inc.

ACKNOWLEDGMENTS

Many people have contributed to this book—too many to thank individually. I would like to acknowledge their help in giving me information I requested, and in answering my varied questions. I would especially like to thank John H. Allan, former editor of *The Bond Buyer* and a former president of the Municipal Forum of New York for preparing the Glossary at the end of the book. Without his help, this book would have been much longer in preparation.

v

CONTENTS

■ Chapter 3
The Federal Reserve System
and How It Affects You

■ Chapter 4
The United States Government
Securities Market: Treasuries

■ Chapter 7
Corporate Bonds

■ Chapter 8
International Bonds

■ Chapter 9
The Secondary Market

■ Chapter 10
E-Trading and the Bond Market

INTRODUCTION

Almost every major corporation and government in the world issues bonds. The bond market dwarfs the stock market, when measured in dollar volume. In addition, while stocks are issued solely in the private sector, both corporations and governments can issue bonds. For governments, issuing bonds or other similar securities is the only way they can borrow money.

In spite of this, the stock market enjoys much greater public visibility. Day and night, television news reports on how the major stock market indices did during the day fill the airwaves, with some news broadcasts dedicated solely to reporting on the stock market. Only relatively recently have news reports also covered the bond market, and then usually only the market performance of the longest United States Treasury bond.

Recent stock market volatility, and a decline in many stocks, especially technology stocks, has caused many stock investors to look for other investment vehicles, either as alternatives to stocks, or simply for balance and diversification. Many are discovering the diverse world of bonds. However, because of the attention historically paid to stock investing, many investors do not understand enough about bonds and bond markets.

This book explains, among other things:

- How a bond differs from a share of stock
- How various kinds of bonds are brought to market
- What the Federal Reserve System (the Fed) does that affects bond prices

- The relationship between bond prices and interest rates in general
- The relationship between bond price and bond yield
- What various people do within a securities brokerage firm when it brings an issue to market
- The different kinds of international bonds
- How much interest you are entitled to when you buy or sell a bond
- New electronic bond trading systems, and how they work
- How to manage your own fixed-income portfolio

This third edition of the popular general introduction to the bond market has been revised to reflect the changes in the bond market since the publication of the previous edition. The chapter on United States Treasury securities, especially, has been extensively rewritten to reflect the changes in that important market. Other chapters have been revised where necessary. In addition, two new chapters have been prepared for this edition: a chapter on electronic trading, and a chapter on international (foreign) securities, reflecting the increasing importance of these two fields.

How the Bond Market Works, 3rd Edition, will give you an illuminating and intriguing description of some of the world's largest and most important markets. It will help you in making bond investment decisions, and it will guide you to sources of information available to you in managing these investments better. You will find *How the Bond Market Works, 3rd Edition*, an excellent introduction to this important investment vehicle.

Riding the Yield Curve

Many people have invested in United States Savings Bonds, Series EE, which are similar to the Series E Savings Bonds, known as War Bonds during the Second World War.

If you buy a savings bond, you have lent money to the United States Government. For example, when you buy a bond at $25, you are extending to the government the use of that money for at least six months. In return, the government gives you a certificate that acts as an IOU. In the agreement on the back of the certificate, the Treasury promises to pay you back twice the amount of the loan, in this case $50. You must hold the loan for a few years to obtain this amount; the date is indeterminate because the interest rate paid varies during the life of the bond. However, you are guaranteed to get this amount in seventeen years. In corporate and municipal loans, this agreement may be called a *trust agreement*, and may be contained in a separate document called an *indenture*.

The Series EE Savings Bond has all the elements of a loan. Original maturity is seventeen years from issue date, and final maturity is thirty years from issue date. The principal amount of the loan is not $25 as you might think, but rather $50, the original maturity amount. However, you may redeem the bond after six months for your purchase price and accrued interest.

This might be confusing, but here's the explanation. With almost any loan, the borrower pays interest to the lender. This interest may be paid in several ways.

1. With a home mortgage, most mortgages have a monthly payment consisting of part interest and part principal.

1

Usually the payments in the early years of the mortgage are mostly interest. In this case, the interest is paid monthly. Note that most monthly payments also include amounts for real estate taxes, and possibly for insurance premiums, but these are not part of the loan repayment schedule.

2. Interest can also be paid in installments over the term of the loan. For example, the United States Government Series HH Savings Bonds make two interest payments each year until maturity, when the Treasury repays the entire principal amount to the owner.

Series HH bonds, incidentally, can be received only in exchange for Series E bonds, Series EE bonds, and United States Savings Notes; they cannot be bought for cash. They are available in denominations starting at just $500. The rate on newly issued HH bonds fluctuates with the market, but once a Series HH bond is issued, the rate does not change for the first ten years. If the HH bond is extended, the rate may change.

All marketable United States Treasury notes and bonds pay interest twice per year.

3. Interest can also be deducted from the principal up front, and this is how Series EE Savings Bonds work. The principal amount, or face amount, of the loan is actually $50. But instead of sending out semiannual checks, the Treasury simply deducts what it would pay in interest payments at the beginning of the term. So the bond buyer pays only half the face amount and is paid the full face amount at maturity. This type of debt instrument is said to be *discounted*.

■ WHAT IS A BOND?

A bond is a long-term debt security. It represents debt because the bond buyer actually lends the face amount to the bond issuer. The certificate itself, if there is one, is evidence of a lender-borrower relationship. It is a security because, unlike a car loan or home improvement loan, the debt can be bought and sold in the open market. In fact, a bond is a loan intended to be bought and sold. It is long-term by definition; to be called a bond, it must generally have a term longer than five years. Debt securities with maturities of less than five years are generally called bills, notes, or other terms.

Since bonds are intended to be bought and sold, all the certificates of a bond issue contain the master loan agreement, if certificates exist. This agreement between issuer and investor, or borrower and lender, is called the *bond indenture* or *deed of trust*. It contains all the information you'd normally expect to see in any loan agreement, including the following:

1. *Amount of the loan.* The face amount, par value, or principal is the amount of the loan—the amount that the bond issuer has agreed to repay at the bond's maturity. A typical face amount is $5,000, although some bonds issued by the United States Government and other issuers have much larger par values.

2. *Rate of interest.* Bonds are issued with a specified coupon rate, or nominal rate, which is determined largely by market conditions at the time of the bond's primary offering. Once determined, it is set contractually for the life of the bonds. However, some bonds have interest rates that fluctuate during the life of the bond; these are called *variable rate bonds,* or *variable rate demand obligations.*

The dollar amount of the interest payment can be easily calculated by multiplying the rate of interest or coupon rate by the face value of the bond. For example, a bond with a face amount of $1,000 and a coupon of 8% pays the bondholder $80 per year ($1,000 times .08).

3. *Schedule or form of interest payments.* Interest is paid on most bonds in the United States at six-month intervals, usually on the first or the fifteenth of the month. In many European countries, interest is paid annually. In other places, interest may be paid at other intervals. In the United States, the $80

of annual interest on the bond in the previous example would be paid in two semiannual $40 installments.

4. *Term.* A bond's maturity, or the length of time until the principal is repaid, varies greatly, but is usually more than five years. Debt that matures in less than a year is a money market instrument, such as a United States Treasury bill, commercial paper, certificate of deposit, or bankers' acceptance. A short-term bond has a maturity of about five years. A medium-term bond has a maturity of about seven to fifteen years. A long-term bond may have a maturity as long as thirty years, and some corporate bonds issued in 1995 have maturities as long as one hundred years. The maturity of any bond is predetermined and stated on the bond certificate, if there is one, and in the bond indenture, if there is one.

5. *Call feature, if any.* A call feature, if specified in the indenture, allows the issuer to call in the bonds and repay them at a predetermined price before maturity. Bond issuers use this feature to protect themselves from paying more interest than they have to for the money they are borrowing. Issuers call in bonds when general interest rates are lower than the coupon rate on the bond, thereby retiring expensive debt and refinancing it at a lower rate. A homeowner does the same thing when refinancing a home mortgage if mortgage rates drop. The former issue is then said to be refunded, or to be called for refunding.

For example, let's say a 10% $1,000 bond is currently paying a full two percentage points more than general interest rates (that is, the rates of interest being paid on other types of debt) and the issuer wants to take advantage of the call feature in the bond's indenture. In this case, suppose the call price is 110, that is $1,100 for the $1,000 bond. The issuer calls the bond at $1,100 and at the same time sells a new issue at 8%. The proceeds of the new issue are used to pay off the old issue. The issuer now enjoys a lower cost for its borrowing.

Some bonds offer call protection; that is, they are guaranteed not to be called for five or ten years. Call features can affect bond values by serving as a ceiling for prices. Investors are generally unwilling to pay more for a bond than its call price, unless there is a great deal of time until the call date (the date when the issuer may call the bond), because they are aware that the bond could be called back from them at a lower price. If the bond issuer exercises the option to call bonds, the bondholder is frequently paid a premium over par for the inconvenience. In the example in the previous paragraph, the call price was 110 and the call premium was 10.

Sometimes, if the bonds are trading below their face amount, the issuer might go into the open market and buy back its own bonds. This transaction is called an *open market purchase.*

6. *The put option, if any.* Sometimes a bond will have an option that allows the owner of the bond to return it to the issuer and demand back the face amount. This is called a *put option,* because the bondholder can "put" the bond back to the issuer. Naturally, the bondholder will do this only if the money can be reinvested elsewhere at a higher rate of return. Series EE Savings Bonds have a put option. The owner can redeem them after six months at cost plus accumulated interest.

7. *Refunding.* If the issuer doesn't have the cash on hand to repay the bondholders when the bonds mature, it may be able to issue new bonds and use the proceeds either to redeem the older bonds or to exercise a call option. This process is called a *refunding.*

8. *Collateral.* If the bond is secured by collateral, just as a home mortgage is secured by the home, the indenture will specify the nature of the collateral. Sometimes the collateral is real property, such as a building, land, or equipment, and sometimes intangibles, such as stocks, bonds, or other securities.

■ DIFFERENT TYPES OF YIELDS

Although the indenture describes the terms of the loan implied in bond ownership, it says nothing about the market price of the security. To know that, you must understand the three basic types of yields.

1. *Coupon or Nominal yield.* As we have seen, if a bond has a face value of $1,000 and pays interest at a rate of 8%, the coupon or nominal yield is 8%. This comes to $80 per year ($1,000 times .08). Because the coupon percentage rate and principal don't change for the term of the loan, the coupon yield doesn't change either. But the second type of yield can change.

2. *Current yield.* Suppose you could buy an 8% $1,000 bond for $800. Regardless of what you paid, you are still entitled to the $80 annual interest. Yet the $80 represents a higher *percentage* yield than the 8% coupon rate. Since you paid only $800 (not $1,000) and still receive $80 return each year, the actual yield is 10% ($80 divided by $800). This is the bond's current yield.

Because this bond is selling at less than its face value, it is said to be selling at a discount. This discounted bond would be quoted at 80, which means $800 for our $1,000 bond, or, more generally, a price of 80% of par. To translate the quote into a dollar price per $1,000, simply multiply it by $10. So a quote of 80½ means $805, that is, 80.5 times $10. Similarly, a quote of 90⅞ means a price of $908.75, or 90.875 times $10. As you can see, each eighth (1/8) in a bond quote equals $1.25, whereas an eighth (1/8) in a stock quote equals 12.5 cents. So:

Dollar Values of 1/8 Increments in Bond Quotes

1/8	$1.25 (= ⅛ × $10.00)
1/4	$2.50
3/8	$3.75
1/2	$5.00
5/8	$6.25
3/4	$7.50
7/8	$8.75

You can see that bond prices are expressed as a percent of par value. Stock prices, on the other hand, are expressed as dollars per share of stock.

If the bond were selling for more than its face value, it would be selling at a premium. For example, suppose that the

8% bond were selling for 110 ($1,100). In that case, the current yield would be 7.3% ($80 divided by $1,100)—lower than the coupon rate. In general, discounts mean an increased current yield and premiums mean a lessened current yield.

3. *Yield to Maturity (YTM).* Current yield does not take into account the difference between the purchase price of the bond and the principal repayment at maturity. Someone who pays $800 for a $1,000 bond will receive $1,000 at maturity, $200 more than the purchase price. That $200 is also considered income, or yield, and must be included in yield calculations. For instance, let's say that the 8% $1,000 has five years left to maturity when it is bought for $800. To include the $200 discount in the yield calculation, divide it by the number of years remaining to maturity. There is a rule of thumb formula to calculate this yield, which is referred to as the Yield to Maturity or YTM. (Actually, the formula for yield to maturity is a bit more complicated than the one we're giving you. It involves mathematical present-value calculations.)

$$\text{Yield to maturity} = \frac{\text{Coupon} + \text{Prorated Discount}}{(\text{Face Value} + \text{Purchase Price}) \div 2}$$

In this case, the only piece of information not immediately available is the Prorated Discount. To get that, divide the discount by the number of years to maturity. In this case, $200 divided by five years equals $40 per year. Let's plug the numbers into the formula and work it out:

$$\text{Yield to maturity} = \frac{\text{Coupon} + \text{Prorated Discount}}{(\text{Face Value} + \text{Purchase Price}) \div 2}$$

$$= \frac{\$80 + \$40}{(\$1,000 + \$800) \div 2}$$

$$= \frac{\$120}{\$900}$$

$$= 13.3\%$$

Thus, this discounted bond has a:

- Coupon yield of 8% ($80 divided by $1,000)
- Current yield of 10% ($80 divided by $800)
- Yield to maturity of 13.3% ($120 divided by $900)

The same yield to maturity formula can be applied to bonds trading at a premium, with two slight changes.

$$\text{Yield to maturity} = \frac{\text{Coupon} + \text{Prorated Discount}}{(\text{Face Value} + \text{Purchase Price}) \div 2}$$

Suppose the same 8% $1,000 bond were selling for $1,100 with five years to maturity.

$$\text{Yield to maturity} = \frac{\text{Coupon} + \text{Prorated Discount}}{(\text{Face Value} + \text{Purchase Price}) \div 2}$$

$$= \frac{\$80 - (\$100 \div 5 \text{ years})}{(\$1,000 + \$1,100) \div 2}$$

$$= \frac{\$80 - \$20}{\$1,050}$$

$$= 5.7\%$$

This bond selling at a premium has a:

- Coupon yield of 8% ($80 divided by $1,000)
- Current yield of 7.3% ($80 divided by $1,100)
- Yield to maturity of 5.7% ($60 divided by $1,050)

Yield to maturity is what bond traders are referring to when they use the word "yield." It is the only one of the three yields shown above that assesses the effect of market value, coupon rate, and time to maturity on a bond's actual yield.

■ WHAT DETERMINES BOND PRICES?

While yield to maturity enables traders and investors to compare debt securities with different coupon rates and terms to maturity, it does not determine price.

Bond prices depend on a number of factors, such as the ability of the issuer to make interest and principal payments, and how the bond is collateralized. Later chapters cover issuer-related influences on prices.

An across-the-board factor that affects bond prices is the level of prevailing interest rates. In previous examples, an 8% bond yielded different rates depending on whether the bond sold at a premium or discount. What was not explained was *why* the bond should sell for more or less than its face value. The reason has to do with interest rates.

Assume the 8% bond was issued five years ago, when prevailing interest rates (on other investment vehicles) were about 8%. Further, assume current prevailing interest rates are about 9%. Why should investors buy a five-year-old bond yielding 8% when they can buy a newly issued 9% bond? The only way the holder of an 8% bond can find a buyer is to sell the bond at a discount, so that its yield to maturity is the same as the coupon rate on new issues.

For example, say interest rates increase from 8% to 10%. With fifteen years to maturity, an 8% bond must be priced so that, when the discount is amortized over fifteen years, it has a yield to maturity of 10%. That discount is a little under $200:

$$YTM = \frac{\text{Coupon} + \text{Prorated Discount}}{(\text{Face Value} + \text{Purchase Price}) \div 2}$$

$$= \frac{\$80 + (\$200 \div 15 \text{ years})}{(\$1{,}000 + \$800) \div 2}$$

$$= \frac{\$93.33}{\$900}$$

$$= 10.4\%$$

The 8% bond with fifteen years to maturity must sell at a little over $800 to compete with 10% issues.

The possibility that interest rates will rise and cause outstanding bond issues to lose value is called *interest rate risk* or *market risk*.

But there is an upside to this risk. If interest rates decline during the five years that the 8% bond is outstanding, the holder could sell it for enough of a premium to make its yield to maturity equal to the lower yields of recent issues.

For instance, should interest rates decline to 7%, the price of the 8% bond with fifteen years to maturity will increase by about $100 to a price of $110:

$$YTM = \frac{\text{Coupon} + \text{Prorated Premium}}{(\text{Face Value} + \text{Purchase Price}) \div 2}$$

$$= \frac{\$80 - (\$100 \div 15 \text{ years})}{(\$1,000 + \$1,100) \div 2}$$

$$= \frac{\$73.33}{\$1,050}$$

$$= 7.0\%$$

All other influences aside, generally bond prices increase when interest rates fall, and decline when interest rates rise.

As a corollary, the prices on longer-term bonds fluctuate more than those of shorter-term bonds in response to the same interest rate change. For example, we know that the 8% bond with fifteen years to maturity has to fall nearly $200 in price to accommodate a rise in rates to 10%.

Under the same circumstances, an 8% bond with five years to maturity requires less of a discount—$80 to be exact.

$$= \frac{\$80 + (\$80 \div 5 \text{ years})}{(\$1,000 + \$920) \div 2}$$

$$= \frac{\$96}{\$960}$$

$$= 10\%$$

Thus, the shorter the term to maturity, the less volatile the price adjustment to the same change in interest rates.

There is a great deal more to bond pricing, as we'll see in later chapters. But the intimate relationship with interest rates is the key to understanding what drives bond prices. When the

United States Treasury, a state or municipal government, a corporation, or any other issuer decides on an offering of bonds, it must weigh, among other things, the effect of interest rates.

When bonds start trading in the secondary market, after they are initially brought to market, they are subject to ongoing interest rate risk. That is, bond prices react to the same factors acting on interest rates. These factors are generally recognized to be the following:

1. *The Business Cycle.* During an upswing, American businesses start borrowing money to buy equipment or raw materials, to build plants, or to develop new services. Would-be borrowers (the demand side) compete for diminished funds (the supply side), driving up the cost of money (interest rates). Banks start raising their lending rates. To attract money into the bond market, yields must rise. As a result, the generally accepted principle is that, as economic activity picks up, interest rates tend to rise.

2. *Inflation.* When the costs of goods rise, lenders must increase their rates of interest to offset their loss of purchasing power. Borrowers pay the higher rates because they expect to use the money profitably and pay back the loan with future dollars of reduced purchasing value. Consequently, interest rates are thought to include borrowers' expectations with respect to inflation. Whether or not that assumption is valid, most economists agree that interest rates (the cost of money) rise with the inflation rate.

3. *Flow of Funds.* At most brokerage firms, economists analyze how capital is flowing through the economy and try to project the future amount of borrowing. When they do this, they attempt to gauge the supply side (amount of credit available) and the demand side (future borrowing) of interest rates. If their analyses are correct, they may be able to project future interest rates.

When it comes to interest rates, the Federal Reserve System plays a major role as it sets and executes the monetary policy of the United States Government. (See Chapter 3 on the Federal Reserve System.)

Fluctuating interest rates also affect a bond's total return. *Total return* is the return based on the reinvestment of interest payments over the term to maturity.

Up to the 1960s, many bond owners, such as university or foundation endowments, simply took their coupon interest payments and spent them. At that time, most bond certificates were printed with coupons attached, a small piece of the certificate representing an interest payment. To receive your interest payment from this type of bond, called a *bearer bond*, you cut off the coupon and presented it to the issuer, usually through a financial intermediary such as your bank or brokerage firm. This practice, known as coupon clipping, became associated with affluent investors under the perception that wealthy people could afford to buy enough bonds to live off the coupon income.

Coupon clipping also reflects a form of simple interest. If a person buys a bond and does not reinvest the coupon payment dollars, then the par amount remains constant, whether the price paid for the bond was at face value, at a premium, or at a discount. The preceding examples of coupon rate and current yield were examples of simple interest because they assumed that the interest was not reinvested.

Once interest dollars are reinvested, however, the bond-holder starts receiving interest-on-interest. For example, suppose a pension fund portfolio manager has in the fund's holdings twenty-five $1,000 8% bonds. Every year these bonds earn $2,000 in interest (.08 times $1,000 face value times 25 bonds). With that $2,000, the manager buys two more of the same kind of bond. In so doing, the manager has converted the $2,000 interest payment into $2,000 of additional principal, on which interest will be paid. The portfolio now contains $27,000 face amount of these bonds, and the following year's interest will be $2,160 ($27,000 times .08). If the $2,160 is used to buy additional bonds, then the next year's principal becomes $29,160. This example, of course, ignores commissions, other costs and tax obligations, and assumes the manager buys the bonds at par.

Interest on interest is a form of compounding. Compound interest can dramatically increase the total return to the bond-holder, sometimes to over half of a bond's total compounded return. For example, suppose our 8% $1,000 bond were bought for $1,000 (face value) at issuance and held for twenty years until maturity. If the bondholder were to clip coupons for twenty years, the total dollar return would be $1,600 ($80 times 20 years). This is an example of simple interest. On the other hand, if for that same term the bondholder reinvests semiannually all the semiannual interest payments for a return also of 8%, the return is much greater. Without going into the somewhat complicated math, the *additional* dollar return over twenty years would be $2,201, for a total compounded return of $3,801 ($1,600 simple interest plus $2,201 interest on interest).

This is not to say that interest has to be reinvested in the same bond. If other investment opportunities present themselves as interest payments are received, all the better. For instance, if the $1,600 in coupon payments were consistently reinvested semiannually in an instrument that returned 10%, the total compounded return would be $4,832, with $3,232 of that being interest on interest.

Understandably, the value of interest on interest diminishes with the time left to maturity. In the preceding example, the interest on interest for an 8% bond held for twenty years was 58% of the total return, or $2,201 of $3,801. If the bond were held for ten years under the same conditions, the interest on interest would be only 33% of the total compounded return: $800 simple interest plus $394 interest on interest, for a total of $1,194. For five years, the total compounded return is only $482: $400 simple interest and $82 compound interest. For one year, the interest on interest is only $1.60, or 2% of the total compounded return.

As you can see, the total compound return, or *total return,* is not the same as yield to maturity (YTM). YTM is simply a number that can be calculated from the bond's price, coupon rate, and time left to maturity. It expresses only the present value of the bond's cash flow, at an assumed interest rate. Total return is calculated from principal, coupon rate, and interest on interest. It assumes that the coupon dollars will be put to work earning additional dollars. While the dollar yields for the two types of calculations may differ, and usually do, the percentage rates of return may be the same under one or more of the following conditions.

First, suppose the bond is a zero coupon bond, so that the interest is deducted from the face amount upfront, as in the case of Series EE Savings Bonds. Since no coupon dollars are received, there is no opportunity to reinvest them. In such cases, the yield to maturity rate on a zero coupon bond would be the same as the rate of total return because the interest has, in effect, already been reinvested at the YTM rate.

Second, if only one payment period is included in the calculation, then there is no opportunity for reinvestment. This would be the case if you were to make a YTM calculation on a bond with only six months to maturity (that is, one interest payment period).

Third, if all coupons are reinvested at the YTM rate, then it would, of course, equal the total return rate. Again, the dollar yield for total return would be higher than that for YTM, but the rates would be the same.

Some people regard the total return rate as a better gauge of market value than yield to maturity for two reasons.

First, the total return rate is more realistic in that it takes into account future changes in reinvestment rates. For instance, if future coupons are reinvested at less than the YTM rate, the total return rate will decrease. If future reinvestment rates are higher than YTM, then the total return rate rises. Yield to maturity doesn't account for any of this.

Second, it enables investors and traders, given a reasonable assumption about future reinvestment rates, to forecast total return more accurately. For example, suppose a portfolio manager expects bond rates to decline over the next year, and decides to invest some of the portfolio's funds at an 8% yield to maturity. Given reinvestment rate assumptions, the manager knows that the actual total return will be less than 8%, and expectations can be adjusted accordingly.

■ THE YIELD CURVE

Given an assumption about reinvestment rates, how do professional traders and portfolio managers make their buy and sell decisions? What general principles do they use with respect to yields, prices, and risk? In a quick answer, their thinking and actions are based on their analysis of what is known as the *yield curve.*

To explain the yield curve and its assumptions, let's assume that the reinvestment rate will stay fixed at 8% until maturity. Given that assumption, the yield to maturity can be depicted simply in a graph as follows:

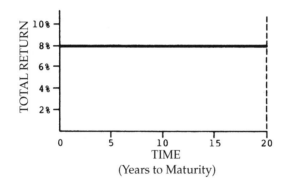

FIGURE 1-1. TOTAL RETURN AT 8% REINVESTMENT RATE

The horizontal line extending from the tic mark for 8% represents the anticipated yield curve for this bond. (It's called a curve even though it's straight.) If the coupons are reinvested consistently at 8% for twenty years, then at maturity the *actual* yield curve will look just like that line. Also, the actual total rate of return will be the same as the yield to maturity, because all reinvested interest will earn interest at 8%. But what if the coupons were reinvested at different rates of return? When that happens, the line for total rate of return diverges from that for yield to maturity. If the coupon reinvestment rate is higher than the YTM rate, the total rate of return will be higher. If the coupon reinvestment rate is lower than the YTM rate, the total rate of return will be lower. The varying rates of return can be depicted as follows:

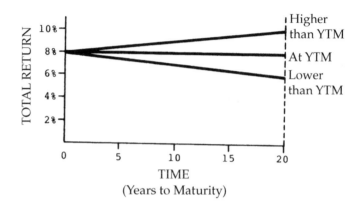

FIGURE 1-2. TOTAL RETURN FOR SEVERAL INVESTMENT RATES

In this figure, the line above the one for the anticipated YTM assumes that the bondholder could put coupon dollars to work in such a way as to earn a rate greater than 8%. Perhaps other bonds or preferred stock were bought at higher YTMs. Investing in another investment does not lessen the compounding effect.

The lower line demonstrates the total rate of return if the bondholder was unable to reinvest at the YTM rate. Maybe some of the coupons had to be applied toward a down payment on a car, in which case the yield on those dollars drops to zero. Perhaps some coupon dollars were put into a 5% or 6% certificate of deposit, in anticipation of paying a tuition bill. In such cases, the total rate of return diverges downward from the YTM rate.

The yield curve is therefore a depiction of bond market rates over time. The curve is supposed to represent the net result of all the buying and selling in the market, and therefore reflect the net effect of supply-and-demand pressures. The curve demonstrates graphically what market participants are willing to pay for short-term, intermediate-term, and long-term debt instruments.

A normal yield curve looks like this:

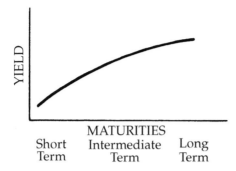

FIGURE 1-3. NORMAL (ASCENDING) YIELD CURVE

This graph is also known as the indifference curve, since it shows that the market is collectively indifferent to accepting one yield at a given maturity along with a different yield at another maturity. This coexistence of various yields for different times to maturity is called the *term structure of interest rates.*

As an example, let's take the preceding yield curve and assign some values to it:

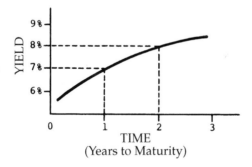

FIGURE 1-4. NORMAL (ASCENDING) YIELD CURVE WITH SAMPLE VALUED ASSIGNED

One-year securities are yielding 7% in this chart, and two-year securities are yielding 8%. The market is indifferent to 7% one-year and 8% two-year instruments in the same market.

That seems strange, but there is a theory that attempts to explain this attitude on the part of investors. The "expectations hypothesis" views the yield curve as a function of investors' expectations of future interest rates. In our example, the holders of a one-year 7% security are content because they expect rates to increase, thereby enabling them to reinvest at maturity in another one-year security yielding 9%. Their two-year yield would therefore be:

7% (one-year) + 9% (one-year) = 8% (two-years)

The yield curve has within itself the expectation that the one-year rate in one year will be 9%. That is why it is called the "expectations hypothesis."

Yields on shorter-term securities are generally more volatile than those on longer-term securities. Given terms of maturity of only several years, changes in price due to a given change in yield are not drastic, and therefore relatively small price changes mean dramatic changes in yield.

An upward sloping yield curve reflects higher future rates. The underlying reasoning is that investors sell longer-term securities and buy shorter-term ones. This is another way of saying that they have a greater liquidity preference. The liquidity preference theory holds that investors attach greater value to shorter-term securities because they are closer to cash.

The horizontal yield curve has buying pressure (demand) on the short-term portion and selling pressure (supply) on the long-term portions.

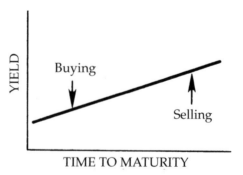

TIME TO MATURITY

FIGURE 1-5. RESULTS OF SHORT-TERM BUYING AND LONG-TIME SELLING PRESSURES

The curve rotates under the pressures of supply and demand, until market equilibrium is restored. This straight line yield curve therefore represents the effects of investors' expectations of future yields and their collective preference for more liquid, short-term investments.

But it does not show the effect of the investors' assessment of risk. The working principle with respect to risk is that prices become more volatile as the term to maturity increases. Thus, to reflect this risk, and assuming interest rates are expected to rise, the prices of longer-term securities tend to be lower than those of comparable shorter-term securities. Since lower bond prices have increased yield to maturity, longer-term maturities are associated with lower prices and higher YTMs.

In addition, changes in price have a lessened effect on longer-term yields. For example, a $100 change in the price of a one-year bond affects the yield by the full amount. For a two-year bond, the annual yield is affected by $50. As the term to maturity increases, a price change is amortized over more years, and its annual effect is diluted. Therefore, prices must change dramatically on long-term securities to have any significant effect on yield. As a result (the mathematical reasons being set aside), the actual normal yield curve is indeed a curve:

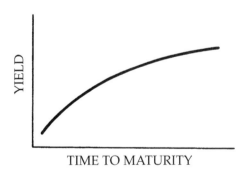

TIME TO MATURITY

FIGURE 1-6. NORMAL (ASCENDING) YIELD CURVE

This is not to say, however, that all yield curves are upward sloping. The assumption in all our examples has been that rates are expected to be higher for longer-term securities. When future rates are expected to decrease, the yield curve descends and becomes flatter or even inverted.

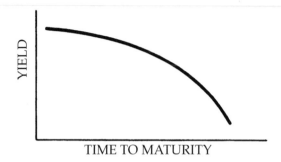

FIGURE 1-7. INVERSE (DESCENDING) YIELD CURVE

In such a case, reinvestment rates and total return will decrease.

Yield curve analysis extends *far* beyond these rudimentary concepts. Professional traders and portfolio managers must understand in complex detail the relationships among price, yield, liquidity, and risk. They must be able to "ride the yield curve"; that is, buy and sell debt securities so as to obtain the greatest total return.

In riding the yield curve, professional traders must be sensitive to many forces at work. Not only must they have sound working assumptions about the future levels of interest rates, but they must be aware of the returns available on other non-bond debt securities. Chapter 2 briefly covers the huge array of fixed-income instruments, and Chapter 3 presents the role of the Federal Reserve System in regulating interest rates.

The Fixed-Income Marketplace

The fixed-income market is so huge and so dynamic that its actual scope is difficult to estimate. Each year United States corporations bring billions of dollars, worth of corporate debt to market. In 2000, they brought 807 billion dollars of debt to market. This compares with only 284 billion dollars of common stock offering sold in the same year. This figure does not take into account short-term corporate debt, such as commercial paper, or bank issues, such as bankers' acceptances.

State and local governments have issued over one trillion dollars of municipal debt, with about 200 billion dollars coming to market each year. In 2000, they issued 200 billion dollars of long-term debt, of which 165 billion dollars were for new money.

The United States Treasury has created over five trillion dollars of direct United States Government debt, and federal agencies have created outstanding additional debt.

The Eurobond and International markets issue many billions of dollars of new debt each year. *(Sources: The Bond Market Association, Securities Data Company, Board of Governors of the Federal Reserve System.)*

■ CAPITAL MARKETS AND MONEY MARKETS

This global arena, in which bonds play a major role, is divided into two major markets: the capital market and the money market.

THE CAPITAL MARKET

In the capital market, long-term debt securities (mostly bonds) are traded, along with stocks (both common and preferred). These are the vehicles by which capital is raised. The bonds traded in this market may be issued by:

- The United States Treasury, through the Federal Reserve System acting as agent for the Treasury.
- Federal agencies, such as the Federal Home Loan Bank, the Federal National Mortgage Association, and other agencies.
- State and local governments, and their agencies and authorities. These are called *municipal bonds*.
- Corporations, both domestic and foreign.
- Foreign governments.

Chapters 4 through 11 cover the capital markets in detail. The rest of this chapter focuses on the money market.

THE MONEY MARKET

The money market consists of short-term, fixed-income vehicles, generally with less than one year to maturity. This market includes bonds whose maturity is now in less than one year, as well as such investments as:

- United States Treasury bills
- United States Government Agency notes
- Municipal notes
- Bank certificates of deposit (CDs)
- Commercial paper
- Federal funds
- Repurchase agreements ("repos")
- Call loans
- Bankers acceptances (BAs)

MONEY MARKET PARTICIPANTS

The money market has no specific location. Instead, it is a collection of markets comprised of:

- Banks in the large money centers, which include New York, London, Tokyo, and some other large cities
- About twenty-seven dealers in United States Treasury securities, known as primary dealers
- A few commercial paper dealers
- A few dealers in bankers acceptances
- A number of money brokers specializing in finding short-term funds from money market lenders and placing the funds with money market borrowers

The most important money market brokers are based in New York and deal in federal funds that represent surplus reserves—money that banks do not need to meet the Fed's reserve requirements. These funds are available for short-term loans, usually overnight.

Money market participants are any political or corporate entities that need to ensure having enough cash on hand to meet their expenses and to operate normally, independent of their cash flow. Participants who at any time need cash may borrow from those who have more than enough cash for their current needs. Thus, the money market provides a pool of cash that, through its trading mechanisms, flows to those participants in need of it. The market is particularly valuable in that the instruments are perceived to have very little risk of default.

At one time, money market investments were available only to the largest financial and commercial institutions. The high interest rates of the early 1980s, however, were too good to ignore. Now, through money market mutual funds, individual investors may enjoy the benefits of the money market: short-term maturities, high liquidity, and relatively low risk. In addition, the United States Treasury has made it easy for individual investors to buy all Treasury securities at periodic auction; individual money market investors may easily buy as many

Treasury bills as most individual investors can want, through the Federal Reserve System, at no cost.

■ MONEY MARKET PRODUCTS

The diverse products traded in this market share one characteristic: They all mature in less than one year. Let's look at the various short-term instruments traded in this market.

UNITED STATES TREASURY BILLS

Probably the best known money market instruments are Treasury bills, or T-bills, short-term discount obligations of the United States Treasury. They do not pay explicit interest, but sell at a discount. The accrual of discount when the bills mature or are sold at a profit is interest income. They are popular investments for institutions because of their short maturities and ready salability. Their market is so large and efficient, and T-bills are so liquid, that they are frequently said to be cash-equivalents.

We'll talk more about T-bills in Chapter 4.

MUNICIPAL NOTES

These municipal securities usually have maturities of less than one year, although very occasionally they may have two- or even three-year maturities. State and local governments, and their agencies and authorities, use such short-term borrowing to bridge gaps in financing, to use for expenses before tax revenues come in, and to use in anticipation of revenues from enterprises run by the issuer. Although notes are sometimes issued at a discount from face value like T-bills, most are issued at about par and bear interest.

The types of notes frequently issued are:

■ Tax anticipation notes (TANs): notes issued in anticipation of receiving tax receipts.

■ Revenue anticipation notes (RANs): notes issued in anticipation of receiving revenues, either from an enterprise run by the government, agency, or authority, or in anticipation of federal or state aid.

■ Tax and revenue anticipation notes (TRANs): notes issued in anticipation of receipt of either taxes or revenues or both.

■ Bond anticipation notes (BANs): notes issued in anticipation of future issuance of bonds.

Often, an issuer finds that he cannot repay the notes at maturity, so he simply sells a new issue of notes to repay the maturing issue. The old notes are said to be "rolled over." Usually, issuers can do this only a limited number of times. For example, frequently notes can be rolled over only four times.

Sometimes notes are used when the issuer's budget hasn't been finished or approved, or when revenues haven't met expectations. In these cases, notes can sometimes be issued regularly, as a usual part of the financing process. For example, for many years New York State issued Tax and Revenue Anticipation Notes (TRANS) in April, and repaid in four installments during the year, with the last payment due the following January.

Don't ever lower your credit standards for notes, or any other fixed-income security, just because they have a short time to maturity. Defaults can occur in short-term securities. One of the most famous recent defaults was New York City's default on about $2 billion in notes in 1975. Although the notes were eventually paid, by an exchange offer for bonds of The Municipal Assistance Corporation for the City of New York, and eventual full payment of those notes that were not exchanged, the results were still unpleasant for the note holders. Some of them had bought the notes planning other uses for the money at maturity; needless to say, the funds were not available as planned. Some holders had to sell the notes, sometimes for as little as 69 cents on the dollar.

CERTIFICATES OF DEPOSIT (CDs)

These certificates are issued by commercial banks and thrift institutions. They represent funds deposited for specified periods to earn fixed rates of interest. Many banks use the description "CD" for savings certificates issued in relatively modest amounts, but the depositor usually can transfer these only with great difficulty, if at all.

Money market CDs are negotiable instruments, issued in minimum denominations of $100,000 or more. When money market CDs trade, the usual round lot trading minimum is $1,000,000 or more. They are quoted on an accrued-interest basis.

The minimum maturity of a CD is seven days, but most are for longer periods. There is no limit on their maturity time, and most mature in one year or less, but a few mature in more than one year. Some banks now offer variable rate CDs with up to five years' maturity.

COMMERCIAL PAPER

This short-term, unsecured promissory note is issued primarily by corporations needing to finance large amounts of receivables. Automobile finance companies, such as General Motors Acceptance Corporation, are among the largest issuers. Paper is sold on a discount basis with maturities ranging from three to 270 days, but most common are thirty to fifty days. Within this range, the buyer has a wide choice of maturities, and can choose an investment to fit any need.

Virtually all commercial paper is rated by one of the major rating agencies, Moody's Investors Service or Standard & Poor's Corporation. This form of debt is generally considered a safe investment, although not as safe as T-bills or bankers acceptances, which tend to have lower rates of return. One of the very rare defaults of commercial paper was that by the Penn Central Corporation in 1970.

FEDERAL FUNDS (FED FUNDS)

Banks that are members of the Federal Reserve System hold their required reserves as deposits with their district Federal Reserve Bank. Since the Fed itself does not pay interest on these deposited reserve funds, banks that have more reserves than they need on deposit with the Fed can lend all or part of their excess to a bank that needs funds to reach its reserve requirement. These are called Federal Funds, and because of the supply/demand dynamics, a market has developed in this area.

The sale of federal funds is called a *straight transaction,* and is usually made on a one-day unsecured basis, although some longer-term transactions are made. The selling bank instructs the Federal Reserve System to charge its account and credit the account of the buying, or borrowing, bank. On the following day, the transaction is reversed. The exchange is made electronically through the Federal Reserve System's communications network, called the *Fed Wire.* No actual physical delivery is made.

REPURCHASE AGREEMENTS (REPOS)

In addition to unsecured loans, money market participants can engage in repurchase agreements. In such agreements, the owner of the securities sells them with a simultaneous agreement to buy them back at some agreed-upon future time and price. The price is set so that, when combined with accrued interest, if any, the buyer receives an adequate return on his investment. In money market transactions, these usually are for only a few days, but some repos can go for much longer periods of time.

A repo is therefore a way of financing securities that are owned, or of converting them temporarily into cash. In economic terms, the buyer of the repo is lending money to the seller, on a short-term basis, frequently overnight. The original seller, when he repurchases the securities, has in effect repaid the loan.

Although economically a repo is a loan, legally it is a sale. Therefore, the credit of the other party is a concern, since, if the other party defaults, the original purchaser might wind up owning the securities. The buyer should also make sure that the securities are not worth less than what was paid for them; in the past, buyers of repos have lost money when the seller defaulted, and the securities were not worth as much as the purchase price the buyer paid for them.

The repo rate is linked to the Federal Funds rate because banks can borrow in both markets, but the Federal Funds rate is usually higher because repos are secured.

A reverse repo is a repo from the point of view of the buyer; it is the purchase and sale of the securities. Its purpose is to lend money to the seller, or to borrow the securities for awhile. This borrowing might be to cover a short sale, or for some other purpose.

Call Loans

These are short-term loans that banks make to securities dealers and brokers. They are considered safe because the brokerage firms put up securities as collateral. The brokerage firms pledge either securities owned by the firm, such as trading inventories, or securities owned by their customers. The customers, of course, have previously agreed to this use for their securities. Most such customer securities so pledged are held in customer margin accounts, where the customers themselves have frequently borrowed money with the securities as collateral.

The name for these loans derives from the fact that either the lender or the borrower can terminate them by giving one day's notice.

Bankers Acceptances (BAs)

This credit instrument is used to finance self-liquidating transactions in both domestic and international markets.

Here is an example of the creation of a bankers acceptance. An American importer buys raw material from an overseas exporter. The exporter shipping the goods without a BA would be paid only when the shipment arrives. Instead, the importer arranges for an American commercial bank to issue, in the name of the exporter, an irrevocable letter of credit, which specifies the details of the shipment. The exporter can then draw a draft on the American bank and take it to an overseas bank for immediate payment. Once the exporter is paid, the bank forwards the draft to the United States for presentation to the bank that issued the letter of credit. The bank stamps the draft "Accepted" and thereby incurs the liability to pay the draft when it matures. Thus, a bankers acceptance is created.

The shipping documents are released to the United States importer against a trust receipt, which allows the importer to obtain and sell the imported goods. The importer is then obligated to deposit the proceeds of the sale at the accepting bank in time to honor the acceptance at maturity, usually 90 to 180 days.

Generally, the accepting bank discounts the new acceptance for the foreign bank and credits the proceeds to the account of the foreign bank. The cost of acceptance financing is the discount charged plus the commission paid to the accepting bank. This cost can be paid by either of the commercial parties involved in the transaction.

The accepting bank may either sell the acceptance to a dealer in bankers acceptances or hold it in its own portfolio. Because a bankers acceptance is an irrevocable primary obligation of the accepting bank, it is considered an extremely safe form of investment. The bank is protected not only by the customer's agreement to pay, but also by the pledge of all the documents evidencing ownership. In fact, in the more than seventy years that bankers acceptances have been used in the United States, there has been no known case of principal loss to investors.

The bond market is only a part of a vast, global trading arena, in which many types of financial instruments are traded. Central to fixed-income trading in the United States—and to one degree or another throughout the world—is the Federal Reserve System. This major player, nicknamed the "Fed," is the subject of the next chapter.

The Federal Reserve System and How It Affects You

The Federal Reserve System (the "Fed"), as the country's central bank, plays a vital role in the management of the national money supply. It has an important function in determining the level of interest rates, bond prices, and business activity. This chapter examines the role of the Fed in the economy, and some of the Fed's activities that you can follow as you manage your investments.

■ THE RICH MAN'S PANIC OF 1907 AND ITS RESULT

In 1900, banks in the United States were hardly systematized and largely unregulated. In the case of a run on one or more banks, there was no central bank to provide reserve capital and to help absorb the shock. Depositors frequently lost their savings, even though with enough time, and with loans to help, the bank might have survived, and the depositors would not have had a loss. Then, in 1907, there was a "Rich Man's Panic," a crash in the securities market that affected only the wealthy. It was severe enough to cause Congress to act. In 1913, Congress founded the Federal

Reserve System (the Fed) for the purpose of guaranteeing the soundness of American banks by holding a reserve of bank capital against all deposits in national banks, and to provide for an improved, safer, and more flexible monetary system. Since its inception, however, the Fed's power, position, and influence have expanded into the central place it occupies today.

The Federal Reserve System affects almost every part of bond investment, and not always in ways that are immediately obvious. If you do any bond investing at all, you should have some understanding of the Fed, what it does, how it does it, and how its actions interact with your bond investments and their management.

■ WHAT IS THE FEDERAL RESERVE SYSTEM?

The Fed is the central bank of the United States of America. Although considered an independent central bank, the Fed is subject to Congressional oversight, because the Constitution, in Article I, Section 8, gives Congress the power to regulate money and control the value of the money. The Fed must work within overall governmental economic and financial policy objectives, but its decisions don't need to be ratified by the President or anybody else.

The Fed is composed of a Board of Governors, located in Washington, D.C., and twelve regional Federal Reserve Banks located in major cities around the country. Figure 3-1 shows the cities, as well as the locations of Fed branches. These components share the responsibility for regulating and supervising certain financial institutions, mostly banks; for providing banking services to depository institutions and the federal government; and for making sure that consumers receive information and fair treatment from the nation's banking system.

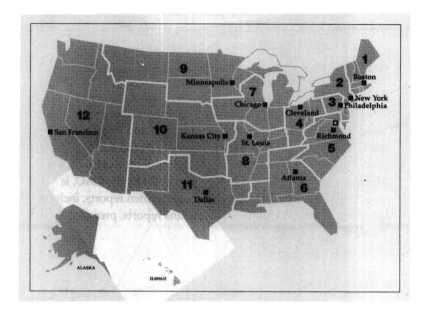

Legend

Both pages
- ▪ Federal Reserve Bank city
- ▣ Board of Governors of the Federal Reserve System, Washington, D.C.

Next page
- • Federal Reserve Branch city
- — Branch boundary

Notes

The Federal Reserve officially identifies Districts by number and by Reserve Bank city (shown on both pages) as well as by letter (shown on the next page).

In District 12, the Seattle Branch serves Alaska and the San Francisco Bank serves Hawaii.

The System serves commonwealths and territories as follows: The New York Bank serves the Commonwealth of Puerto Rico and the U.S. Virgin Islands; the San Francisco Bank serves American Samoa, Guam, and the Commonwealth of the Northern Mariana Islands.

Source: Federal Reserve System

FIGURE 3-1. THE FEDERAL SYSTEM CITIES AND BRANCHES

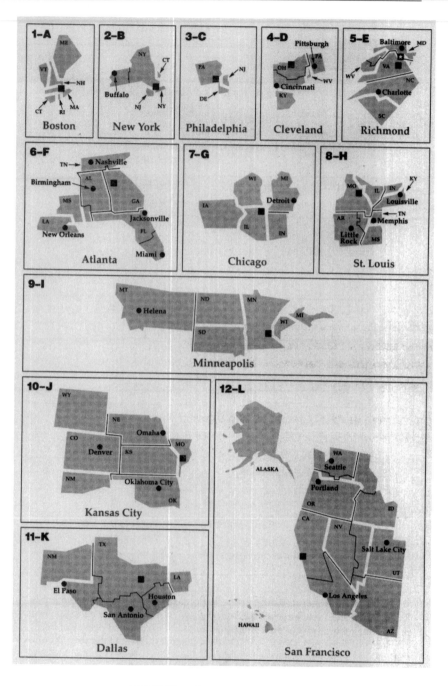

FIGURE 3-1. (CONTINUED).

Number	Letter	Bank	Branch
1	A	Boston	
2	B	New York	Buffalo, NY
3	C	Philadelphia	
4	D	Cleveland	Cincinnati, OH Pittsburgh, PA
5	E	Richmond	Baltimore, MD Charlotte, NC
6	F	Atlanta	Birmingham, AL Jacksonville, FL Miami, FL Nashville, TN New Orleans, LA
7	G	Chicago	Detroit, MI
8	H	St. Louis	Little Rock, AR Louisville, KY Memphis, TN
9	I	Minneapolis	Helena, MT
10	J	Kansas City	Denver, CO Oklahoma City, OK Omaha, NE
11	K	Dallas	El Paso, TX Houston, TX San Antonio, TX
12	L	San Francisco	Los Angeles, CA Portland, OR Salt Lake City, UT Seattle, WA

The Federal Reserve Bank of New York maintains an operations center in East Rutherford, New Jersey.

Source: Federal Reserve System

FIGURE 3-1. (CONTINUED).

■ WHAT DOES THE FED DO?

The Fed performs the following four major functions:

1. It maintains the financial system's stability.
2. It conducts monetary policy.
3. It supervises and regulates banking institutions.
4. It provides financial services to the United States Government, the public, financial institutions, and foreign official institutions.

All of these affect you in some way, some more directly than others. Maintenance of the system's stability is a prerequisite for any systematic national investment and investment policy. Financial services affect you directly in your investment activities by allowing you to buy Treasuries directly at auction. Monetary policy conduct affects you in the area of trading and investment policy. Bank regulation and supervision affect you when you do business with one of the nation's banks.

■ MAINTAINING THE STABILITY OF THE MONETARY SYSTEM

The Fed maintains the financial stability of the monetary system by ensuring that funds are available for the conduct of business. Monetary policy has this as one of its purposes. One reason for conducting open market operations, setting discount rates, and establishing reserve requirements, is to ensure the stability of the monetary system.

Maintaining monetary system stability is possibly the most important of the Federal Reserve functions, and one that you as an investor may usually assume is effective.

■ HOW THE FED CONDUCTS MONETARY POLICY

Monetary policy consists of increasing or decreasing the money supply as needed to achieve government policy objectives.

Usually, these objectives are stable money value, reasonable interest rates, and enough money available for the conduct of the nation's transactions.

The Fed conducts monetary policy in three ways:

1. By open-market operations (usually buying and selling United States Treasury securities)

2. By setting the discount rate, which is the rate charged commercial banks and other depository institutions when they borrow from the Fed

3. By setting reserve requirements for the nation's banks and other depository institutions

How the Fed Conducts Open-Market Operations

The Fed manages money supply most often by open-market operations, conducted by the Federal Open Market Committee (FOMC). The FOMC is composed of the Board of Governors, the President of the Federal Reserve Bank of New York and the presidents of four other Federal Reserve Banks on a rotating basis. Open-market operations are buying and selling securities— almost always United States Treasury securities—in the securities markets.

The FOMC meets eight times per year, and more often if needed. The minutes of its meetings are available to the public six weeks after each meeting. The FOMC oversees the open-market operations and uses them to implement monetary policy, and to ensure that money market conditions and money and credit growth are best for the country.

Sale of securities by the Fed reduces the money supply, since the buyer must pay for them; buying securities increases the money supply, because the Fed must pay for the securities it buys. Therefore, when the Fed sells securities, it restricts the money supply because it absorbs money from the money supply; buying securities loosens the money supply because it increases the amount of money available. Restricting the money supply causes prices to remain stable or even to go down, and causes interest rates to increase, because less money is available for lending and for purchasing goods and services. Increasing the money supply causes prices possibly to increase, and interest rates to decrease, because more money is available for lending and for purchasing goods and services. The Fed tends to restrict money supply in times of inflation or business boom, and tends to increase money supply in times of business recession or when inflation is not a concern.

Most of the FOMC's transactions are in short-term securities. Open-market operations affect the money supply almost immediately, because the trades must be settled in three business days.

The Fed does not announce open-market operations, but the minutes of the Open Market Committee are made public six weeks after the meeting, and are available for public inspection. The actions and the minutes are frequently reported in the newspapers. However, persons active in the bond markets, especially the United States Treasury securities market, are aware of Fed operations almost immediately. Bond traders talk to each other all the time, so almost every active trader is informed within a matter of a few minutes. Major news wire services also report Fed open-market operations promptly.

The Fed also conducts open-market operations by using repurchase agreements, and occasionally uses reverse repurchase agreements. (Repos and reverse repos were discussed in Chapter 2.)

When the Fed needs to absorb reserves only temporarily, it conducts a matched book operation, which consists of the immediate sale of securities with an agreement to repurchase them later. The immediate sale draws reserves from the banking system; these reserves are replaced when the purchase occurs later. The time period for a matched book normally does not exceed seven days, and usually these sales and purchases are done with Treasury bills. The Fed invites competitive bids from dealers, and accepts the best bids.

How Discount Rate Changes Work

A second way of managing monetary policy is by changing the discount rate, which is the rate the Fed charges banks and other depository institutions that wish to borrow from the Fed. Raising the discount rate increases the costs to the banks of borrowing money from the Fed, and as a result tends to raise interest rates generally throughout the economy. This results in a decline of economic activity, due to decreased demand for money because of the higher cost of borrowing.

Lowering the discount rate works in the opposite direction. It lowers the cost of money to the banks, and therefore tends to lower the cost of borrowing by individuals and businesses. This results in an increase in economic activity, because money is easier and cheaper to obtain.

Discount rate changes are not announced ahead of time, although frequently rumors circulate widely. They are announced after the close of United States trading and are well reported in the major newspapers, especially those with business news sections.

How Bank Reserve Changes Work

A third way of conducting monetary policy is by changing the reserve requirements for the nation's banks. Banks set up reserves to make sure that they have enough funds for special requirements, including emergency requirements. Banks are also required to deposit special reserves at the Fed. The Fed sets the size of the reserves and holds them without interest. The reserves therefore remove money from the money supply because they are not available for lending or spending. Increasing required reserves reduces the amount of money available and therefore tends to tighten money and increase interest rates. Reducing required reserves increases the amount of money available and therefore tends to loosen the money supply and decrease interest rates. Banks with excess reserves can lend them, and banks that need reserves can borrow them. (These are Federal Funds, discussed earlier in Chapter 2.)

The Fed rarely changes reserve requirements, and when it does, these changes also are widely reported in the press. Usually, reports of both discount rate changes and particularly reserve requirement changes are accompanied by extensive commentary and analytical reporting.

■ KEEPING UP WITH DISCOUNT RATE AND RESERVE REQUIREMENT CHANGES

If you do any fixed-income investing at all, you should be aware of discount rate changes and reserve requirements changes. The business sections of almost all major newspapers will provide extensive reports. The same papers will also report Federal Reserve open-market operations in their daily bond market reports. You should follow these reports, at least for background for your bond-investment management.

■ HOW MONETARY POLICY DIFFERS FROM FISCAL POLICY

Don't confuse monetary policy with fiscal policy. Fiscal policy consists of setting United States Government taxing and spending policies to control business activity and inflation. Monetary policy consists of increasing or decreasing money supply, for the same reasons. For example, when the United States Government raises or lowers taxes, or raises or lowers government spending, that is fiscal policy. When the Fed buys or sells United States Treasury securities, that is monetary policy.

■ HOW THE FED SUPERVISES AND REGULATES DEPOSITORY INSTITUTIONS

The Fed supervises and regulates certain banking institutions. Supervision and regulation are not the same thing. *Supervision* means overseeing the actual operations of an institution, to make sure that it complies with the applicable laws and regulations, and conducts its business in a sound way. *Regulation* means the creation of laws and rules to ensure that, when followed, the nation has a banking system that is financially sound and able to meet the country's banking requirements. When the Fed promulgates a new regulation for banks, which all banks must follow, this is called *regulation*. When representatives of the Fed visit a bank to make sure that the regulations are being followed, and that the bank is financially sound and follows good banking procedures, this is called *supervision*. Fed regulations apply to all banks. The Fed actually supervises only about 1,000 of the nation's banks, those that are chartered by the states, but are members of the Federal Reserve System. These are called *state members*.

The Fed also writes and interprets regulations for consumer protection, and enforces consumer protection laws.

■ WHAT THE FED DOES FOR THE UNITED STATES GOVERNMENT AND THE PUBLIC

The Fed provides a variety of financial services to the Treasury, the investing public, and many others. For you as an investor, the Fed service acting as agent for the United States Treasury Department is the most important. The Fed acts as agent for the United States Treasury Department in the sale, by auction, of new issues of Treasury securities. The Fed offers the Treasury Direct system, which provides a convenient method for investors of all sorts to buy Treasury securities, at fair prices, with little or no cost. (Treasury Direct is discussed more in Chapter 4 on United States Treasury securities.) It allows investors to buy Treasury securities at the auction, at prices determined by the competitive bids for these securities. Investors may also enter bids directly or through an agent, usually a bank or broker. These agents usually charge a fee, frequently about $50. If you use the Treasury Direct system, you are using a service of the Fed.

Other Fed services include issuance of currency and coin, bank check processing and clearance services, electronic funds transfer services, the automatic clearinghouse (another electronic funds transfer service), net settlement services, and international services.

■ THE CHANGING CONDITIONS IN EARLY 2001

In early 2001, several developments in government finances caused some changes in the Fed's approaches to implementing monetary policy, Federal Reserve lending policies, and possibly other policies as well.

For several years, Federal Government tax revenues had increased, mostly due to an expanding economy. At the same time, government spending had not increased as much, due at least in part to governmental policy, as well as a political inability to agree on the type and amount, if any, of tax reduction and federal spending changes. The boom times also increased Social Security taxes, increasing the Social Security imputed surplus. The result, and the only place the money could really be used, was national debt reduction. The Treasury sold fewer securities while also purchasing outstanding securities, mostly long-term, high-coupon bonds. And in late 2000, the Treasury ended the monthly auction of one-year Treasury bills. Later, the Treasury ended the sale of 30-year bonds.

The Fed has usually conducted monetary policy by doing transactions in Treasury securities, although certain Federal Agency securities were also occasionally used. In 1999, the Fed Board of Governors granted temporary authority to use mortgage-based securities issued by two federal agencies, the Federal National Mortgage Association (FNMA, also called Fannie Mae) and the Federal Home Loan Mortgage Corporation (FHLMC, also called Freddie Mac), as well as Government National Mortgage Association (GNMA, also called Ginnie Mae) securities. With the reduction in outstanding marketable Treasuries, the Fed found it more difficult to conduct monetary policy using only Treasuries, and started to use these other securities in addition to Treasuries and regular Federal Agency bonds. This temporary authority was extended in early 2001.

Another possible change is the list of securities eligible for collateral for primary dealers. The shortage of Treasuries has led the Federal Reserve Board to consider allowing other securities besides Treasuries as collateral. These possible changes include accepting certain state and local debt and the obligations of certain foreign governments. The Fed always had the authority to accept these securities, but has never done so. No decisions have been made on this (as of March, 2001), and the Fed will consult with Congress before making any decisions, but clearly some changes are being considered.

Another possible change is in the use of the discount window to make it easier for banks to use it to get loans. In early 2001, banks rarely used the discount window because of a possible stigma attached to using the Fed as a lender of last resort. The Fed is considering possible changes to make use of the discount window more attractive to banks.

The United States Government Securities Market: Treasuries

Some of the most influential money decisions in the world are made every day in the U.S. Government securities market. Hundreds of billions of dollars change hands against a background of deal-making phone conversations, automated quotation and trading systems, and blinking telephone lights.

Before seeing how trading in this vast market is conducted, however, you must know the array of government securities available. These fall into three categories:

1. Treasury securities
2. Government agency issues
3. Derivative instruments

Governments have always had to borrow to get by. It's not that they are more profligate than the rest of us; it's just that large masses of people, or their elected representatives, have always found it easier to spend money for the public good than to pay the necessary taxes. In times past, such lenders and investment bankers as the Fuggers and the Rothschilds have financed the public debt privately, and this gave them inordinate political power. The United States has taken a different tack in funding the public debt.

In this country, more than any other, evidence of a government's indebtedness has become legal tender, a reservoir of savings, and the basis of the largest securities market in the world. By preserving political stability, and by giving the Federal Reserve the power to oversee the government securities market, the U.S. Government has found itself in the enviable position of being regarded as the premier issuer of debt securities, even though it has no demonstrable ability to repay them and no collateral behind them. Worldwide trading markets exist in United States Treasury securities. You can trade Treasuries at any hour of the day or night, with good prices offered to you, and at low transaction costs.

Whatever the reason, the Treasury is able to issue many billions in new securities every year and refund many billions more, all at yields below those on the highest quality corporate securities. With all this issuing to do, the Treasury has had to adopt a regular schedule of auctions, so that the market can prepare itself to absorb each issue in turn. The regular rhythm of Treasury auctions is one of the most important constants in the government securities market.

The Treasury issues a very wide range of securities, maturing from a few days after issue up to twenty years after issue. By tradition, Treasury issues are grouped into three classes: bills, notes, and bonds. Let's look at these three classes in detail.

■ TREASURY BILLS

Treasury bills (T-bills) are securities that have a year or less to maturity at the time they are issued. T-bills do not have a coupon; instead, they are sold at a "discount from par value." The owner earns interest when the bills mature at par, or are sold for more than the purchase price. Bills are traded at a "discount yield," which determines the size of the discount and the price of the bill. The amount of the discount varies at the time of issuance.

For example, investor Starr buys a $100,000 13-week bill, priced at a discount yield of 6%. She will pay approximately $98,500 for the bill. After 13 weeks, the bill matures for $100,000. The $1,500 difference represents interest of $6,000 annually. If Starr held a $100,000 6% debt instrument for one year, she would earn $6,000 in interest ($100,000 times 6%). Since she held the bill for only a quarter of a year (13 weeks), she is entitled to one quarter of the annual interest income ($6,000 times .25), or $1,500.

If you are given the discount yield, you can compute the amount of the discount. To make this computation, dealers use the exact number of days to maturity based on a theoretical 360-day year:

$$\text{Discount} = \frac{\text{Days to maturity}}{360} \times \text{Rate (\%)}$$

(per $100 of maturity value)

The Rate shown in the equation is the discount yield. To find the price, use the following formula:

Price ($) = $100 − Discount (per $100 of maturity value)

As an example, let's find the dollar price for a T-bill that is due in 147 days and trades on a 5.32% discount yield basis.

First, find the discount:

$$\begin{aligned} D &= (M/360) \times R\ (\%) \\ &= (147/360) \times (.0532) \\ &= 2.1723\ \text{full discount} \end{aligned}$$

In other words, the investor receives a discount of $2.1723 per $100 of maturity value. For a $100,000 bill, the discount is $2,172.30 ($2.1723 times 1,000).

The next step is to calculate the price:

$$\begin{aligned} P &= \$100 - D \\ &= \$100 - \$2.1723\ \text{per}\ \$100 \\ &= \$97.8277 \end{aligned}$$

The dollar price of the T-bill is equal to $97,8277 for every $100 of face (or maturity) value. So a $100,000 bill sold on a 5.32% basis would cost $97,827.70, and mature at $100,000 after 147 days.

The discount yield is the pricing mechanism for T-bills. For example, a discount of 6% on a one-year bill would produce a price of about 94 (100 − 6), but the same discount on a 13-week bill (maturing in 90 days) would produce a price of 98.5 (100 − 6/4); the bill matures in one-quarter of the 360-day year.

BOND EQUIVALENT YIELD

The true yield, or bond yield, would be higher than the discount yield on each of these bills because the bill buyer receives yield return on less than the par amount of the bills. For example, the true annual yield on our hypothetical one-year bill at a 6% discount yield would be 6.383% (= 6/94) because the owner earns 6.00 on an investment of only 94. On the hypothetical 13-week bill, the true yield would be approximately 6.094% (= [1.5/98.5] × 4) because the owner earns 1.5 in three months on an investment of 98.5. This true yield is also called *bond equivalent yield,* because it is the bond yield equivalent of the discount yield. Note that in the actual mathematics, the true bond yield for the one-year bill would actually be 6.2843%, because the bond business quotes rates as nominal annual rates, but they are compounded semiannually.

NEW ISSUES OF T-BILLS

On Friday, March 14, 2001, an issue of T-bills maturing on June 14, 2001, was quoted as 4.42 bid, 4.40 asked. The 4.42 discount bid gives a dollar price of about 98.8704 ([92/360] × 4.42 = 1.1296 = discount, and a price of 98.8704). The 4.40 discount yield gives a dollar price of about 98.8756.

This is a difference of about $52 between the bid and ask prices on a $1,000,000 lot of T-bills.

Underlying this pricing system is a system of "basis points." There are 100 basis points in each percentage point, so a basis point is one one-hundredth of a percent. For example, if a 13-week T-bill's discount drops from a 5.17 to a 5.10 discount yield, the yield has declined 7 basis points. The dollar value of the decline is $175 per $1,000,000 par amount of bills (.0007 × .25 × $1,000,000).

The Treasury usually issues bills with two maturities: 13 weeks and 26 weeks. The first bill is known when it is issued as the "three-month bill," and the second as the "six-month bill," although they actually conform to those exact time periods for only one day. The Treasury also issued 52-week bills each month, but no longer does so as of late March 2001. The last one-year bills were sold in February 2001.

Thirteen-week bills and 26-week bills are auctioned off each Monday. Bids may be submitted at any Federal Reserve Bank or branch (except Helena, Montana), or at the Bureau of the Public Debt in Washington, D.C. The bids, or *tenders* as they are called, must be submitted by 12:00 noon Eastern time. All bills auctioned off on Monday must be delivered and paid for the following Thursday, and they mature on Thursday the specified number of weeks later. If a bank holiday falls on a Thursday, the bills are delivered, or mature, the next day, Friday. This regular issuing procedure has been going on for years, and is ingrained in the market.

Occasionally the Treasury issues bills that mature at other times, often on dates of expected tax receipts. These are called "cash management bills." There is no regularity about their issuance.

The buyer of a bill does not receive a certificate. Ownership is recorded on the computer at the buyer's clearing bank, whose ownership in turn is recorded on the computers at the Federal Reserve System. This system, called a *book entry system,* means that billions of dollars' worth of bills can trade every day without the shifting of countless pieces of paper. Instead, the Fed computer records every sale and the new owner's bank acts as custodian for the new owner. Each owner, of course, gets periodic statements from the bank stating the bills owned.

Because of the intense interest in Treasury bills, they actually trade before they are issued by the Treasury. From around 4:00 P.M. on Tuesday of the week before they are auctioned, when the amount of the next week's bills is announced, they are traded on a "when issued" basis. These "when issued" bills are very important, because traders in the bill market use them to offset positions in bills that have already been issued. When-issued bills are also important because they don't have to be paid for until the Thursday of the following week. Depending on the customer's margin arrangements with a Primary Dealer, when-issued bills give the opportunity to participate in the market on very high leverage.

Treasury bills are sold at auction, either by competitive bid or by noncompetitive tender. A bidder in a competitive bid submits the bid for the amount of bills desired, and the price he or she is willing to pay. A person making a noncompetitive tender simply states the number of bills desired and will get them, up to the legal limit, at the average price of the competitive bids accepted.

When bids are closed, the Fed has already determined how many bills it wishes to sell. The Fed next figures the total amount of noncompetitive tenders it has received, and subtracts that amount from the total amount of bills to be sold. The remaining bills will be sold by competitive bid.

The Fed then starts to award bills to the competitive bidders, highest price (lowest discount yield) bids first. It fills these bids until it has awarded all the bills it wishes to sell competitively. The lowest successful bids will receive only a partial award; this could be as little as less than 1% of the amount they bid for, or as high as more than 99% of the amount they bid for.

The Fed then awards the bills at this lowest price, up to the legal maximum. For bills, in early 2001, this was $1,000,000 face amount for noncompetitive tenders.

If you are an individual investor, you may purchase bills at the auction. You may enter a competitive bid if you wish, but almost all individual purchasers of bills enter noncompetitive tenders. You will get your bills in the amount you wish to buy up to the legal maximum. If you can't enter the bid yourself at the Fed, you can enter it by mail, or your local bank or your broker will enter it for you; a common charge for this service is $50.

Many individual investors use a system called *Treasury Direct* to purchase their Treasury securities at auction. The Treasury Direct system is run by the Fed. The buyer of Treasury securities has an account at the Fed, used to buy Treasury securities at auction. Interest income and proceeds of maturing securities are sent directly to the investor's account at the investor's bank. The security buyer can check the account status at any time. This makes the purchase of Treasury securities at auction about as easy as it can possibly be.

Purchases of T-bills represent an attractive alternative to money market funds and bank CDs for many investors, since the interest income is exempt from state income taxes, and the bills may be either sold easily or rolled over into a new issue of bills when they mature, if so desired.

Bills are traditionally purchased and traded by large investors, either institutions or very wealthy individuals. They are also traded in very large volume. In early 2001, total daily trading volume in Treasury securities at Primary Dealers was around $200 billion, and possibly half that trading volume was in bills. In addition, each individual transaction is usually very large. In fact, the usual round lot in the bill market is $5,000,000. But since bills are issued in minimum amounts of $1,000, with multiples of $1,000 over the $1,000 minimum, these odd lots exist in the market, and they trade at somewhat disadvantageous prices when compared to round lots. Investors who get quotes on round lots and then try to execute an odd lot order may be in for a small surprise. However, small lots, even down to the $1,000 minimum, are easily traded at relatively modest cost.

■ TREASURY NOTES

Securities issued by the Treasury with maturities from one to ten years are defined as *notes*. Unlike bills, notes have coupons and pay interest every six months. All notes are noncallable by the Treasury. There is a very wide range of note issues outstanding, with maturities ranging from a few days to as long as ten years, and, in early 2001, with coupons ranging from 4.25% to 8%.

The Treasury issues notes in regular cycles, like T-bills, but much less frequently. In 2001, the Treasury offered two-year notes monthly, and five-year and ten-year notes quarterly. As in bids for T-bills, both competitive bids and noncompetitive tenders may be made for notes. The Fed, acting as agent for the Treasury, awards competitive bids in decreasing order of price, highest prices first. Noncompetitive tenders are awarded in full, up to the maximum allowed (in early 2001) of $5,000,000, at the average of the awarded competitive bids. All are awarded at the lowest accepted bid.

If you wish to buy notes, you can easily and conveniently buy them at the auction. You can submit your bid yourself, in person or by mail, or you can ask your bank or broker to submit it for you; a common charge for this service is $50. For many investors, notes are a convenient investment, and the income is exempt from state income taxes. Almost all individual investors submit noncompetitive tenders, although you can submit a competitive bid if you wish. If you submit a noncompetitive tender, you will get your notes, up to the $5,000,000 maximum, at the award price. The Treasury Direct system is used for this as well as for Treasury bills.

Treasury notes are actively quoted, along with Treasury bonds, in the financial news. Most major daily papers carry at least some Treasury security quotations, and many of them carry complete market quotations.

Treasury notes are quoted in prices denominated in percentage points and 32nds of a percentage point. These are percentages of par amount. Although prices are written using a decimal point, the number to the right of the decimal point is expressed in 32nds. Thus, a price of 98.16 would be 98 and 16 32nds of par, or 98½% of par, or $985,000 per million dollars of par amount. Each 32nd is equal to $312.50 per million dollars of par amount. Occasionally, issues are quoted in 64ths of a percentage point, which is equivalent to $156.25 per million dollars of par amount.

A million-dollar par amount is considered a round lot in the Treasury note market, just as $5,000,000 is considered a round lot in the T-bill market. However, much smaller lots of notes can be easily bought and sold, at relatively small expense. Notes are available in minimum amounts of $1,000 and multiples of $1,000. Notes are now in book entry form only, like T-bills.

You can see that notes are easily available in amounts closely suited to your investment needs, even if you are a relatively small investor. Many investors find Treasury notes a suitable short- to medium-term obligation. They are easily available at auction or in the secondary market, may be easily sold with a modest transaction cost, and the interest income is exempt from state income taxes.

Most Treasury notes are owned by commercial banks, Federal Reserve Banks, United States Government agencies, and government trust funds. These notes permit holders to arrange their portfolios with coupons and maturities spaced over a limited period of years, giving automatic liquidity and attractive average yields.

Treasury notes and bonds pay interest to holders semiannually, almost always on the anniversary date of the issue date. Interest accrues on notes and bonds during the period between payments. The buyer of a note or bond pays, and the seller receives, accrued interest when the securities are sold. Thus, an investor who buys notes or bonds after a coupon payment date and sells them before the next coupon payment date receives the bond interest for the period during which he or she held the securities.

For example, let's say on June 15 you bought one million dollars par value of a 5% note, with coupon dates of May 15 and November 15, and held it until October 15. When you bought the note, you would have paid 31 days of accrued interest (there are 31 days from May 15 to June 15, counting exact days) at $135.87 per day. There are 184 days from May 15 to November 15, and the note earns $25,000 of interest during that six-month period; $25,000 divided by 184 = $135.87, which is the amount of interest earned each day. The total accrued interest therefore would be $4,211.96.

When you sold the note, you received accrued interest for 153 days, also at $135.87 per day, for a total of $20,788.11. The person who bought it from you, assuming it was held until the November 15 interest payment date, would receive a check for $25,000, half a year's interest.

You can see that no matter when you buy a note or bond, you will receive back the accrued interest you paid when you bought it, and receive your interest earnings as well for the time you hold the note or bond.

■ TREASURY BONDS

Treasury securities with more than ten years to maturity at the time of sale are called *Treasury bonds,* or *T-bonds.* They are similar to notes, but there are a few important differences.

Treasury bonds are sold by an auction process similar to the auction process for notes, and they are traded on a dollar price basis, with accrued interest calculated in the same manner as that for notes. The Treasury Direct system is used for Treasury bonds just as for T-bills and Treasury notes. New issues of Treasury bonds are only in book entry form, but some older bonds, issued years ago, may be in bearer or registered form.

Treasury bonds have a minimum amount of $1,000, with multiples of $1,000 over that minimum amount.

Some Treasury bonds have a call feature; they may be called by the Treasury at par five years before the maturity date and at any interest payment date thereafter. Thus, you can guess that if a bond is trading substantially above 100, it may have a call feature that will cause it to have an effective maturity date up to five years shorter than the stated maturity date. That change in maturity date can affect the bond's price performance, making it less volatile than it otherwise would be.

For example, in early 2001, the Treasury had a 7⅝% bond outstanding, maturing in February, 2007. However, the bond also had a call feature, so that the Treasury could call it at par in February, 2002. This meant that the bond, in early 2001, was trading at a three-point premium over par instead of the approximate fifteen-point premium over par it would have been trading at if it were not callable; the call feature had effectively reduced the price of the bond by about twelve points, and the bond owners will probably have their bond called away from them in February, 2002.

In the past, the Treasury has issued thirty-year and twenty-year bonds, but in 2001 discontinued the sale of the thirty-year bonds.

Treasury bonds can quickly and easily be sold at a low transaction cost. This is shown by the small spread between the bid and ask prices in the offering sheets. Treasury bonds, like Treasury notes, are quoted in dollar prices, in 32nds of a point. For example, if a $1,000 Treasury bond is quoted at 96.6, this means that the price is 96⁶/₃₂, or 96.1875 percent of par.

T-bonds are quoted in the financial press. The reports show both notes and bonds together, but identify the notes with a code in the description. Reports also show the bid price, the ask price, and the change in price from the previous day's close as well as the bond yield to maturity.

A look at the report shows that each issue may have different prices and a different yield to maturity, which is used for comparing different Treasury securities, as well as other fixed-income securities.

MARKETABLE TREASURY INFLATION-INDEXED SECURITIES

Marketable Treasury Inflation-Indexed Securities offer interest and principal payments based on a consumer price index. This may protect the investor, to some extent, against inflation. The principal amount is adjusted for inflation, based on the U.S. City Average All Items Consumer Price Index (non-seasonally adjusted), for all urban consumers (CPI-U), which is published monthly by the Bureau of Labor Statistics. (If this index is discontinued, provision is made for a replacement by an alternative index.)

The coupon rate stays the same for the life of the security, but is paid semiannually on the adjusted principal amount. At maturity, the investor receives the greater of the adjusted principal amount or par amount of the original issue.

Coupon rates range from 3½% to 4¼%. In early 2001, there were a total of eight inflation-adjusted securities, with final maturities ranging from July 15, 2002 to April 15, 2029. The Treasury offers these securities using the same single-price auction system that is used for all of the Treasury's marketable securities.

These are a relatively new security, first offered by the Treasury in 1997. They still have not been widely accepted, accounting for about $74.7 billion, or about 1.3%, of the public debt of the United States. They are widely reported, and may grow in popularity with investors seeking some protection against inflation, at least for part of their portfolios. However, the cost of this protection is a lower rate of coupon return, and a varying principal amount, which might even decline if consumer prices go down and the security was purchased at more than the original principal amount (par).

How to Read a Treasury Market Report

If you are at all active in bond investment, or any sort of investment, for that matter, you should know how to read a Treasury bond market report. There are several reasons for this. First, the Treasury market is the most important fixed-income market in the world, and the leader in setting worldwide interest rates. Many other securities trade in some relation to Treasury rates; they are said to "trade off" Treasuries. For example, many investment managers compare the yields on mortgage-backed securities and municipal securities to yields of Treasuries of comparable maturity. Many derivative securities have their terms set in relation to Treasury yields. Treasuries are widely held and widely traded; worldwide trading markets exist in these securities. Even with the recent decline in the outstanding amounts of marketable Treasuries, they are still important.

How to Read a Treasury Bond and Note Report

Suppose you read the following in your Treasury market report:

Feb 26   k   6   107.18   107.20   +0.12   5.43

Here is a description of the entries and their meanings.

Feb 26: The maturity month and year of the bond. In this case, the bond matures in February 2026. The day is usually omitted. Almost all Treasury bonds and notes mature on either the 15th of the month or on the last day of the month. In this case, the bonds mature on February 15, 2026.

k: This is a Treasury bond, nonresident aliens exempt from withholding tax. No tax is withheld from the interest payment. Years ago, an interest equalization tax was withheld, but this was repealed in 1974. A *p* in this position means that the security is a Treasury note, also nonresident aliens exempt from withholding tax.

6: Coupon rate on the bond. This bond pays $60 annually per $1,000 principal, in two $30 payments on February 15 and August 15.

107.18: The reported bid side of the market for this bond. Remember, bond prices are expressed as percent of par. The digits after the period are 32nds of a point, so this price is 107 and 18/32 percent of par, 18/32 = 9/16 = .5625. The price of the bond, in decimal form, is therefore 107.5625. A $1,000,000 par amount will cost $1,075,625.00 at this price.

107.20: This is the reported ask side of the market for this bond. The same comments above on the bid side apply here also, except the price willbe 100.625 (percent of par).

+0.12: This represents the change in price from the previous day's close, expressed in 32nds of a point. Here, 0.12 = 12/32 = 3/8 = .375.

5.43: This is the yield to maturity of the bond.

Some Treasuries have a call feature. Here is an example of how this would be noted:

Nov 09-14   k   11¾   147.11   147.12   +.08   4.95

This means that the bonds mature in November, 2014 (on November 15, in this case), and may be called at par on November 15, 2009 and on any interest payment date thereafter. The other information is interpreted similarly to the bond shown above.

How to Read a Treasury Bill Report

Suppose you read the following in your Treasury bill report:

Feb 28 02   4.00   3.98   -0.01   4.16

This is how it would be interpreted.

Feb 28 02: The bills mature on February 28, 2002.

4.00: The bid is 4.00 discount yield, as reported by the news service.

3.98: The ask is 3.98 discount yield.

-0.01: The change in discount yield from the previous day.

4.16: The bond equivalent yield.

THE PUBLIC DEBT OF THE UNITED STATES

Figure 4-1. shows the public debt of the United States, as of June 30, 2001, as reported by the Federal Reserve Board, and adjusted. This is reported in the monthly Federal Reserve Bulletin, and some other places.

Public Debt of the United States As of 06/30/01		
	Amount (Billions)	Percent
Marketable		
Bills	620.1	10.8
Notes	1,441.0	25.2
Bonds	616.9	10.8
Inflation indexed	129.3	2.3
Total	2,822.3	49.3
Non-Marketable		
Savings bonds	178.4	3.1
SLGS	153.3	2.7
Other	24.0	0.5
Total	355.7	6.2
Total held by public	3,178.0	55.5
Government Account Series	2,474.7	43.2
Total interest-bearing debt	5,682.8	99.2
Other	44.0	0.8
Total	5,726.8	100.0

Source: Federal Reserve Bulletin, adjusted. Totals may not add due to rounding.

FIGURE 4-1. PUBLIC DEBT OF THE UNITED STATES

At the time of this report, the debt's size was about $5,727 billion. Almost all of this was interest-bearing debt. The very small amount of non-interest-bearing debt is mostly matured debt on which interest has stopped accruing.

A little over half of the debt is held by the public, mostly as marketable securities. These are the bills, notes, bonds, and inflation indexed securities discussed elsewhere.

About 6% of the total debt is held by the public in the form of nonmarketable securities. Most of these are savings bonds and state and local government series (SLGS). Most investors are familiar with savings bonds, which have been offered to the investing public since the 1930s. State and local government series bonds are issued to state and local governments and their agencies and authorities when these issue new bonds, so that the issuers don't violate the Internal Revenue Service arbitrage regulations. Most individual investors don't need to concern themselves with these specialized issues.

About 43% of the debt is held by government accounts, mostly the Social Security Trust fund and the federal retirement system. These securities are specially designed and issued for their specific holders. They are not offered to the public, and are held by their government agency holders for long-term investment purposes.

■ TREASURY STRIPS

United States Treasury Separate Trading Registered Interest and Principal Securities (STRIPS) were created by the Treasury in 1986 to meet the demand for zero coupon obligations. A zero coupon bond has no interest payment during the life of the bond. Instead, all the interest due is paid at the maturity of the bond. The best known zero coupon bond is a United States Savings Bond.

The Treasury does not issue STRIPS. Instead, the Treasury declares that certain issues of Treasury notes and bonds are eligible for the STRIPS program. These eligible notes and bonds, and no others, may be split up into separate interest and principal payments, with each payment trading as a separate security. This splitting up, or "stripping" of the issue, is done by government bond dealers and others, not by the Treasury. Each such separate security receives its own CUSIP number for security identification. (A CUSIP number is one that identifies each unique security.) The STRIPS may also be reassembled to recreate the original security.

Zero coupon bonds automatically reinvest the interest earnings at the same yield basis at which the investor originally bought the bond. This guaranteed compounding feature is attractive enough so that investors are sometimes willing to pay higher prices (lower yields) for zero coupon bonds than for regular coupon bonds. However, Internal Revenue Service regulations may require the bond owner to report this earned, but not paid, interest income on an income tax return, and pay the appropriate taxes. As a result, most buyers of these securities are those who are exempt from federal income taxes. They include pension funds and individual pension accounts, such as IRAs and Keogh plans. If you have an IRA or a Keogh plan, you should at least look at Treasury STRIPS as an investment. You won't have to worry about reinvesting interest income; it will automatically be reinvested for you at the rates at which you originally bought the STRIPS.

■ ORIGINAL ISSUE DISCOUNT SECURITIES, MARKET DISCOUNT SECURITIES, AND THEIR TAX TREATMENT

This type of security is said to be an Original Issue Discount (OID) security. An OID security is issued at a large discount. The discount is accrued as income over the life of the bond, and reported as income on the owner's federal income tax return. The Internal Revenue Service has issued regulations covering the tax treatment of original issue discount, and the definition of original issue discount securities. Any security issued at a discount, whether or not it has a coupon, may be an original issue discount security, with the annual accrual of discount subject to federal income taxes. For example, a bond with a 3% coupon that was originally issued at a price of 50 would probably be an original issue discount security.

Sometimes a security is bought in the market at a price lower than par and lower than its issue price. This discount may be considered "market discount" and the accrual of market discount during the period until maturity may be reported and taxed as interest income.

If you own bonds such as these, you should consult with your tax advisor or accountant about the correct tax treatment of these issues.

■ OTHER SECURITIES SIMILAR TO STRIPS

Older zero coupon issues, secured by Treasuries held by a trustee, may still exist, but none have been issued since the mid-1980s, due to the STRIPS program. Many of these securities have names such as TIGRS (Treasury Investment Growth Receipts), CATS (Certificates of Accrual on Treasury Securities), and other similar names, many of them feline in character. These too may be original issue discount securities, most of which will have matured by now.

STRIPS are traded on a bond yield basis. Many, not all, leading newspapers report prices for all STRIPS, but most report prices for at least a few.

■ REASONS FOR DIFFERENT YIELDS

What causes different issues to have different yields to maturity? A common reason is difference in perceived credit quality; the higher the perceived quality, the lower the yield. Thus, one would expect Treasuries to yield less than bonds issued by agencies of the United States Government, such as the Federal Home Loan Bank; agencies to yield less than AAA-rated corporate bonds; and AAA-rated corporate bonds to yield less than lower-rated corporate bonds.

Sometimes, however, that expectation isn't quite valid. We need then to explain yield differences between securities with the same issuer, such as Treasury securities. In these cases, we must look for other reasons.

One such reason is differences in term to maturity. This is so common that it has given rise to the phrase "yield curve," which describes the changes in yield as time to maturity for like issues increases. When the yield increases as the maturity lengthens, the yield curve is called *normal*. When the yield decreases as the maturity lengthens, the yield curve is called *inverted*. Some traders are so concerned with the shape of the yield curve and the exact yield differences between maturities that it is virtually the only thing that dictates their trading.

Another factor that can explain yield differences, especially between issues with identical or nearly identical maturities, is coupon and dollar price. In general, the higher the coupon, and thus the higher the dollar price, the higher the yield. This is partly because this factor tends to bring the after-tax yields closer, and partly because of compounding considerations. Also, investors tend to prefer bonds trading at around par, and insist that bonds with high premiums offer a higher yield.

A last reason for yield differences is the technical market condition of the securities. An issue in which a dealer is trying to cover a large short position will often trade at a lower yield than one in which the dealer has a long position, which he is trying to sell. The buying effort raises prices (lowers yields), while the selling effort lowers prices (raises yields).

A special case of the technical condition aspect has to do with the Treasury's auctions of securities. The Treasury does not pay Primary Dealers a selling concession to market its issues, and the Primary Dealers must bid on all Treasury auctions. For this reason, in the days before the auctions, dealers tend to go short the issues with maturities near those of the issues to be auctioned. This short position allows the dealer to propose that customers swap out of the issues the dealer has just sold short into the issues the dealer expects to buy in the auction. (A *swap* is a sale of a security combined with a purchase of a similar security.) This also hedges the dealer against a fall in general market prices while he is long the securities he has just bought because a loss in the issues he has just bought will be offset by a gain in the issues he has just sold short. It also has the effect of making the existing issues yield more, temporarily, than they otherwise would yield.

A great deal of trading in the marketplace, by both customers and Primary Dealers, is based on the idea that there is an equilibrium yield spread between any two issues. Whenever that spread gets out of line, one issue is sold and the other is bought. Then the trader waits for the spread to go back to its equilibrium level. That is good trading strategy, as long as the equilibrium spread is not in the process of changing. If it is, one can be left with losses instead of the expected profits.

■ TAXATION OF TREASURY SECURITIES

The interest income paid to investors on Treasury securities is subject to federal income taxes, but is exempt from state and local income taxes. However, this exemption applies only to "direct" obligations of the United States Government. Many obligations of federal agencies may be subject to state and local income taxes. (See Chapter 5 for a fuller discussion of this.)

While Treasury securities make for a huge market, they are not the only securities related to the federal government. A wholly different trading arena consists of securities issued by federal government agencies, securities backed by pools of mortgages, and financial futures and options. These are explained in the next chapter.

5

United States Agency Securities, Mortgage-Backed Securities, and Bond Futures and Options

American voters, and thus the American government, have had longstanding commitments to several sectors of the economy. These include the family farmer, the family homeowner, and students. A contrary but equally longstanding perception is that direct government assistance to these or to any other sectors is unfair and undesirable. The conflict between these two viewpoints gave rise to a separate class of securities—those issued or guaranteed by agencies of the federal government.

Agencies are not always part of the federal government; they are sometimes owned by the constituencies they serve. Yet they perform the governmental functions of giving assistance and regulation to these constituencies.

Agencies are divided into two categories. First are Federally Related Institutions. These are actually arms of the federal government, and in general don't issue securities directly into the market. Instead they usually borrow from the Federal Financing Bank, which was created in 1973 to consolidate borrowing by a number of institutions that had previously borrowed in relatively small amounts, resulting in somewhat higher borrowing costs. However, the Tennessee Valley Authority occasionally borrows from the public. Its securities are not guaranteed by the United States Government, but are exempt from state income taxes. The Government National Mortgage Association (GNMA) is an agency with the Department of Housing and Urban

Development and is discussed later in this chapter. It issues an important type of pass-through mortgage-backed security.

The second type of agency consists of Government Sponsored Entities (GSEs). There are eight such agencies which issue two types of securities: bonds and discount notes. The bonds are sold with maturities of more than two years. The discount notes range up to one year in maturity.

The eight agencies are:

■ Federal Farm Credit Bank System
■ Farm Credit Financial Assistance Corporation
■ Federal Home Loan Bank
■ Federal Home Loan Mortgage Corporation (frequently called Freddie Mac)
■ Federal National Mortgage Association (frequently called Fannie Mae)
■ Student Loan Marketing Association (frequently called Sallie Mae)
■ Financing Corporation
■ Resolution Trust Company

The Federal Farm Credit Bank System (FFCBS) provides credit and related services to the farm sector. It has three parts: the Federal Land Banks, Federal Intermediate Credit Banks, and Banks for Cooperatives. Before 1979, each of these issued its own securities. Now their debt is issued by the Federal Farm Credit Bank System, on a consolidated basis. The FFCBS issues discount notes. In early 2001, the FFCBS had securities maturing from May, 2002 through December, 2002.

The Farm Credit Financial Assistance Corporation (FACO) was set up in 1987 to help the FFCBS, which faced financial problems due to the farmers' difficulties in making loan payments. FACO bonds are guaranteed by the United States Treasury, unlike the bonds issued by the other federally sponsored agencies.

The Federal Home Loan Bank System (FHLBS) is an independent federal agency. Most of its debt is issued on a consolidated basis by its members, the twelve Federal Home Loan

Banks. In early 2001, FHLBS had securities outstanding maturing from 2002 to 2008.

The Federal Home Loan Mortgage Corporation (FHLMC or Freddie Mac) has a federal charter, is subject to some federal oversight, and is considered a federal agency. But it is actually a public company owned by its stockholders that issues and guarantees mortgage-backed securities.

The Federal National Mortgage Association (Fannie Mae) also has a federal charter, some federal oversight, and also is considered a federal agency. But it is a company owned by its stockholders. Like FHLMC, it issues and guarantees mortgage-backed securities. Stocks of both FNMA and FHLMC are traded on the New York Stock Exchange.

The Student Loan Marketing Association, known as Sallie Mae, provides money for entities lending under the Federal Guaranteed Student Loan Program, the Health Education Assistance Loan Program, and the PLUS loan program. Sallie Mae has issued discount notes, floating-rate securities, long-term fixed-rate securities, and zero coupon bonds.

The Financing Corporation (FICO) was set up by Congress in 1987 to help with the problems caused by the failure of many savings and loan institutions and the resulting difficulties for the Federal Savings and Loan Insurance Corporation.

The Resolution Trust Company (RTC) was formed in 1989 to continue helping FICO to cope with the problems caused by the ongoing failures in the savings and loan industry. RTC gets its funding from the Resolution Funding Corporation (REFCORP) which can issue long-term bonds. REFCORP has issued 30-year and 40-year obligations.

■ HOW AGENCIES HELP THEIR CONSTITUENTS

Agencies assist their constituencies in two ways. Some borrow in the marketplace by issuing securities themselves and lending the proceeds to their constituents. When they do this, they substitute their high-quality credit for the lower-quality credit of the farmer, homeowner, or student.

Other agencies guarantee the timely payment of interest and principal on the securities issued by their constituents, thereby enhancing their credit. Some agencies do both. Some issues guaranteed by agencies also have the guarantee of the United States Treasury, and some do not.

In diversity, quality, liquidity, and trading volume, agency securities fall between the homogeneous world of Treasury securities and the heterogeneous world of corporate securities. Some of the diversity of agency securities was eliminated when the agricultural agencies banded together to issue securities under the umbrella of the Federal Farm Credit System, incorporated as Federal Farm Credit Funding Corporation, New York, Fiscal Agent.

Agency securities also differ in method of issuance. Some securities are issued directly by the agency, following an issuing procedure that falls between a Treasury auction and a corporate underwriting. Several agencies issue or guarantee mortgage-backed securities that are issued in a less-controlled process.

■ HOW AGENCY SECURITIES ARE QUOTED AND TRADED

Agency securities are traded in an over-the-counter market, just like United States Treasury obligations, and usually by the same dealers. However, spreads are somewhat wider, so it is more costly to trade in this market than in the Treasury market.

The agency discount securities are similar to Treasury bills, and like T-bills are quoted on a discount yield basis. The interest is paid at maturity, similar to T-bills. Time to maturity goes out to one year.

Long-term agency securities are coupon securities, like United States Treasury notes and bonds, and, like them, pay interest semiannually. Similarly, they are quoted in dollar prices.

Agency securities are not obligations of the United States Treasury, with a few exceptions. However, few people believe that the United States Government will allow any federal agency actually to default on its obligations. Agencies are considered a perfectly safe investment. Their interest income is subject to federal income tax, but may be exempt from state income taxes.

INVESTING IN AGENCY OBLIGATIONS

If you buy agency obligations, you are buying a security that is not quite as safe as a United States Treasury security and is harder and somewhat more expensive to trade. Price quotations may be somewhat more difficult to obtain. In exchange for this, you should receive a somewhat higher yield. Agency securities should be quite satisfactory investments as long as you understand these constraints. Be sure to consult with your tax advisor on the tax status of the interest they pay.

■ MORTGAGE-BACKED SECURITIES

One of the most spectacular developments in the government and other securities markets since the early 1970s has been the development of mortgage-backed securities. In order to understand these securities, we must first look at the underlying mortgage contract. Its features affect all mortgage-backed securities and have led to the development of special mortgage-backed securities.

■ HOW A HOME MORTGAGE WORKS

A mortgage, of the sort we are considering here, is a loan that is secured by real estate. In the mortgages we are looking at, the real estate is a one- to four-family home, where the owner is a resident. Usually these are single-family homes, and the mortgage is taken out by the owner to buy the property. However, often the mortgage will be a refinancing instead, especially when interest rates have just fallen. A refinancing occurs when a homeowner who already has a mortgage on a house finds that borrowing is available at a somewhat lower interest rate than the rate of the present mortgage. For example, a homeowner might have a mortgage with a 9% interest rate. Suppose interest rates fall and she can now borrow at 7%. Naturally the homeowner would do that, assuming that she qualifies for a new loan. The homeowner borrows (takes out) a new mortgage and uses the proceeds simultaneously to pay off the old mortgage. The saving will be 2% each year, less the cost of the transaction. On a $200,000 mortgage, that would be a $4,000 annual interest saving (2% of $200,000), worthwhile for most individuals.

During the Great Depression of the 1930s, many homeowners could no longer pay even the interest on their mortgages, and sometimes lost their homes. Sometimes they had lived in their homes for years, and if they had made even small principal payments periodically, their mortgages would have been paid off. This led to the creation of the monthly level-payment amortizing mortgage. Almost all home mortgages are now of this sort and have the following general characteristics:

1. The homeowner makes a monthly payment of interest and principal, and usually taxes and sometimes insurance as well. Common times to maturity for mortgages are fifteen and thirty years; these are equivalent to 180 and 360 monthly payments.

2. The monthly payments are made to a firm, called a *mortgage service firm*, that in turn makes the interest and principal payments to the owner of the mortgage, after deducting a fee for its services. The owner could be the mortgage service firm itself, but usually the mortgage has been sold to a permanent holder of (investor in) the mortgage.

3. The payments for taxes and insurance go into an escrow fund, from which the mortgage service firm makes the appropriate payments. These payments are no longer part of this discussion.

4. The owner has the right to pay all or part of the mortgage ahead of time, almost always without significant prepayment penalty. This is the equivalent of a call feature on a bond and gives the mortgages, and any pool that the mortgages may be put into, an uncertainty not present in many other fixed-income investments.

5. Often the borrower pays "points" when he takes out the mortgage. Points are a deduction from the proceeds of the mortgage loan. They may be considered a sort of call premium if the owner pays off the loan ahead of time, because the full face amount of the mortgage loan is paid, not the reduced amount actually lent to the owner because of the points. This is the case even if the borrower pays off the loan soon, such as within a year or two.

6. Partial mortgage prepayments reduce the principal due, but do not reduce the monthly payment. Instead, the number of payments is reduced, and the mortgage is paid off earlier than planned.

7. Often mortgages are made under one of several programs offered by a United States Government agency. For example, both the Veterans Administration (VA) and the Federal Housing Administration (FHA) offer mortgages to qualified home buyers; their mortgages are insured by the agency as to eventual payment of principal.

■ WHAT IS DONE WITH THE MORTGAGES AFTER THEY ARE MADE?

Most mortgages are not kept by the firm that originally makes them, but instead they are sold. Many of these are put together in a collection of mortgages, called a *mortgage pool.* All the mortgages in a particular pool will have the same interest rate, the same period to maturity, the same kind of insurance (if they are insured), the same kind of property (in the cases we are considering, usually single-family home property), and other features as well. These other features can include the ratio of the payment to the borrower's income, the ratio of the mortgage to the value of the house, and the actual size of the mortgage. Sometimes these mortgage pools themselves are insured in addition to any insurance carried by the individual mortgages in the pool.

Thus, a mortgage pool will have the same characteristics as the underlying mortgages, and can be said to have a coupon rate, a final maturity date, possibly a form of insurance, and other features.

Each mortgage pool then forms the basis for securities, with the pool itself as the source for the payments due on the securities. The payments made by the original borrowers are sent on to these security holders according to one of several possible methods. The pool is assigned a pool number, and the securities issued for the pool are assigned CUSIP numbers, like any other security.

Although several different pools may have the same characteristics, such as interest rate and time to maturity, the actual payments made by different pools will almost always differ somewhat because the borrowers whose mortgages are in the different pools may make somewhat different prepayments. The uncertainty of the prepayments by the individual borrowers on their mortgages in turn gives uncertainty to the payments of the mortgage pools. We'll talk about what this does to the pools, but first we must talk about the two different kinds of securities created by these pools.

■ WHAT KINDS OF SECURITIES CAN BE CREATED FROM THESE POOLS?

Two different kinds of securities can be created from these pools: *pass-throughs* and *pay-throughs*, or collateralized mortgage obligations (CMOs). A pass-through security simply sends along to each security owner his or her pro-rata share in the payments received, according to the particular interest in the pool. For example, if an owner owned 1% of the pool, that owner would receive 1% of the total payments of interest and principal received by the pool.

A CMO distributes the payments to individual security holders according to a predetermined schedule of payments. Some security holders will receive principal payments before others, according to the agreement set up ahead of time.

Here is an example to show the main features of these two different forms, and how they work.

Suppose Bill has borrowed $4,800 on a mortgage on his home, and he agrees to pay $100 each month on the principal, starting in one month, with interest at 6% per year. Bill has scheduled 48 monthly payments of $100 each, with interest starting at $24 in the first month and going down by $.50 each month. Thus, Bill's first scheduled payment, due in one month, will be $124, and the last scheduled payment, due in 48 months, will be $100.50 which will pay off the mortgage. Each payment is made to a trustee who receives Bill's payments and in turn sends the money along to the owners of the right to receive the payments.

Of course, in the real world, Bill's payments would be the same, and not decrease month by month; the trustee would also be paid for any services. In this example, we have simplified things somewhat to get a more understandable explanation.

Suppose Bill's mortgage has four owners, John, Mary, Sally, and Jim. Suppose that they agree to share equally each payment Bill makes. The trustee will send to each of them a one-quarter share of each payment. Thus, the first payment each will receive will be $31, representing one quarter of Bill's first payment of $124, and the last payment each will receive, in month 48, will be $25.13, representing their one-quarter share of Bill's last payment of $100.50.

Now suppose that in month 3 Bill includes an extra $40 payment on the principal. The trustee receives the extra payment, and sends the share to each of the four investors, or $10. In future months the interest income of each will be reduced by $.05, because of the prepayment. Bill will continue to make the monthly $100 principal payment, so each of the four will continue to receive a $25 share, until the last month, when Bill's payment will be only $60 (assuming he has made no additional prepayments), and each of the four will receive a final payment of $15, together with the interest on the last payment.

This is a pass-through security. Each payment, including the extra payment, was distributed to the four participants according to each one's share in the pool; each got one quarter of the payments Bill made.

But suppose the participants don't want to do this. Suppose, for example, that each will still invest $1,200, but John wants his principal returned during the first year, Mary wants her principal returned during the second year, Sally wants her principal returned during the third year, and Jim is willing to wait until the fourth year to get his principal back. The loan could be structured in the following way: Each investor gets his interest on the amount owed to him, but all principal payments go to John first, then to Mary when John is fully paid, then to Sally when Mary is fully paid, and finally to Jim when Sally is fully paid. Thus, during the first year, John receives $100 in principal payments each month, while the other three get only their interest, which would be $6.00 per month. John's interest would start at $6.00, but go down $.50 per month. At the thirteenth payment, John is paid off, and Mary starts to receive her monthly $100, with her interest declining each month by $.50. After two years, Mary is paid, and Sally receives her $100 monthly, and finally during the fourth year, Jim receives his monthly $100. A CMO has been created, and the four different classes of ownership, represented by the four different actual owners in this example, are called *tranches.*

Note that in the first case each owner received the same payments, and each owns the same security. Each security would have the same description and the same CUSIP number, and would receive the same pro-rata payments. In the second case, four different securities were created, each with a different principal repayment plan. Each of these four securities would have a different description and a different CUSIP number.

Now suppose Bill makes his extra $40 payment in the third month. All of this extra payment will go to John, because he gets repaid first. John will continue to get his $100 monthly payments, but his interest will be reduced by $.20 per month because he was repaid the additional $40 in the third month. At the twelfth month, John will receive only $60, because he got the extra $40 earlier, and the remaining $40 of the payment will go to Mary, because she gets all the principal payments next. At the twenty-fourth month, Mary in turn will receive only $60, while Sally will receive a $40 payment, and at the thirty-sixth month, Sally will receive only $60, while Jim will receive his first principal payment of $40. At month 48, Jim will receive a final payment of only $60, because he received $40 in month 36.

Of course, in the real world of CMOs, these would have annual maturities, not monthly maturities, and owners of later maturities, such as Sally and Jim, would receive a higher interest rate than owners of earlier securities, such as John and Mary, because their securities mature later. For example, John and Mary might receive a 5.5% interest rate and Sally and Jim might receive a 6.5% interest rate. But this example shows the general principles of CMOs' operation.

You can easily see that Bill's prepayment caused everyone's payments to change. This is called a *plain vanilla* or *sequential pay* prepayment system. But you can also easily see that quite complicated repayment systems can be devised. For example, Bill's $40 prepayment might go to Jim, along with any other prepayments Bill might make. In this case, the cash flows of John, Mary, and Sally would remain unchanged, unless Bill prepaid more than $1,200 during the first three years, while Jim's payment schedule might change a lot. Or Bill's $40 prepayment might go to Sally, so that the payments of John and Mary would not change, but the payments to Sally and Jim would change. A very large number of prepayment schemes could be devised, even for this simple case. In actual practice, the schemes can become quite complicated.

You can also see that Bill's decision to prepay the $40 changes at least one schedule of payments, and may change everybody's schedule of payments. Therefore, the prepayment decisions of the people whose mortgages are in the pool will make a big difference in the actual payments to the security holders. This requires a look at how prepayments are measured and the effects of prepayment rate on the mortgage-backed securities.

■ PREPAYMENT RATES AND HOW THEY ARE MEASURED

People prepay mortgages for a wide variety of reasons. These include a move to another location; a sudden source of funds, such as from a bonus or inheritance, which allows paying down or paying off of the mortgage; a simple desire for additional savings, which are channeled into additional monthly principal payments; and other reasons.

■ REFINANCING A MORTGAGE

Refinancing the mortgage can be an important additional reason for prepayment. Refinancing depends almost entirely on the level of interest rates, because refinancing doesn't pay unless it can produce a big interest saving.

Not everybody can refinance a mortgage even if interest rates have dropped. A main reason may be that the borrower no longer qualifies for a mortgage loan: Family income may be down, other family loans may have increased, or the borrower may not personally qualify for other reasons. In cases like these, the borrower can only continue making the required payments and hope that the situation will change. The value of the house may have dropped so that the new loan can't be large enough to pay off the old loan. Real estate prices dropped during the period from 1986 to 1996, hampering some unlucky owners.

■ PREPAYMENT RATES AND MODELS

For individual borrowers, prepayments can't easily be predicted; but for large groups of borrowers, they can be predicted with reasonable accuracy. These lead to the construction of prepayment schedules and ideas. If you know the prepayment rates of the mortgages in the pool, then you can predict the actual flow of funds, and better evaluate the mortgage-backed securities because you have a better idea of what their flow of funds will be.

In early 2001, the standard prepayment model was the one published by The Bond Market Association (TBMA), formerly the Public Securities Association. TBMA is the bond market trade association composed of firms and banks active in any of the areas of debt securities. These include United States Government securities, federal agency securities including mortgage-backed securities, municipal bonds, corporate bonds, and money market instruments.

TBMA, located in New York City, with an office in Washington, D.C., has a number of important education and information services on all aspects of debt securities. The association publishes statistics and engages in lobbying for the debt securities industry. Anyone interested in this field can obtain information directly from TBMA.

TBMA's Standard Prepayment Model starts at an annual prepayment rate of .2% during the first month, rises by .2% each succeeding month, and levels off at 6% at 30 months. Thus, in the tenth month, the prepayment rate will be (.2%) × (10) = 2% annually. TBMA's model has replaced previous widely used models. These previous models include a 12-year prepaid life (previously widely used for GNMA securities), the Constant Prepayment Rate (CPR) model, and Federal Housing Administration (FHA) experience. Most major Wall Street brokerage firms have also developed their own econometric models for use by their customers and themselves.

Mortgage prepayment rates, in early 2001, were given as percentages of Prepayment Speed Assumptions (PSAs). For example, 100% PSA means that the prepayment rate is exactly the same as TBMA's Standard Prepayment Model; 200% of PSA means a rate twice the 100% PSA rate; that would mean a starting rate of .4% per month, increasing in a straight line fashion by .4% each month until it reaches 12% annually in the thirtieth month, where it remains. In another example, 150% PSA means one and one-half times the PSA model.

■ PASS-THROUGH SECURITIES AND HOW THEY WORK

Pass-through securities all have fundamentally the same structure, illustrated by our simple example above. Mortgages, all with the same characteristics, are placed in a pool, given a pool number, and the securities are given a CUSIP number. All cash flows from the mortgages in the pool are passed along to the security holders according to their share in the pool, after subtracting the fee for servicing the mortgages. However, there are minor differences between the various kinds of pass-throughs offered by the three federal agencies that offer them, and by the private firms that also sometimes offer them.

Three different Federal agencies offer pass-through securities: the Government National Mortgage Association (GNMA), part of the Department of Housing and Urban Development (HUD); the Federal National Mortgage Association (FNMA);

and the Federal Home Loan Mortgage Corporation (FHLMC or "Freddie Mac").

GNMA pools are composed solely of mortgages with FHA or VA insurance. These pools are assembled by private concerns, approved by GNMA, and sold to the public. GNMA securities also have a United States Treasury guarantee of interest and principal payments. FNMA and FHLMC pools are mostly composed of conventional mortgages, although there are a few with FHA or VA insurance. Also, FNMA and FHLMC pools do not have a Treasury guarantee of payments. However, the agencies themselves guarantee payment, and there is no reason to doubt the overall quality of these securities. The underlying mortgages of each pool must pass strict quality requirements before they are put into a pool. As a result of the Treasury guarantee, GNMA securities tend to sell for somewhat lower yields than FNMA and FHLMC pass-throughs, although there is no reason to doubt the soundness of the last two. The FHA and VA insurance guarantees that the mortgages will be paid; it just doesn't guarantee that interest will be paid currently while you wait, in case of a mortgage payment delay or default.

All of these pay monthly interest and principal. Interest payments will decrease each month as principal is repaid, but principal payments will fluctuate monthly. Generally, principal payments should increase as interest payments decrease, because interest is paid on smaller principal amounts, but principal payments will reflect prepayments as well as the scheduled regular principal amortization payments. Because of these prepayments, principal payments on these securities can fluctuate widely month by month. Each individual security holder should keep records on his own payments.

■ COLLATERALIZED MORTGAGE OBLIGATIONS (CMOS) AND HOW THEY WORK

The previous example shows the general principles of operation of a CMO. The mortgages or mortgage pass-through securities are placed in a pool, and the funds received from the mortgage payments are distributed by a trustee who follows the plan set up when the CMOs were originally sold. The pool receives a number, and the securities backed by the mortgages in the pool receive CUSIP numbers. A large number of different securities could be issued based on this pool, whereas with a pass-through security, only one type of security is issued.

The wide variety of possible securities available from the one pool allows the underwriter of these securities to offer them to a wider variety of investors. In our example earlier, John wanted securities maturing in one year, while Jim wanted securities maturing in four years. By structuring the loan in tranches, the underwriter could give both John and Jim (and Mary and Sally) securities that met their needs. In this way, the underwriter has greatly expanded the market for mortgage-backed securities. The whole point of this diversity of CMO offerings is precisely this market expansion. In theory, and to some extent in practice, this expansion benefits everybody: The issuer gets a wider market for the securities, the investor has a wider choice of offerings to meet her needs, and the underwriter (or middleman) earns more money.

The wider diversity of securities has also removed from some of them a little of the uncertainty about the exact time of repayment, but has increased this uncertainty in others. Another price paid for this diversity is that these offerings are more complicated, and in many cases harder to understand and to evaluate.

The first and simplest CMO was a simple tranche, as outlined in the example above. In that case, four tranches were created, and the principal of each tranche was paid in full before principal payments started on the next tranche. However, each tranche received current interest payments on the amount outstanding. Thus, John was paid in full before anybody else because he owned the first tranche, but everybody received interest payments when due. This system is called a *plain vanilla tranche.*

Note that each tranche will have a planned average life, but the prepayments will affect that average life. In the first CMO offerings, all the securities were plain vanilla tranches.

Z Bonds and How They Work

The first change to wholly plain vanilla tranches was the introduction of Z bonds. These are not zero-coupon bonds, but rather receive their interest in the form of additional principal amount of bonds. Only when the bonds in the preceding tranches have been paid off do the Z bonds start receiving interest payments in cash, as well as principal amortization. This allows the interest, which would normally go to the Z bonds, to flow to the previous tranches, so that these tranches will be paid off somewhat earlier than would otherwise be the case. In our example, if Jim's bond were a Z bond, he would receive no interest payments, and the interest earned on his bonds would retire the bonds of John, Mary, and Sally. Jim would, however, receive additional principal amount instead of interest. Only after Sally's tranche was paid (the last tranche before Jim's bonds) would Jim start to receive interest and principal payments. Jim's interest would be paid on his total principal accrual, including the bonds paid to him as interest.

The accretion on Z bonds can also be used to pay down another set of tranches. This gives these other tranches a well-defined maturity, so they are called *Very Accurately Defined Maturity* (VADM) tranches.

Planned Amortization Classes and How They Work

Planned Amortization Classes (PACs) are another kind of CMO that can be used in structuring a CMO deal. PACs are set up so that they have a high degree of certainty as to principal repayment. First, the sinking fund is determined so that it won't change within a wide range of prepayment arrangements. Second, the PAC can make payments on principal at the same time as some (or all) of the other CMO classes. Thus, the PAC will receive its scheduled repayments no matter what the status of the other classes. This increased cash flow certainty makes the PAC more attractive.

The uncertainty doesn't go away; it is simply reassigned to other CMO classes. In our previous example, we could make John's repayments more sure by having all prepayments during the first year go to reduce Mary's loan, rather than John's loan. Thus, John would get his scheduled repayments, while the $40 prepayment would go to Mary.

Another way to do this would be to split John's loan in two parts, say $600 each. Imagine that John owns $600, and Josette owns the other $600, and that all prepayments go to Josette, not to John. When Bill makes his $40 prepayment in the third month, Josette gets the whole $40 in addition to her planned principal payment; John gets only his planned principal payment. Josette has absorbed all the uncertainty of prepayments for the first year. This kind of tranche (owned by Josette) is variously called a *non-PAC*, *companion*, or *support tranche*. Return and average life are much more variable in this kind of tranche, because companion bonds absorb much or all of the variability of prepayment. Almost any type of bond can be a support to other tranches by appropriately arranging the flow of funds when the entire CMO deal is set up. For example, Josette's companion bond could have a planned maturity schedule of four years, but absorb all the prepayments made on the entire issue (at least until Josette's bonds are paid off). How could anyone predict the actual lifetime of Josette's companion bonds?

PAC bonds can be set up with amortization depending on the level of prepayment of the issue. They could be structured so that no change to the planned amortization schedule occurred unless the prepayments were at a certain predetermined level of PSA. For example, the arrangement could be that no additional payment would be made unless the issue's prepayments were outside a range of 200% around PSA, at which point extra principal payments would occur. Perhaps no principal payments would be made unless prepayments were outside the range of 75% of PSA to 275% of PSA. Another PAC might have a 100% range, say from 100% of PSA to 200% of PSA. Clearly the second case would be less secure than the first because prepayments are more likely to move outside the 100% range than outside the 200% range. The first case would be called a PAC I and the second case a PAC II. Maturity schedules of PAC I bonds would be more certain than those of PAC II bonds. Additional classes of PACs would be possible.

OTHER CMO SECURITIES

Targeted amortization classes (TAC) bonds receive their planned maturity schedule only if prepayments are at a predetermined level. If prepayments are at a different level, TAC bonds may receive principal payments earlier or later than planned.

Interest Only (IO) and Principal Only (PO) securities, as their names imply, receive a share of only the interest or principal, when it is paid. If interest is not paid, the Interest Only securities will not receive any payment; extensive prepayments could result in an actual loss on IO securities. PO securities will receive their principal when that is paid; prepayments are beneficial to them, because they will receive principal sooner than planned. Both these securities are sold at deep discounts from their principal amounts (for PO securities) and their "notional" amount (for IO securities).

Sometimes a Z bond may have interest payments start early, based on a trigger event, such as a high prepayment rate or a large change in bond yields. These are called Jump Zs. Jump Zs that continue paying interest even if the trigger event stops are called "sticky" Jump Zs, while "non-sticky" Jump Zs return to their original payment schedule. Not many of these have been issued recently but some may still be outstanding in the market.

Residuals are securities that receive payment after all the other securities in the issue have been paid in full. This gives residuals a wide range of possible values.

■ INVESTMENT IN MORTGAGE-BACKED SECURITIES

These securities are complicated and are not for everybody. Even the simplest of them requires extra effort to understand; many require extra accounting for receipt of principal and interest; the tax treatment can be more complicated; they are harder to trade; and they have wider spreads when you do trade them. Many of them have relatively high market risk. Why would anyone want to buy them?

More money, that's why. They yield a higher return than standard Treasury bonds, but in many cases have almost the same guarantee. GNMAs, for example, are guaranteed as to payment of interest and principal by the United States Treasury, and many others have insurance by an agency of the United States Government, such as the Veterans Administration or the Federal Housing Administration. Historically, GNMA obligations have returned from .8% to 1.5% more than United States Treasury obligations of comparable maturity, a very worthwhile income increase. GNMAs are fully subject to state income taxes, but for investment accounts that are exempt from income taxes, such as IRAs, Keogh plans, and other deferred or retirement accounts, investments in CMOs can be quite worthwhile.

However, if you invest in these, you should have a complete description of your securities and keep it in a safe place. The Official Statement or Prospectus would have such a complete description; make sure you get one. The issue's trustee can also answer additional questions. You should also consult with your tax advisor before making any proposed investment.

Most individual investors should probably stick with the more common and straightforward investments in mortgage-backed securities. These include GNMA and other pass-throughs and the more standard CMOs. They probably would be well-advised to avoid the more exotic CMO issues, and many well-regarded brokerage firms won't even deal in them.

■ FINANCIAL DERIVATIVES

One characteristic of the fixed-income markets since the late 1960s has been a high degree of interest-rate volatility. The reasons for this have been subjects of endless debate—as well as more than a few political campaigns—but the markets have had to adapt to it nonetheless. Along with the volatility came large budget deficits and a large volume of Treasury securities issues. More recently, budget surpluses and a declining volume of Treasury issues have replaced the budget deficits.

The Primary Dealer community, which underwrites these new Treasury issues, had limited capital with which to distribute this large volume of securities, and that shortage of capital had been exacerbated by the volatility. Clearly, the dealers had to find a way to reduce part of their very high risk.

The solution turned out to be *financial derivatives,* or investment products whose price performance is derived from another instrument. The best-known derivative products to average investors are probably the call option and the put option on common stocks, which have their value based on the value of a common stock. For bonds, a wide variety of derivatives has also been developed. The best known are financial futures, but the market has also developed options, both exchange-traded and over-the-counter. Collectively, these derivative products have changed forever the face of the fixed-income markets, especially the United States Government securities market.

FINANCIAL FUTURES

The original derivative product in the fixed-income markets was a *financial futures contract.* Futures contracts have traded for many years in the agricultural and metals arenas. They are bilateral agreements to make and take delivery of a physical item at some agreed future time, at some agreed price. Originally, agricultural and metal products traded for future delivery on an over-the-counter basis. However, because of the predictable seasonal nature of agricultural demand and supply, trading for future delivery became larger than trading for immediate delivery. Futures exchanges were founded to bring order to a chaotic marketplace and to standardize the contracts, thereby enabling buyers to unwind their positions without going back to the original sellers. This unwinding of a position is called *closing out* a position; a position in a future, either long or short, is called an *open position.* If a person has purchased a future, that is, has promised to buy the commodity traded, that person is said to be *long* and to have a *long position.* The person who has sold the commodity is said to be *short* and to have a *short position.* Clearly the long and the short position must offset each other. The total open position is a measure of the popularity of the contract and the extent of its trading activity.

Futures markets exist for wheat, corn, rye, cocoa, cotton, coffee, tin, gold, silver, oil, pork bellies, and a wide variety of other commodities. These markets are reported in the financial pages of most major daily newspapers.

What worked for wheat and corn would also work for debt securities. In 1970 the Chicago Board of Trade (CBT) began trading in futures on GNMA pass-throughs, and in 1975 the same exchange began trading in futures on Treasury bonds. If the daily trading volume in Treasuries is so much larger than the trading volume in GNMAs, why was the GNMA contract started first? Simply because there was already a liquid market in GNMA securities for forward delivery, and the CBT wanted to give a new concept every chance to succeed. CBT delisted the GNMA futures in the 1980s, but in March, 2001, the CBT introduced a new mortgage security futures and options contract.

Succeed it did, beyond their wildest imaginations. For many years, the bond futures contract traded a larger volume than any other financial futures contract, and was by far the most important one. In terms of representative dollar volume, it traded more than any other single exchange-traded instrument. Stock index futures and options, which were introduced in the early 1980s, trade more contracts on a daily basis, but each contract represents only a fraction of the principal, and risk, of the CBT bond contract. Often the liquidity provided by the traders in the CBT bond pit has been essential to the smooth functioning of the bond market itself.

However, in early 2000, the Treasury bond yield curve became humpbacked, with the 10-year Treasury yielding somewhat more than the long bond. At the same time, the Treasury began a program of buying in longer term Treasury bonds, so that fewer long-term Treasury bonds were outstanding. Later, the Treasury also stopped new issuance of the 30-year bond.

As a result, traders and investors began to take more interest in the 10-year Treasury security as the main trading vehicle. As a result, the 10-year began to equal or exceed the bond contract in terms of daily trading and open interest. For example, in early March, 2001, the long-term Treasury future had an open interest of about 525,000 contracts, while the 10-year Treasury had an open interest of about 555,000 contracts. On one trading day, the trading in the long bond was about 251,000, while the trading in the 10-year Treasury was about 191,000, somewhat lower than the trading volume of the long bond. However, frequently this ratio is reversed, as the 10-year trading exceeds the long bond trading volume. This interest in the 10-year Treasury has continued, although in early 2001 the long-term bond once again yielded more than the 10-year Treasury, as the yield curve resumed its normal shape.

The primary reason for its trading success is that the CBT bond contract is a proxy for the entire long-term Treasury bond market. That is, at expiration of the futures contract, almost any Treasury bond with more than twenty years to maturity can be delivered in satisfaction of the contract. Furthermore, as opposed to delivery of a commodity, such as wheat or copper, delivery of Treasury bonds is easy and convenient, and done electronically. Obviously, some mechanism was needed to equate, for delivery purposes, all the deliverable issues, with a variety of coupons, maturities, and yields.

The mechanism chosen by the CBT is the creation of an imaginary bond that the futures contract represented: a 6%, 30-year bond. Thus, the price at which the futures contract trades is the one at which a 6%, 30-year bond would be delivered when the contract expires. Other coupons and maturities are equated to the imaginary security through the use of *conversion factors,* which adjust the principal amounts of bonds to be delivered. Bonds with coupons higher than 6% and maturities longer than thirty years have conversion factors higher than one. When $100,000 is divided by the conversion factor, the deliverable amount of securities is determined, and that amount can be delivered at the futures price. (The first contracts assumed a rate of 8%; this was later changed to 6%.)

The equivalent delivery price and the current price for the security are almost never the same, even for the "cheapest to deliver" security. Why? When bonds can be carried at a profit, the futures price is always lower than the equivalent delivery price, and when the yield curve is inverted, the futures contract is always higher. This phenomenon, called *convergence,* is purely a function of the cost of carry.

If you could buy a bond to yield 12%, finance it at 8%, and sell it in three months for today's price, you could lock up a 4% profit per year, or 1% per quarter. In such a case, the futures contract should decline in price for each quarterly expiration by approximately the cost of carry divided by the conversion factor.

If you were to buy the bond, finance it, sell the futures contract, and deliver the bond at futures expiration, you should realize 8%, the short-term yield. This relationship, which is basic to the futures markets, is still not comprehended by many bond market participants, who still think that they can buy bonds, sell futures, and realize the full-bond yield.

OTHER BOND FUTURES

Other bond futures are also traded. Municipal bond futures are traded on the CBT, but here there is not even a bond to deliver. The municipal future is based on appraisals of recently issued municipal bonds that meet the requirements for inclusion in the index. As such new bonds are issued, they replace bonds previously in the index. The index is based on appraisals only, and subject to change in the bonds included, so it is not possible actually to deliver any security at settlement date. All futures transactions are closed out on settlement day if they have not been closed out earlier. Trading in the municipal bond future is less than one-tenth of trading in the near T-bond future, although the municipal index is still an actively traded future.

Futures also exist on 2-, 5-, and 10-year Treasury notes, on 30-day Federal Funds, and on 5- and 10-year Federal Agency notes.

INTEREST RATE OPTIONS

If the theory surrounding financial futures is relatively straightforward, the one surrounding options is anything but simple. Whereas a futures contract is a bilateral agreement requiring both sides to perform at expiration, an option is the right to institute a transaction at any time before expiration. More precisely, the owner of an option has the right, but not the obligation, to exercise the option on or before the option's expiration date (in the United States). For example, if you own an option to buy 100 shares of AT&T common stock at a price of $25 per share on or before March 15, you own a call option. You may, if you wish, exercise the option, on or before March 15, and buy the AT&T common stock. Similarly, a put option gives the owner of the option the right to sell the underlying security, which may be a stock, a bond, or any other security, at an agreed-upon price, on or before an agreed-upon date.

If the buyer and seller of a futures contract share equal status, the buyer of an option has a decidedly better position than the seller.

Not surprisingly, then, the option buyer pays the seller a price for that better position. That price, called the *premium*, is a function of several factors:

- *Strike price:* The price at which the option buyer can execute the transaction.

- *Term:* The number of days until the option expires.

- *Investment yield:* The yield to the holder of the security that underlies the option.

- *Alternative yield:* The yield to the holder of a risk-free instrument that matures at the same time as the option expires.

- *Price volatility:* The historical or implied volatility of the price of the item that underlies the option.

Based on this information, you can calculate (or buy a computer program to calculate) the "theoretical value" of any option. *Theoretical value* is the premium level at which a theoretical investor would be indifferent between owning the option and the equivalent position in the underlying instrument. For a *call*, or the right to buy the instrument, the equivalent position would be owning the instrument itself. For a *put*, or the right to sell the instrument, the equivalent position would be short the instrument itself.

Obviously, however, from even this basic information, the risk inherent in the positions isn't at all the same. When you buy the instrument and the price falls 10 points, you are out the full 10 points. Had you bought a call on the instrument for 2 points, you could lose only those 2 points, no matter how far the instrument itself fell. On the other hand, should prices remain relatively the same, the option's value would most likely decline until, at expiration, most or all of the 2 points would have disappeared.

This property has caused options to be termed *wasting assets*, which has given them a connotation that they do not deserve. Options have often been regarded by regulators as speculative, or inherently inferior, investment vehicles, for two reasons:

- They afford higher leverage than is currently available in common stocks, but lower leverage than is generally available in government securities. The reason for this is that common stocks have higher requirements for borrowing against them (called *margin*) than government bonds.

- They are wasting assets.

This image has probably done more to obscure the true nature of options than any other possible misconception. The true value of options, and of futures, is that they can change the nature of the underlying instrument, and thus afford the portfolio manager a much wider range of management tools. These can be used for both hedging and speculative purposes.

Used in conjunction with positions in the underlying security, derivative instruments can add or subtract volatility, increase or decrease risk, and enhance or reduce total return. Certain combined positions have become relatively well known among options professionals:

- *Covered call:* This is the sale of a call against the holding of the underlying instrument. Here the manager is selling the potential for large gains in the future in exchange for cash today.

- *Married put:* This is the purchase of a put against the holding of the underlying instrument. The manager is buying insurance against catastrophic market decline, with the cost to be subtracted from the instrument's total return.

- *Cash-secured put write:* This is the sale of a put against the holding of a cash-equivalent instrument. The manager is selling the potential to profit from a rise in rates in exchange for cash today.

■ *Money-market call (90/10):* This is the purchase of a call against the holding of money-market instruments. The term "90/10" comes from the practice of investing 90% of the funds in short-term instruments and 10% of the funds in calls, but the description is somewhat outdated. Here the manager reduces substantially the risk of owning the underlying instrument, with the cost of that risk reduction being subtracted from the total return of the short-term portfolio.

Other option strategies may be appropriate, depending on the manager's market outlook and the relative cost of various options. Choosing among them requires you to know some basic rules about options and options markets.

An option's theoretical value is made up of two parts:

1. *Intrinsic value,* or the option's value if exercised immediately, and
2. *Time value,* or the value of being able to delay the decision to exercise or not.

Intrinsic value will be positive if the call's strike price is lower than the trading price of the underlying instrument. For example, if the strike price is 101, and the bond is trading at 102, the option has a positive intrinsic value. It will be negative if the strike price is higher than the trading price. An option with positive intrinsic value is called *in-the-money;* one with zero intrinsic value is called *at-the-money;* and one with negative intrinsic value is called *out-of-the-money.*

Time value is made up of the premium minus the intrinsic value. Obviously, when an option is out-of-the-money, the negative intrinsic value is added to the premium to produce the time value.

It is important to remember that:

■ *The higher the intrinsic value, the lower the time value.* In other words, the options with higher premiums, and thus higher intrinsic values, will hold their prices better over time than those with lower premiums.

■ *Unless the premium is very high, options do not move as fast as the underlying instruments.* The percentage of the underlying instrument's move that an option moves is called the *delta,* or *hedge ratio.* The delta of an at-the-money option is usually about .5 and it rises or falls as the intrinsic value rises or falls.

■ *An option's premium does not increase as much as the term increases.* For an at-the-money option, the premium will increase by the square root of the increase of the term. Thus, if a three-month option has a premium of one point, you would expect the six-month option to have a premium of 1.414.

Call and put options exist on Treasury bonds and several different issues of Treasury notes. The most active option is on Treasury bonds. They are traded on the Chicago Board of Trade, and are quoted in most major financial daily newspapers.

THE BLACK-SCHOLES OPTIONS PRICING FORMULA

A full discussion of options includes a presentation and discussion of the Black-Scholes options pricing formula (or model). This model was developed several decades ago, and has become a standard for the industry. Several variations of this model exist, and there are other models as well.

The Black-Scholes equation is related to, and can be derived from, the partial differential equation for heat transfer. Understanding this equation requires an understanding of probability and statistics, including the normal distribution, and of partial differential equations. These are far beyond the scope of this book.

Municipal Securities

In 1975, New York City seemed to be going broke. After rapidly increasing its outstanding debt for more than ten years, the city defaulted on a note issue, although not on any of its bond issues. Suddenly the market prices of its other debt obligations—rated A by the rating agencies until then—declined dramatically. The city was in trouble. Not only were its existing debt issues losing value in the fixed-income market, but its looming bankruptcy cast a shadow over the entire municipal bond market. After ten years of sometimes painful austerity, the city regained its former high ratings and became a "going concern" once again. Yet its troubled times made it impossible to regard the quality of local debt as unimpeachable.

New York City, however, was not the first municipal issuer to encounter rocky times. Ancient historical documents tell of occasional defaults as long as 2,000 years ago.

■ DEFINING MUNICIPAL SECURITIES

Municipal securities are debt securities issued by states, cities, townships, counties, political subdivisions, and United States Territories, and their authorities and agencies. The capital raised by these securities is used to do such things as build a new high school, construct a water purification plant, extend a state highway spur through a rural area, erect a multisport center, and sometimes just refund old debt. "Munis" provide the finances that fuel growth and that generate income for local government.

93

In the United States, municipal debt has a history almost as long as that of the country itself. In the 1820s, booming cities needed money to grow, and they raised funds by issuing bonds. By 1843, when the first records were kept, outstanding municipal debt was at about $25,000,000. Spurred by the needs of a sometimes violently growing nation, particularly by the building of the railroads and the development of the West, state and local governments issued more and more debt. The Panic of 1873 and the depression of 1893 took the momentum away for only a few years, and by 1900 the outstanding municipal debt level had reached $2 billion.

In 1913, the introduction of the federal income tax was to have profound effects on just about all aspects of living in America. With respect to municipal bonds, it raised a states' rights question: May the federal government tax income from state and local debt? Two landmark cases of the 1800s laid the groundwork for a decision in this area: The Supreme Court cases of *McCulloch* vs. *Maryland* (1819) and *Pollock* vs. *Farmer's Loan and Trust Co.* (1895) made states all but immune to interference by the federal government. As a result of these cases, interest on municipal bond debt was completely exempt from federal income taxes until the Tax Reform Act of 1986 was passed.

Even then, however, some people, including even some municipal bond attorneys, privately believed that there was in fact no real constitutional basis for exemption of municipal bond interest from federal taxation, and moves to impose a tax go back at least to Depression times. In the mid-1930s the Roosevelt administration tried to tax this interest, but failed.

In 1983, Congress required municipal bonds to be in registered or book entry form for the interest income to be exempt from federal income taxes. The state of South Carolina brought suit, claiming that this was an unconstitutional invasion of states' rights. The state lost, and the Supreme Court added in its opinion that Congress had the right to tax municipal bond interest income if it wished to. Congress has not done this so far, but the right of Congress to do this is now clear, and the exemption of municipal bond interest income from federal income tax now clearly has no constitutional basis whatever.

However, the Tax Reform Act of 1986 (TRA) did subject some municipal bond interest to possible income tax—the federal Alternative Minimum Tax.

This Act distinguishes between municipal bonds issued before August 15, 1986, and those issued after that date, with a few exceptions. Munis issued before this date retain their tax-exempt features. Any municipal bond issued after this date falls into one of three categories, depending on its purpose:

- *Public purpose bonds,* issued directly by the state or local government, are used for traditional municipal projects, such as a new school building or highway improvement program, projects that are clearly the responsibility of government. These munis are tax-exempt.
- *Private activity bonds,* even if they are issued by the state or local government or an agency, supply funds for "private" projects, like a sports arena, shopping mall, or civic center. These bonds may be subject to federal taxation, but they may be exempt from state or local taxes in the states in which they are issued. Note that even if a bond has mostly a public purpose, even a small private purpose may make it into a private purpose bond. This could happen if a private concern used part of a public facility. For example, if a school were built that included a cafeteria for the children, and a private catering concern actually provided the food, this might be enough to convert the issue into a private purpose issue.
- *Nongovernmental purpose bonds* raise funds for "nongovernmental" (but not "private") uses, such as housing or student loans. These are tax-exempt but the TRA puts a cap on the amount that a municipality may issue of such bonds and the income is treated as a preference item for purposes of the alternative minimum tax.

As a result, the phrase "municipal bonds" is no longer synonymous with the term "tax exempts." Although a tax-exempt municipal bond's interest payments (usually on a semiannual basis) are exempt from federal taxation, any profit from its purchase or sale is not exempt. Likewise, they are not exempt from personal property or estate taxes.

Because of the tax-free feature, municipal bonds generally carry lower interest rates than corporate or United States Treasury bonds. Investors in higher tax brackets may actually achieve higher dollar returns with the lower yields. Suitability is partly determined by asking: What precise taxable bond yield would the investor need to equal the tax-exempt return of the muni being considered? To answer this question, you must convert the tax-free yield into the equivalent taxable yield. The formula is:

$$\text{Taxable equivalent yield} = \frac{\text{Tax-free yield (\%)}}{100\% - \text{Tax bracket (\%)}}$$

For example, an investor is in the 28% tax bracket. She purchases a municipal bond paying a tax-free rate of 6%. She is also considering a corporate bond with a yield of 7.5%. Which bond—the muni or the corporate—offers her the greater yield after taxes?

$$\begin{aligned} \text{Taxable equivalent yield} &= \frac{\text{Tax-free yield (\%)}}{100\% - \text{Tax bracket (\%)}} \\ &= \frac{6\%}{100\% - 28\%} \\ &= 8.33\% \end{aligned}$$

To get the same after-tax yield as the muni, the corporate would have to offer an 8.33% return. The investor buys the muni.

In some instances, the interest payments are also free of state and local income taxes, usually on the condition that the bondholder live in the same state as the issuer. (A few states, however, tax the income from their own bonds.) This triple exemption is always a feature of some issues, such as those of Puerto Rico, the U.S. Virgin Islands, and other territories.

If anything, the introduction of the income tax into the American way of life had the effect of fostering interest in municipal bonds. Although the Great Depression of the 1930s certainly set the market back, defaults were not as severe as after 1873. During World War II, outstanding municipal debt levels actually dropped because the country's resources were being

used to win the war. After the war, however, new issues prolif-
erated. From $14 billion outstanding in 1945, the 1980s saw lev-
els of $400 billion, and by early 2001, outstanding tax-exempts
had reached about 1.5 trillion dollars.

■ THE PRIMARY MARKET

When a municipality needs more money than it receives from
tax and other regular revenues, it has the option of "borrowing"
against future tax revenues. That loan takes the form of a municipal bond issue. In effect, the state or local government, or the
authority or agency, promises to pay lenders the face value of the
bond (the principal amount of the loan) at maturity, out of future
tax or revenue dollars. Given that a municipality chooses to take
such a loan, how is it arranged?

The Federal Reserve System brings United States Treasury
bond issues to the market through the primary dealers. Is there
such an agency that does the same for state and local issuers?
There is no agency, but there are brokerage firms that specialize
in "underwriting" municipal bond issues—that is, bringing
them to market.

THE MUNICIPAL BOND DEALERS

The many new municipal issues—or "primary offerings"—have
fostered a vast underwriting industry. Of the several thousand
securities dealers and commercial dealer banks registered with
the SEC, only about a third are active underwriters. Many of
them are regional underwriters that handle their communities'
business and even some major state issues. Still, over half of the
total volume in municipal underwriting is conducted by fewer
than thirty firms in New York, in Chicago, and on the West Coast.

The community of municipal bond dealers is varied. Most
major brokerage houses have departments devoted to underwriting and trading municipal securities. Other smaller firms
specialize in municipals, sometimes even in particular types of
munis, such as housing bonds. Some "retail" dealers trade
munis largely or solely with individual investors. Commercial

banks that are dealer banks, also members of the dealer community, under the provisions of the Glass-Steagall Act, must limit themselves to underwriting general obligation bonds, with a few exceptions.

These dealers and dealer banks take care of the distribution of the new bonds, through their sales forces, to traditional muni bond investors. Households, property and casualty insurance companies, and commercial banks account for over 90% of all municipal bond purchases. Pension funds don't buy municipal bonds because they are already tax-exempt and buy higher-yielding corporate and Treasury bonds instead.

THE FINANCIAL ADVISOR

The issuer's first step may be to seek the services of a financial advisor. Most state and local governments are not adequately staffed or experienced to offer a bond issue without such "outside" advice. These issuers rarely come to market, and have no reason to develop this skill. This financial advisor's role is more often assumed by the relatively small regional underwriter than by the major dealer. The smaller regional dealer has financial advisor specialists who may undertake service in this capacity on a fee basis. Some firms do only financial advisory work.

One of the first decisions that the advisor helps the issuer make is the type of bond to be offered. Municipals can be divided into two broad categories:

1. General obligation (GO) bonds, which include limited tax bonds and special assessment bonds.
2. Revenue bonds, which include industrial development bonds, special tax bonds, and public housing authority bonds.

Any of these types may or may not be tax-exempt depending on their date of issuance and purpose.

GENERAL OBLIGATION BONDS

General obligation bonds may be issued by states, cities, towns, or counties. All GO bonds are, in one way or another, backed by the taxing power of the issuer. Therefore, only an issuer with the power to tax may issue GO bonds. Hence, these bonds are also referred to as *full faith and credit bonds*. Defaults are rare, and principal and interest are paid regularly.

Generally, states have greater taxing powers than their political "local" subdivisions—cities, towns, villages, school districts, counties—and they usually rely on personal and corporate income taxes, as well as on sales and gasoline tax or highway use taxes as security for the bonds. Usually without the taxing powers of states, local issuers have to rely on ad valorem (assessed valuation) taxes to back their GOs. Such taxes, the most common source of security revenue, are often levied in mills per dollar of assessed valuation (a mill equals one tenth of one cent). For example, if a property is assessed at $100,000 and the tax rate is 8 mills, the tax due is $800 ($100,000 × .008). Often, however, local governments share in state taxes, such as sales taxes.

LIMITED TAX BONDS

When a legal limit is imposed on the taxing power of the issuer, general obligation bonds are then called *limited tax bonds;* in other words, taxes may not be raised indefinitely to cover the debt. Bonds not restricted in this way are called *unlimited tax bonds*.

SPECIAL ASSESSMENT BONDS

Special assessment bonds are secured by an assessment on those who benefit directly from the project. For example, if sidewalks are put in with the proceeds of the issue, the residents of the area in which the sidewalks were installed are assessed.

REVENUE BONDS

Revenue bonds may be issued by an agency, commission, or authority created by legislation in order to construct a "facility," such as a toll bridge; turnpike; hospital; university dormitory; water, sewer, and electric districts; or ports. The fees, taxes, or tolls charged for use of the facility ultimately pay off the debt. Governments with the power to tax also issue revenue bonds, but restrict the debt service funds to only those funds from the governmental enterprise that generates these revenues; the government itself does not pledge its own credit to pay the bonds. Examples are water and sewer revenue bonds. In the late 1990s, about two-thirds of municipal new issues were revenue bonds. Because the municipality itself doesn't back such bonds, they are sometimes riskier than general obligation bonds, and frequently pay a correspondingly higher interest rate. Defaults, while not frequent, can occur.

In some cases, especially with respect to sewer and electric system special assessment bonds, the underlying municipality or state assumes liability for the debt service if the income from the project is insufficient. Such issues are thus more like GOs than revenue bonds, and they are referred to as *double-barreled issues.*

INDUSTRIAL REVENUE OR INDUSTRIAL DEVELOPMENT BONDS

Industrial revenue or industrial development bonds enjoyed a vogue in the 1960s, but legislation has since curtailed them somewhat. With this type of issue, an authority created by a municipality would float a "tax-exempt" bond, construct a factory or other project with the proceeds of the bond issue, and then enter into a long-term net lease agreement with an industrial corporation. The "rent" would pass through the authority to the bondholders as tax-exempt income. In effect, the corporation constructed a new plant at municipal borrowing rates, which are lower than corporate borrowing rates due to the tax-free nature of the interest income. Smaller issues (below $10 million) may still be offered, and issues already outstanding in the secondary market are not affected. They may, however, be subject to the federal alternative minimum income tax as tax preference items. New issues are essentially restricted to those that improve civic services, such as airports, harbors, mass transit, or pollution control facilities. The security behind any industrial revenue or development bond is the lease entered into by the corporation and the issuer, and the ability of the corporation to pay its bills.

NOTES

Notes are short-term instruments, usually issued with maturities of less than a year. They are discussed in Chapter 2 under Money Market Products. Notes are issued under a different set of laws than bonds. Sometimes the security offered by bonds is better than the security offered by notes; for example, when New York City defaulted on its notes, it continued to pay interest and maturing principal on its bonds.

CERTIFICATES OF PARTICIPATION (COPs)

Certificates of Participation (COPs) are usually paid from lease revenues of real property or equipment that is used by the issuer. Examples of these include office buildings, trucks, and computer equipment. Debt service payments require annual appropriation by the issuer's governing body. If the appropriations are not made, the debt service may not be paid. This can give COPs an element of risk not present in regular bonds.

SPECIAL TAX BONDS

Special tax bonds are frequently paid for by an excise tax on items such as liquor or tobacco.

PUBLIC HOUSING AUTHORITY (PHA) OR
NEW HOUSING AUTHORITY (NHA)

Public Housing Authority (PHA) or New Housing Authority (NHA) bonds offer United States Government backing to locally issued housing project bonds to assist in constructing low-income housing. The revenues (rents) are expected to pay the debt service, but if they do not, the full faith and credit of the United States Government provides the ultimate security through the Housing and Urban Development Department (HUD). Investors get tax-exempt income plus a government guarantee. PHA or NHA bonds are among the very few tax-exempt bonds that have a United States Government guarantee. They have not been issued since 1974, but the issues had maturities of up to forty years, and these bonds are still available in the secondary market.

In addition to determining the type of bond to be offered, the advisor also helps the issuing municipality to set up a repayment schedule. Issuers have three options: serial bonds, term bonds, or an offering of both serial and term bonds.

Usually, general obligation bonds are issued in serial form. They mature in stages, usually with annual maturities. The issuer's purpose is often to maintain level debt service.

When a serial municipal bond issue comes to market, the managing underwriter writes a new issue scale that lists (1) the par amount maturing each year, and (2) the offering price of each maturity, stated as a percentage of par or as a yield basis. If the yields are lower for the shorter-term bonds than for the longer-term bonds, it is known as a *normal scale*, just as the ascending yield curve is called a *normal yield curve*. If the shorter-term yields are higher than longer-term yields, the scale is said to be *inverted*.

Term bonds all mature on the same date, and usually have a mandatory sinking fund that will pay off part or all of the bonds before final maturity. Term bonds are usually quoted in dollar prices, not yields, and are referred to as *dollar bonds*. Sometimes a particular new issue will have more than one term bond maturity.

A Split Offering

A split offering combines serial and term bonds in a single offering.

Regardless of type, municipal bonds are usually callable before maturity, often with 10-year call protection. For example, a common call feature in the late 1990s was callable in ten years at 102, in eleven years at 101, and in twelve years or more at 100. If the entire issue is not called, frequently it will be called in part in inverse order of maturity; that is, the longest maturities are called first. If an entire maturity is not called, the bonds will be chosen by lot within the maturity.

Besides the financial advisor, the issuer often calls on other specialists for expert help in such fields as engineering, architecture, ecology, and other aspects of the issue.

The Bond Counsel

The legal "specialist" is the bond counsel, who is responsible for the legal opinion that accompanies almost every municipal bond issue. In preparing the opinion, the bond counsel addresses two key legal needs: One is that the requirements of local laws, the state constitution, judicial opinions, and enabling legislation or procedures are all met, and the bonds are legally issued and are valid obligations of the issuer. The second is that the interest income is exempt from federal income tax (if it is so exempt) according to federal laws and regulations, and exempt from state income taxes (if it is so exempt). There is also at least an implication that the counsel has done some work to make sure that nothing important has been omitted and that all statements are truthful and correct.

The bond counsel collects all the documents that ensure the legality of the issue into what lawyers call a *transcript of proceedings*. The transcript is given to the underwriter before the bond issue is distributed to investors. The counsel also makes sure that the bonds are issued properly and in accordance with the law, and usually checks signatures and terms on the final documents.

Years ago most of the bond counsel work was done by a relatively few firms; now many law firms do this. The importance of this work has not generally been recognized by individual investors, but institutional investors always check the legal opinion and the law firm that issues it. Figure 6-1 on pages 105-107 shows a sample legal opinion, which you should study.

MUNICIPAL BOND INSURANCE

Municipal bond insurance started in the early 1970s when AMBAC and MBIA started offering municipal bond insurance policies, but it became important in the mid 1980s, when the percentage of new issues insured rose to over 20%. In the late 1990s, the percentage of new issues insured was between 40% and 50% each year.

Municipal bond insurance guarantees that the insurer will pay interest and principal on the insured bonds, as they become due, if the issuer fails to make the payments. It doesn't matter why the issuer fails to make the payments, it only matters that he or she doesn't pay. The insurer will also make mandatory sinking fund payments if they are not paid by the issuer. These are the only payments the insurer will make.

Most municipal bond insurance is sold as part of the new-issue process. The bonds are insured at issue, the insurance becomes part of the bond description, the insurance policy is printed on the bond certificate (if a bond certificate exists), and the insurance premium is paid when the new issue of bonds is delivered.

Bond insurance has become an important part of the municipal new issue business, and an important part of the municipal bond business. In 2000, about 39.6% of municipal new issue was insured. This was down from the mid-1990s, due to a combination of high premiums and more stringent underwriting standards. Since some new issue was of such high quality as to make bond insurance uneconomical, and other new issue was of such low quality as to be uninsurable, the percentage of eligible new issue was even higher.

Bond insurance offers municipal bond investors three advantages:

- the improved security given by the resources of the insurance company
- an Aaa/AAA/AAA rating from the rating agencies
- market homogeneity due to the insurance

Most of the bond insurers, and all the largest ones, have a AAA rating from at least one major rating agency. The buyer of bond insurance gets a higher rating for his or her bonds.

Buyers of insured bonds don't usually care much about the actual issuer; they only care about the insurance. The buyer of an insured bond owns "insured paper," which trades in its own market as an insured bond. As a result, the bond belongs to a much wider pool of similar paper, increasing its desirability, and as a result, increasing its salability. The owner of insured paper is likely to receive a better price for such a bond when the time comes to sell it.

Bond insurers also provide insurance to secondary market bonds, but this is a small part of their overall business, about 10.3% in early 2000.

Bond insurance is mostly bought by retail (individual) investors. No one knows for sure what percentage of insured new issue is bought by individual investors, either directly or through unit investment trust or mutual funds, but one informed estimate puts it at about 80%. In about twenty-five years, bond insurance has achieved an important place in the municipal bond new-issue business. See Figure 6-2 for a sample bond insurance policy. You should read and study this insurance policy.

APPENDIX 1

Form of Opinion of Hawkins, Delafield & Wood

March 29, 2001

Long Island Power Authority
333 Earle Ovington Blvd.
Uniondale, NY 11553

Ladies and Gentlemen:

We have examined a certified record of proceedings relating to the issuance of $300,000,000 Electric System General Revenue Bonds, Series 2001A (the "Series 2001A Bonds") of the Long Island Power Authority (the "Authority"), a corporate municipal instrumentality of the State of New York (the "State") constituting a body corporate and politic and a political subdivision of the State.

The Series 2001A Bonds are issued under and pursuant to the Constitution and statutes of the State, including the Long Island Power Authority Act, being Title 1-a of Article 5 of the Public Authorities Law, Chapter 43-A of the Consolidated Laws of the State of New York, as amended (herein called the "Act"), and under and pursuant to proceedings of the Authority duly taken, including a resolution adopted by the Trustees of the Authority on May 13, 1998 entitled "Electric System General Revenue Bond Resolution", as supplemented by a resolution of said Trustees adopted on March 1, 2001 (collectively, the "Resolution").

The Authority has heretofore issued bonds (the "Outstanding Bonds") under the Resolution. The Resolution provides that the Authority may issue additional Bonds (as defined in the Resolution), and incur Parity Obligations (as defined in the Resolution), thereunder from time to time on the terms and conditions and for the purposes stated therein. The Outstanding Bonds, the Series 2000A Bonds, such additional Bonds, if issued, and such Parity Obligations, if incurred, will be equally and ratably secured under the Resolution, except as otherwise provided therein.

The Series 2001A Bonds are dated, mature, are payable, bear interest and are subject to redemption, all as provided in the Resolution.

We are of the opinion that:

1. The Authority is duly created and validly existing under the laws of the State, including the Constitution of the State and the Act. Under the laws of the State, including the Constitution of the State, and under the Constitution of the United States, the Act is valid with respect to all provisions thereof material to the subject matters of this opinion letter.

2. The Authority has the right and power under the Act to adopt the Resolution and to perform its obligations thereunder, including its rate covenant relating to the establishment and maintenance of System fees, rates, rents, charges and surcharges. The Authority has received all approvals of any governmental agency, board or commission necessary for the adoption of, or performance of its obligations under, the Resolution, including the approval of the New York State Public Authorities Control Board. The approval of the Public Authorities Control Board of the acquisition of the Long Island Lighting Company by the Authority directs the Authority to obtain the approval of the New York State Public Service Commission prior to implementing certain rate increases.

3. The Resolution has been duly and lawfully adopted by the Authority, is in full force and effect, is valid and binding upon the Authority, and is enforceable in accordance with its terms. The Resolution creates the valid pledge which it purports to create of the Trust Estate (as defined in the Resolution), subject only to the provisions of the Resolution permitting the application thereof for the purposes and on the terms and conditions set forth in the Resolution.

App. 1–1

FIGURE 6-1A. FORM OF OPINION

4. The Series 2001A Bonds have been duly and validly authorized and issued in accordance with the laws of the State, including the Constitution of the State and the Act, and in accordance with the Resolution, and are valid and binding special obligations of the Authority, enforceable in accordance with their terms and the terms of the Resolution, payable solely from the Trust Estate as provided in the Resolution. The Authority has no taxing power, the Series 2001A Bonds are not debts of the State or of any municipality thereof, and the Series 2001A Bonds will not constitute a pledge of the credit, revenues or taxing power of the State or of any municipality thereof. The Authority reserves the right to issue additional Bonds and to incur Parity Obligations on the terms and conditions, and for the purposes, provided in the Resolution, on a parity of security and payment with the Series 2001A Bonds and the Outstanding Bonds.

5. Any registration with, consent of, or approval by, any governmental agency, board, or commission that is necessary for the execution and delivery and the issuance of the Series 2001A Bonds has been obtained.

6. The adoption of the Resolution, compliance with all of the terms and conditions of the Resolution and the Series 2001A Bonds, and the execution and delivery of the Series 2001A Bonds, will not result in a violation of or be in conflict with any term or provision of any existing law, or of any approval by any governmental agency, board or commission necessary for the adoption of, or performance of the Authority's obligations under, the Resolution.

7. The Financing Agreement, dated as of May 1, 1998, between the Authority and Long Island Lighting Company d/b/a LIPA (as successor by merger to LIPA Acquisition Corp.) (the "Subsidiary") has been duly authorized, executed and delivered by the Authority and the Subsidiary and is a valid and binding obligation of the parties thereto, enforceable in accordance with its terms. You have received a separate opinion of Clifford Chance Rogers & Wells LLP, New York, New York, the Disclosure Counsel to the Authority and the Subsidiary, dated the date hereof, as to the valid existence of the Subsidiary and as to certain other matters relating to the Subsidiary, all of which we have assumed, without further investigation, in rendering the opinions in this paragraph 7.

8. Under existing statutes and court decisions and assuming continuing compliance with certain tax covenants described herein, (i) interest on the Series 2001A Bonds is excluded from gross income for Federal income tax purposes pursuant to Section 103 of the Internal Revenue Code of 1986, as amended to the date hereof (the "Code"), and (ii) interest on the Series 2001A Bonds is not treated as a preference item in calculating the alternative minimum tax imposed on individuals and corporations under the Code; such interest, however, is included in the adjusted current earnings of certain corporations for purposes of calculating the alternative minimum tax imposed on such corporations. In rendering the opinions in this paragraph 8, we have relied on certain representations, certifications of fact, and statements of reasonable expectations made by the Authority and the Subsidiary in connection with the Series 2001A Bonds, and we have assumed compliance by the Authority and the Subsidiary with certain ongoing covenants to comply with applicable requirements of the Code to assure the exclusion of interest on the Series 2001A Bonds from gross income under Section 103 of the Code.

9. The original issue discount on the Series 2001A Bonds, if any, that has accrued and is properly allocable to the owners thereof under Section 1288 of the Code is excludable from gross income for Federal income tax purposes to the same extent as other interest on the Series 2001A Bonds.

10. Under existing statutes, interest on the Series 2001A Bonds is exempt from personal income taxes imposed by the State or any political subdivision thereof, and the Series 2001A Bonds are exempt from all taxation directly imposed thereon by or under the authority of the State, except estate or gift taxes and taxes on transfers.

The opinions expressed in paragraphs 2, 3, 4 and 7 above are subject to applicable bankruptcy, insolvency, reorganization, moratorium and other laws heretofore or hereafter enacted affecting creditors' rights, and are subject to the application of principles of equity relating to or affecting the enforcement of contractual obligations, whether such enforcement is considered in a proceeding in equity or at law.

App. 1–2

Source: Long Island Power Authority.

FIGURE 6-1B. FORM OF OPINION

Except as stated in paragraphs 8, 9, and 10, we express no opinion regarding any other Federal or state tax consequences with respect to the Series 2001A Bonds. We render our opinion under existing statutes and court decisions as of the issue date, and assume no obligation to update our opinion after the issue date to reflect any future action, fact or circumstance, or change in law or interpretation, or otherwise. We express no opinion on the effect of any action hereafter taken or not taken in reliance upon an opinion of other counsel on the exclusion from gross income for Federal income tax purposes of interest on the Series 2001A Bonds, or under state and local tax law.

We express no opinion as to the accuracy, adequacy or sufficiency of any financial or other information which has been or will be supplied to purchasers of the Series 2001A Bonds.

This opinion is issued as of the date hereof, and we assume no obligation to update, revise or supplement this opinion to reflect any facts or circumstances that may hereafter come to our attention, or any changes in law, or in interpretations thereof, that may hereafter occur, or for any other reason whatsoever.

Very truly yours,

App. 1–3

Source: Long Island Power Authority.

FIGURE 6-1C. FORM OF OPINION

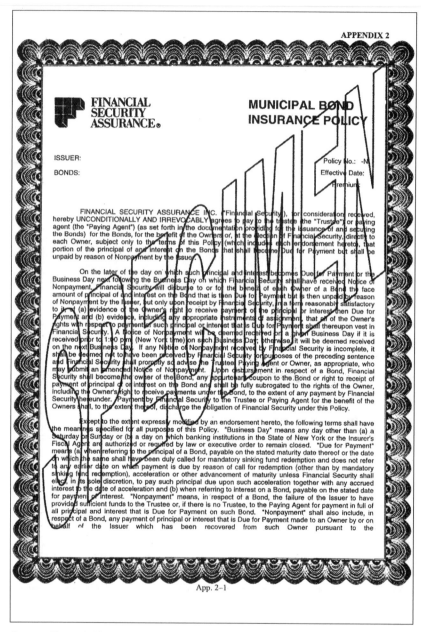

Source: Financial Security Assurance Inc.

FIGURE 6-2A. MUNICIPAL BOND INSURANCE POLICY

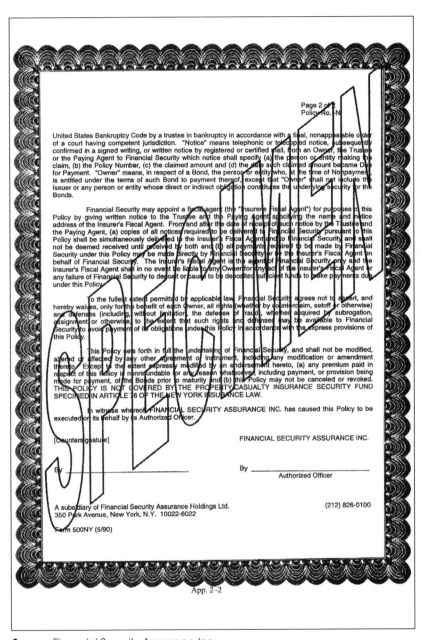

Page 2 of 2
Policy No. -N

United States Bankruptcy Code by a trustee in bankruptcy in accordance with a final, nonappealable order of a court having competent jurisdiction. "Notice" means telephonic or telecopied notice, subsequently confirmed in a signed writing, or written notice by registered or certified mail, from an Owner, the Trustee or the Paying Agent to Financial Security which notice shall specify (a) the person or entity making the claim, (b) the Policy Number, (c) the claimed amount and (d) the date such claimed amount became Due for Payment. "Owner" means, in respect of a Bond, the person or entity who, at the time of Nonpayment, is entitled under the terms of such Bond to payment thereof, except that "Owner" shall not include the Issuer or any person or entity whose direct or indirect obligation constitutes the underlying security for the Bonds.

Financial Security may appoint a fiscal agent (the "Insurer's Fiscal Agent") for purposes of this Policy by giving written notice to the Trustee and the Paying Agent specifying the name and notice address of the Insurer's Fiscal Agent. From and after the date of receipt of such notice by the Trustee and the Paying Agent, (a) copies of all notices required to be delivered to Financial Security pursuant to this Policy shall be simultaneously delivered to the Insurer's Fiscal Agent and to Financial Security and shall not be deemed received until received by both and (b) all payments required to be made by Financial Security under this Policy may be made directly by Financial Security or by the Insurer's Fiscal Agent on behalf of Financial Security. The Insurer's Fiscal Agent is the agent of Financial Security only and the Insurer's Fiscal Agent shall in no event be liable to any Owner for any act of the Insurer's Fiscal Agent or any failure of Financial Security to deposit or cause to be deposited sufficient funds to make payments due under this Policy.

To the fullest extent permitted by applicable law, Financial Security agrees not to assert, and hereby waives, only for the benefit of each Owner, all rights (whether by counterclaim, setoff or otherwise) and defenses (including, without limitation, the defense of fraud, whether acquired by subrogation, assignment or otherwise, to the extent that such rights and defenses may be available to Financial Security to avoid payment of its obligations under this Policy in accordance with the express provisions of this Policy.

This Policy sets forth in full the undertaking of Financial Security, and shall not be modified, altered or affected by any other agreement or instrument, including any modification or amendment thereto. Except to the extent expressly modified by an endorsement hereto, (a) any premium paid in respect of this Policy is nonrefundable for any reason whatsoever, including payment, or provision being made for payment, of the Bonds prior to maturity and (b) this Policy may not be canceled or revoked. THIS POLICY IS NOT COVERED BY THE PROPERTY/CASUALTY INSURANCE SECURITY FUND SPECIFIED IN ARTICLE 76 OF THE NEW YORK INSURANCE LAW.

In witness whereof, FINANCIAL SECURITY ASSURANCE INC. has caused this Policy to be executed on its behalf by its Authorized Officer.

[Countersignature]

FINANCIAL SECURITY ASSURANCE INC.

By _____

By _____
Authorized Officer

A subsidiary of Financial Security Assurance Holdings Ltd.
350 Park Avenue, New York, N.Y. 10022-6022

(212) 826-0100

Form 500NY (5/90)

App. 2-2

Source: *Financial Security Assurance Inc.*

FIGURE 6-2B. MUNICIPAL BOND INSURANCE POLICY

THE SYNDICATE

Neither the financial advisor nor the bond counsel, however, actually brings the issue to the market. That is the work of the underwriter, or more specifically, the syndicate. A syndicate is a temporary partnership of dealers under the direction of a senior manager. It has been set up to underwrite and sell a particular issue of bonds. Usually the syndicate has a life of about 30 days, although it may be disbanded if it sells the bonds sooner, or if it is unsuccessful in winning them to sell.

The makeup of syndicates varies. For example, one co-manager might be a major dealer with branches from coast to coast, and the other co-manager could be a regional firm with extensive distribution channels in the issuer's locale. Another dealer/member of the syndicate might specialize in sales to institutional clients, and still another in sales to individual investors.

Competitive syndicates almost always have a historical basis. That is, the same groups, with the same members, spring to life again to bid on new issues of certain issuers whenever these issuers come to market. Members of the underwriting department of municipal bond dealers check the competitive "Sealed Bids Invited" section of *The Bond Buyer* each day to see whether they head up syndicates that bid on these issuers. If they do, they start the process going again by writing a syndicate letter and sending a copy to the prospective syndicate account members. Usually they also telephone the account members. Sometimes old account members drop out, are no longer in business, and sometimes new dealers want to join the account. Occasionally members want to increase their participations as well.

The dealer involved in competitive bid syndicates may bid on five or more underwritings in one day and actually participate in that many winning bids per week. The staff involved are used to keeping up a fast pace and making spur-of-the-moment decisions.

Syndicates can have as few as two members or as many as one hundred or more. They can have more than one manager (that is, they may have co-managers), but only one manager, the "senior" or "lead" manager, actually "runs the books of the account."

Syndicates are held together by the "syndicate letter" or contract, which states the conditions and obligations of membership and specifies the details of the underwriting, the amount of the bonds, bid and offering terms, names of the managers and members, priority of orders, and similar information. The syndicate letter, following Municipal Securities Rulemaking Board (MSRB) regulations, also describes the priority of orders received by the syndicate. Usually this priority order is as follows:

- *Presale orders*—Orders received by the syndicate before the actual bid is submitted.
- *Group account orders*—Next filled are orders for the group as a whole. These are usually at the net offering price. They are credited to each member according to each member's participation.
- *Designated orders*—Next filled are orders that specify which syndicate members will receive a credit. They are usually also at net prices, but a special credit is given only to members designated by the customer, for par amounts designated by the customer.
- *Member takedown orders*—Orders from members for sale to the members' own customers. These are taken from the account at the full takedown price; the member will receive the entire full takedown upon sale of the bonds to retail customers.

Each account member has a share in the account, called *participation,* and shares in the profits (and losses, if any) of the syndicate according to this participation. Each member of the syndicate is responsible for selling bonds, and when all the bonds are sold, the syndicate profits are then split according to each member's participation. Sometimes the bonds in the account are distributed to each member, once more according to participation. The bonds, most likely term bonds, are then said to be "split up among the members."

Syndicates may be involved in two types of underwriting mechanisms: *competitive bids* and *negotiated offerings.*

In both types of underwriting, the essential business structure is the same. The syndicate buys the bonds from the issuer at one price and resells them at a slightly higher price for a profit.

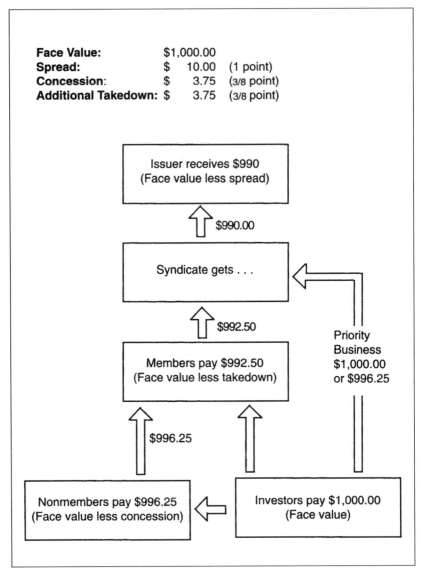

FIGURE 6-3. TAKEDOWN AND OTHER SYNDICATE SALES

The firms charge no commissions on the sales of the bonds because they are acting as "dealers" or as "principals." Either term means that they buy and sell for their own accounts. They may charge a commission only when they execute trades on behalf of clients, that is, when they act as "brokers" or as "agents."

The difference between the price at which the syndicate buys the bonds and the price at which the bonds are sold is called the *spread* or maximum gross operating profit in the municipal underwriting. The manager allocates the bonds to syndicate members at the *takedown* price. The takedown price is typically about 1/2 point, or about $5.00 per $1,000 par amount of principal below the offering price. The bonds are then sold to the public.

As an example, the syndicate purchases each bond in an offering at a 1-point discount. For each $1,000 it pays $990 to the issuer. The spread is therefore 1 point, or $10. If the full takedown is 3/4 point, each syndicate member purchases its bonds at $992.50 each ($1,000 − $7.50), and then offers them to the public at par. Thus, the managing underwriter keeps 1/4 point per bond in the account, and each member keeps 3/4 point (see Figure 6-3 on page 112).

Sometimes a dealer not in the syndicate has a client order to fill and buys from the syndicate members to fill it. The nonmember's compensation is the *selling concession* or simply *concession*. It is included in the takedown. For example, in a typical breakdown between the member and the nonmember dealer, if the takedown is 3/4 point, and the selling concession is 3/8 point, the nonmember makes $3.75 on the sale and the member makes the other $3.75. Recently, some large issues don't have concessions.

In a negotiated offering, the issuer approaches the underwriter directly; a competitive underwriting involves many more steps, the first of which is for the issuer to make its intentions known to prospective underwriters.

By law, *competitive bidding* must be used for the sale of many general obligation bonds. To solicit bids, an issuer publishes an "official notice of sale" in the financial news and in some general publication as well. Active issuers also generally send copies of the notice to dealers they have worked with in the past.

An ad in the municipal bond industry's trade paper, *The Bond Buyer,* is a must. Anyone involved with munis reads this paper, especially people in the syndicate departments of dealer firms. The paper itemizes most negotiated and competitive issues in one of three sections: "Sealed Bids Invited," "Negotiated Offerings," and "Official Bond Sale Notice Advertisements." A related company offers a new issue worksheet service online, a successor to a service, "The Bond Buyer's Worksheets," that was long accepted throughout the municipal bond industry. Complete presale and post-sale information is offered on both competitive and negotiated new issues. *The Bond Buyer* reports on bond sales, shown in the sections "Negotiated Bond Sales" and "Competitive Bond Sales."

With the word out about an upcoming competitive offering, the initiative rests with the dealers. To understand how dealers conduct a competitive bid, however, you need to know who does what inside the firm's municipal bond department.

■ WHO DOES WHAT INSIDE THE MUNICIPAL SECURITIES DEALERS

Within the dealers, the municipal department is normally composed of six areas:

1. The underwriting, or syndicate, area consists of one or more people who decide on and conduct underwritings. They set prices and yields on new issues, sit in on pricing meetings, coordinate with other dealers, and keep the firm's traders and sales staff current on upcoming offerings.

2. The *traders* do not actively participate in selling a new issue. Instead, they buy and sell the bonds in the "secondary" market, after the primary offering is complete. Nevertheless, they need to be informed of pending issues in order to prepare for maintaining an inventory of the bonds later on. Larger trading sections have traders who specialize in types of munici-

pal bonds. In smaller firms and regional branches of large firms, the trading and underwriting functions may be done by the same person.

3. The *sales* personnel become very involved in primary offerings. While the syndicate staff will evaluate the salability of a new issue and price it, the salespeople are the ones who actually make the calls and make the sales. The salespeople also give the underwriting staff valuable presale information on who will buy the prospective new issue, how much they will pay, what maturities they are interested in, and, in some cases, how to structure the new offering in terms of serial or term arrangements, and the preferred coupon rate on the new bonds.

The large brokerage houses with a retail (or individual investor) orientation may even locate a special group of people, called the *marketing* or *liaison* group, near the trading desk at the main office. As the branch salespeople call in orders to the sales group at the main office, the orders are passed on to the traders for execution. In other firms, instead of installing a "liaison" sales group with the main office traders, traders are located at each of the branch offices.

The syndicate, sales, and trading people all sit in a large room that is equipped for trading. Before them are quotation consoles and phone systems that link them with customers and other members of the municipal bond dealer community. The offering itself, if priced properly and sold aggressively, is often sold out within the day.

Most dealers now use computer systems to show their municipal bonds to their salespeople, who, in turn, show these bonds to their customers.

4. The *public finance* group has the task of drumming up new negotiated underwriting. Occasionally, they may also offer their services as financial advisors for a fee, but their main emphasis is getting negotiated underwriting business. This involves a great deal of travel and calling on prospective bond issuers.

Commercial banks may also have a public finance group, but the emphasis is frequently on financial advisory work. However, they can work on prospective negotiated underwriting of GO bonds, and frequently housing and educational revenue bonds.

5. *Municipal research* assumed greater importance when it became apparent that municipal issuers could default. At one time the rating agencies were the sole source of credit information on state and local issues, but now municipal research sections have come to be increasingly vital to successful underwritings. Generally this department prepares a concise opinion before the dealer makes a commitment in a negotiated offering or a bid in a competitive deal. Like other research, this opinion may be made available to the institutional and individual clients of the firm.

6. *Operations* processes orders, issues payment checks, takes and makes deliveries of securities, and performs other required recordkeeping functions. This area, also known as the "back office," is responsible for "clearing" the trades that the firm makes with or on behalf of its customers and other dealers.

Each of these six areas has an important role to play in both negotiated and competitive underwritings.

■ HOW A COMPETITIVE UNDERWRITING WORKS

As the firm bids on upcoming bond issues, the syndicate people keep the salespeople up-to-date, usually in a Monday morning meeting. At these meetings, each issue is received and a sales strategy devised. Usually, the salespeople work a little harder on upcoming negotiated offerings because they are certain that their firm will have them for sale. Figure 6-4 shows a diagram of how a competitive bid works.

The actual competitive bidding process on a particular issue begins with an opinion from the research staff. While municipal

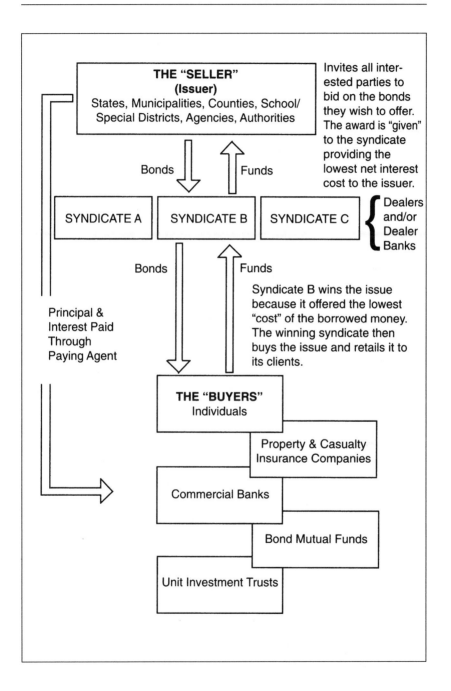

FIGURE 6-4. COMPETITIVE BIDS

issuers call on rating agencies to rate their offerings, the syndicate staff in the brokerage firm generally wants an independent evaluation. If this opinion is strong enough, the firm may put in an aggressive bid, on the assumption that, given an assurance of selling out the issue, they can offer a lower-interest cost to the issuer. Of course, if the research department's analysis is weak, the dealer may not even submit a bid.

To come up with a competitive bid, syndicate members hold several price discussions, with the manager leading. These used to be actual price meetings, and some meetings are still held, but most discussions, especially in cases of small syndicates, are held by phone. For other messages, the manager may communicate with members by means of the *The Bond Wire*, a newswire run by the *Bond Buyer* organization, using the Internet, that may also be used to send information only to specified clients of the service.

Preliminary price meetings or phone conferences, usually held the day before the sale, are low-keyed. Members of the syndicate discuss the salability of the upcoming offering—spread, prices, yields, and other information. One important topic is the "reoffering scale," which is the array of prices and yields for each maturity in the issue. See Figure 6-6 for the cover of an Official Statement for a new issue, which includes reoffering prices and yields. (Note, however, that this is a negotiated new issue.) These prices and yields are distributed to the firm's sales staff.

The overall goal is to reach agreement on a set of yields for the new bonds that balances two objectives. One is to keep the yields high enough to attract investors and to make the issue salable. As input on this score, the syndicate group gets the feedback of its sales and trading people, who advise the group on what yields investors are looking for. The second objective is a low enough issuer cost to win the bid. To issuers, interest represents cost, so the lower the interest, the better. That is why competitive bids are awarded on the basis of interest cost; that is, whichever syndicate offers to buy the issue at the lowest interest cost to the issuer wins the bid. Two different measures are used, "net interest cost" (NIC) and "true interest cost" (TIC), which is also sometimes called "Canadian interest cost" (CIC). Both measure the interest cost to the issuer, but use different calculation methods.

About an hour before the bid is due, the manager convenes the final price meeting or telephone conference, which is usually more tense than the first. It begins with the presentation of the proposed scale, perhaps suggesting the spread, and a report on orders and on the latest developments in the municipal bond market. Then discussion is opened. Members suggest other scales, often disagree, and even occasionally drop out of the syndicate. While orders continue to come in, with some issues sold out before the meeting is over, members argue for perhaps a wider spread or a lower scale. Another item discussed is the "order period"—the time during which all orders will have equal priority in execution. Usually the order period is one hour.

Only minutes before the deadline, the final scale is calculated by the firm's computer and the bid phoned to the person who is to deliver it to the issuing municipality or an advisor. The manager is responsible for ensuring that the sealed bid is delivered, usually by hand, to the municipality. With the bid goes a good-faith check, usually for about 2% of the total value of the issue. The municipality may use the good-faith money if the dealer should fail to deliver the proceeds of the sale and pick up the bonds. This rarely happens.

After the bidding deadline, the issuer computes the interest cost of each bid, and awards the bonds to the winning bidder. The winning bidder does not actually own the bonds until the issuer has awarded them to him. The actual award could take place hours or even days later, but usually the bonds are awarded promptly.

The apparent winner is known within several minutes of the bidding deadline, when the competing syndicates generally reveal their bids to one another. (Almost always the apparent winner is also the real winner, but on rare occasions a mistake is made in the bid submission or interest cost calculation, and the apparent winner turns out not to have won the bonds after all.)

If their syndicate is the apparent winner, the salespeople start selling immediately. By the time the selling commences, the senior manager has released a letter to syndicate members describing the bonds, their coupons and reoffering yields, the selling concessions, and other information. The senior manager also sends this information for distribution over *The Bond Wire* and other wire services.

Orders are awarded according to the priority stated in the syndicate letter. All orders are considered "when-issued" orders and are contingent on the actual delivery of the bonds. Most municipal bonds are arbitrarily dated the first or the fifteenth of the month of issuance. The *offering date* is the date on which the bonds are sold to the public. For competitive offerings, this is also the date of sale. However, the bonds must be printed (if they will have certificates), arrangements must be made with Depository Trust Company, and legal work must be done before the bonds can be delivered. This usually takes about one month, so until then the bonds are sold and traded on a *when, as,* and *if issued* basis. (If the bonds are not issued, the trades are canceled.) The firm will sell and deliver the bonds *when* they are issued, *as* they are issued, and *if* they are issued. Usually, the bonds are delivered about four weeks after the offering date. Interest accrues to the seller from the dated date and up to, but not including, the settlement date. (The dated date is the date the bonds start to accrue interest.)

During the selling period, the manager performs a number of other duties. He keeps the books for the syndicate and confirms orders over the phone after the order period.

Hot issues—that is, issues in great demand—can sell out in a couple of hours. Usually, however, bonds are left after the order period, and orders are taken on a first-come, first-served basis. The syndicate is disbanded when the issue is sold out. Most syndicates run for about thirty days, but the members can renew if necessary. Few offerings run that long, however. When an issue does not sell in thirty days, the syndicate can change the terms of the offering. This usually requires the majority consent of the members, voting according to their participations.

If the issue still cannot be sold, the bonds can be distributed among the members, or given to a "bond broker."

A bond broker (or "broker's broker") trades only with other municipal bond dealers. These firms do not deal directly with investors. Of the approximately four to six such brokers in the country, almost all are located in New York City.

Municipal bond dealers turn to these brokers when they want to either sell or buy bonds for their inventory; the brokers are another source of both bids and offers. When selling, bond brokers gather bids from other brokers and municipal bond dealers; this is called the "bid-wanted" business. When buying, they circulate the fact that they are willing to buy a particular bond at a stated yield or price.

When an issue proves to be particularly difficult to sell, the remaining bonds can be given to one broker or to a group. The brokers then "put the bonds out for the bid." Syndicate members, like any other dealer, can bid for the bonds. Whoever has the best bid for the group of bonds gets them, although the manager has the right to reject all the bids. Brokers get a commission of as much as 1/8 point ($1.25 per bond), but usually less, for completing this transaction.

There are some differences between competitive bids and negotiated deals, which is the subject of the next section.

■ HOW A NEGOTIATED UNDERWRITING WORKS

Competitive offerings provide excitement, romance, and glamour, but most municipal new-issue volume is brought to market by a somewhat different type of underwriting, called a *negotiated* underwriting. In the late 1990s, negotiated underwritings accounted for about three-quarters of total municipal bond new-issue volume. Figure 6-5 shows a diagram of how a negotiated sale works.

A negotiated underwriting has a syndicate that underwrites and sells the bonds, but it is created in a totally different way from those for competitive bids. In the case of a negotiated underwriting, the lead manager, usually the other managers, and sometimes even the syndicate members are chosen by the issuer.

Municipal bond investment bankers compete for this business. They will call on prospective new issuers of bonds, hoping that the issuers will choose their firm to bring the issuer's bonds to market when the issuer decides to sell bonds. Investment bankers may call on an issuer for years before any bonds actu-

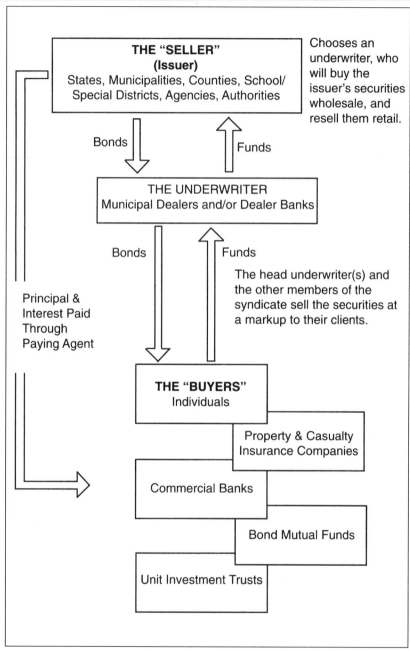

FIGURE 6-5. Negotiated Sale

ally come to market, and even then, that firm may not get the business.

When the issuer decides to sell bonds, it usually interviews many prospective investment bankers before it decides which firms to employ to bring the bonds to market. Based on the results of the interviews, the issuer selects the lead manager, the joint managers, and sometimes even the actual syndicate members. Several considerations enter into the selection process. These include the underwriter's record of selling the issuer's bonds in previous issues, the location of the underwriter (is the underwriter located in the issuer's region?), advice the firm has given in previous issues, personal relationships built up over the years, and other factors.

When the syndicate has been formed, a *syndicate letter,* or agreement among underwriters, provides a contractual basis for its operation.

The lead manager and the joint managers then negotiate with the issuer the terms, structure, timing, and placement of the issue. They advise the issuer on when the issue should come to market; if the market is unfavorable, they may advise the issuer to withdraw temporarily the issue from the market. They will advise the issuer on whether to use serial or term bonds, or some combination of these; whether to use bond insurance on some or all of the maturities; what the coupon rates and reoffering yields should be, especially whether to offer zero coupon bonds; and other features of the issue. They will also negotiate the total spread for the issue, and even the components, which include takedown, expenses, underwriting fee, and management fee. The management fee, which is shared only by the managers—with the lead manager usually getting by far the largest share—is the reason that investment bankers compete for this business in the first place.

When the terms of the issue have been decided, the underwriters offer the bonds for sale. Based on the market's response, they may change the terms of the offering. If the issue has good acceptance in the market, the underwriters may be able to raise the offering prices (lower the offering yields). If the issue has not sold well, the underwriter may lower the prices. Underwriters do not often have more than one repricing.

The lead underwriter, when satisfied with the sales performance, calls the issuer, reports on the issuer's status, and asks, "Do we have a deal?" The issuer responds favorably (the underwriter hopes), and the agreement is informally made; this is called the "handshake." The handshake is not legally binding. The underwriter owns the bonds only after the issuer has formally awarded them; usually this does not take long.

The underwriter publicizes the new issue and its terms, sending notices over the newswires and by other means of communication. The sales force, of course, is actively marketing the bonds. The lead manager keeps the syndicate members informed on the progress of the deal in the marketplace. At this point, in most respects, the negotiated underwriting and the competitive underwriting become similar.

■ AFTER THE OFFERING

About one month elapses between the time that the issue is first brought to market and the bonds are actually delivered and paid for. During that time, the certificates are being printed (if the issue will be in registered form and have certificates), or arrangements are made with Depository Trust Company (DTC) (if the issue will be in pure book-entry form). There are other depositories, but almost all municipal new-issue depository business goes to Depository Trust Company. DTC is a cooperative owned by its members and operated for their benefit. The legal work is finished, and the legal opinion and the bond insurance contract, if the bonds are insured, are printed on the certificates.

At the same time, the manager has to wrap things up and sends a letter to syndicate members stating the "reoffering terms," that is, the terms by which the bonds are to be reoffered to investors and other buyers. Such terms include the spread, takedown, and concession. The letter also explains how the issue will be advertised and how members will be represented in the ad. (Syndicate members are generally listed in accordance with the size of their participation, with the greater participants closer to the top of the ad.)

When the bonds are ready for delivery, all payments are made. To pay the issuer, the manager arranges a loan from a commercial bank. If the manager or any other member of the syndicate is a bank, it may make the loan. The check to the issuer is for the amount agreed upon less any good-faith deposit. The bonds are then delivered and distributed to the members who pay for them. The members in turn fill orders and receive payments for their orders. The manager retires the loan, later distributes the profits among the members, and sends the members a final statement of participations, expenses, and profits.

All this takes a few days.

At about the same time, the issuer makes available a disclosure statement on the new issue, called an *official statement* (OS). This document is not required by federal law, but almost every issuer provides one. The Municipal Finance Officers Association (MFOA) encourages state and local governments to disclose primary offering information. Moreover, the Securities and Exchange Commission (SEC) now requires underwriters to make sure that issuers agree to provide continuing financial information if they want to underwrite the bonds; this accomplishes the same thing. Larger issues frequently have a preliminary official statement, which is distributed to prospective buyers before the sale, and contains substantially the same information as the final official statement, except, of course, the final terms of the issue. Figure 6-6 shows the cover page and inside cover page of an OS.

An official statement includes all the legal, financial, and other types of information that investors need to make intelligent investment decisions about the new municipal bond issue. The cover page of the official statement summarizes the issue. It shows information on ratings, authority for issuance, delivery date and place, security for the issue, and, of course, maturity amounts, dates, coupon rates, and reoffering yields or prices. The document is also sent to various municipal bond information storage and retrieval centers.

MSRB regulations require that a final official statement be sent to every person who purchases a new-issue bond during the underwriting period, which is generally the period from the date

NEW ISSUE—Full-Book-Entry

In the opinion of Bond Counsel to the Authority, under existing statutes and court decisions, and assuming continuing compliance with the tax covenants described herein,(i) interest on the Offered Securities is excluded from gross income for Federal income tax purposes pursuant to Section 103 of the Internal Revenue Code of 1986, as amended to the date of delivery (the "Code"), and (ii) interest on the Offered Securities is not treated as a preference item in calculating the alternative minimum tax imposed on individuals and corporations under the Code; such interest, however, is included in the adjusted current earnings of certain corporations for purposes of calculating the alternative minimum tax imposed on such corporations. See "Tax Matters" in Part 1 of this Official Statement. In addition, in the opinion of Bond Counsel to the Authority, under existing statutes, interest on the Offered Securities is exempt from personal income taxes imposed by the State of New York or any political subdivision thereof, and the Offered Securities are exempt from all taxation directly imposed thereon by or under the authority of the State of New York, except estate or gift taxes and taxes on transfers.

$300,000,000

LONG ISLAND POWER AUTHORITY

Electric System General Revenue Bonds, Series 2001A

Dated: Date of Delivery   Maturity: September 1, as shown on inside cover page

The Electric System General Revenue Bonds, Series 2001A (the "Offered Securities") will be issued only as fully registered bonds registered in the name of Cede & Co., as nominee of The Depository Trust Company, New York, New York, which will act as securities depository for the Offered Securities under the book-entry-only system described herein. Individual purchases of beneficial ownership interests in the Offered Securities may be made in the principal amount of $5,000 or any integral multiple thereof. Beneficial Owners of the Offered Securities will not receive physical delivery of bond certificates. United States Trust Company of New York, New York, New York, is the Trustee under the Resolution.

The Offered Securities are being issued for various capital purposes as described herein.

Interest on the Offered Securities is payable on September 1, 2001 and semiannually thereafter on each March 1 and September 1.

The Offered Securities are subject to optional redemption and mandatory sinking fund redemption prior to maturity as described herein.

The scheduled payment of principal of and interest on the Offered Securities maturing on September 1, 2027 and September 1, 2028 (the "Insured Bonds") when due will be guaranteed under an insurance policy to be issued by FINANCIAL SECURITY ASSURANCE INC. concurrently with the delivery of the Offered Securities.

ℙ FSA

MATURITY SCHEDULE — See Inside Cover Page

The Offered Securities are special obligations of the Authority payable principally from the revenues generated by the electric system owned by its subsidiary, LIPA, after the payment of operating expenses of the System, on a parity with other Electric System General Revenue Bonds and other Parity Obligations of the Authority. The Offered Securities shall not be a debt of the State of New York or of any municipality, and neither the State of New York nor any municipality shall be liable thereon. The Authority shall not have the power to pledge the credit, the revenues or the taxing power of the State of New York or any municipality, and neither the credit, the revenues nor the taxing power of the State of New York or any municipality shall be, or shall be deemed to be, pledged to the payment of any of the Offered Securities. The Authority has no taxing power.

The Offered Securities are offered when, as and if issued and accepted by the Underwriters, subject to the approval of legality by Hawkins, Delafield & Wood, New York, New York, Bond Counsel. Certain legal matters with respect to the Authority and LIPA will be passed upon by Stanley B. Klimberg, Esquire, General Counsel to the Authority and LIPA, and by Clifford Chance Rogers & Wells LLP, New York, New York, Disclosure Counsel to the Authority and LIPA. Certain legal matters will be passed upon for the Underwriters by Nixon Peabody LLP, New York, New York, counsel to the Underwriters. It is expected that the Offered Securities will be available for delivery in book-entry-only form through The Depository Trust Company in New York, New York on or about March 29, 2001.

Salomon Smith Barney

	Bear, Stearns & Co. Inc.	Goldman, Sachs & Co.
	Lehman Brothers	UBS PaineWebber Inc.

ABN AMRO Inc.	Advest, Inc.	M♦R♦Beal & Company
CIBC World Markets	Dain Rauscher, Inc.	eBondTrade, LLC
A.G. Edwards & Sons, Inc.	First Albany Corporation	First Union National Bank
Jackson Securities Inc.	Raymond James & Associates, Inc.	Lebenthal & Co., Inc.
David Lerner Associates, Inc.	McDonald Investments, Inc.	Merrill Lynch & Co.
JPMorgan	Prager, McCarthy & Sealy	Quick & Reilly, Inc.
Ramirez & Co., Inc.	Roosevelt & Cross Incorporated	Siebert Brandford Shank & Co., LLC

Dated: March 22, 2001

Source: *Long Island Power Authority*

FIGURE 6-6A. COVER PAGE OF OFFICIAL STATEMENT

Maturity Schedule

$300,000,000

LONG ISLAND POWER AUTHORITY

Electric System General Revenue Bonds, Series 2001A

Maturity (Sept. 1)	Principal Amount	Interest Rate	Yield
2013	$ 435,000	4.60%	4.65%
2013[1]	1,325,000	5	4.65
2014	310,000	4.70	4.75
2014[1]	1,090,000	5	4.75
2015	100,000	4.80	4.85
2015[1]	910,000	5	4.85
2016	595,000	4.90	4.93
2017	410,000	5	5.00
2019	6,195,000	5	5.16
2020	5,620,000	5	5.19
2021	305,000	5⅛	5.22
2021[1]	4,665,000	5⅛	5.22

$ 75,645,000 5⅜% Term Bonds due September 1, 2025 — Yield 5.28%[1]

$112,035,000 5% Term Bonds due September 1, 2027 — Yield 5.16%[2]

$ 37,965,000 5¼% Term Bonds due September 1, 2028 — Yield 5.10%[1,2]

$ 52,395,000 5⅛% Term Bonds due September 1, 2029 — Yield 5.33%

---

[1] Priced to first par call on September 1, 2011.
[2] Insured by Financial Security Assurance Inc.

Source: Long Island Power Authority

FIGURE 6-6B. INSIDE COVER PAGE OF OFFICIAL STATEMENT

the issue is first offered to the public to the date the bonds are delivered and paid for. This must be sent, even if the buyer did not buy the bonds from a member of the underwriting syndicate; the buyer's own broker has the responsibility of sending the final OS.

As the syndicate disbands, the bonds become available for purchase and sale in what is known as the "secondary market," which is the subject of Chapter 9. In the next chapter, we will see how corporate bonds are created and marketed.

Corporate Bonds

Corporations can raise capital in a number of ways. For short periods—that is, for less than five years—they can raise funds through commercial bank loans, promissory notes, or certificates, whether offered publicly or privately. Most banks, however, will not tie up funds in a loan for more than five years, because they are exposed to interest-rate risk along with anyone else in the fixed-income market. If, for example, a bank extends a loan at 8% for more than five years, what revenues would it lose if interest rates were to rise above 8% during the term of the loan? Its money should be earning greater returns.

To gain the use of capital for more than five years, corporations may turn to sources other than commercial banks. Borrowing from other financial institutions, such as pension funds or insurance companies, is one possibility. An alternative is distributing stocks or bonds.

Bonds offer issuing corporations several advantages over stocks. Issuing stock, or shares of ownership, can weaken the control of the company's founders over decision making and policy setting. Bonds, on the other hand, do not dilute the equity of the current shareholders.

Bonds are also preferable to bank loans because they provide capital at rates of interest that may be lower than bank rates. A commercial bank takes deposits from its customers, pays them one rate of interest, and lends the money to, among other clients, corporations in need of capital. When a company sells bonds directly to investors, it effectively cuts out the bank acting as a middleman—and a tier of interest rates. The borrowing process thus becomes more efficient and less expensive.

Bond issues are even more efficient in that the corporation is spared the burden of having to negotiate a separate loan agreement with every potential creditor. Large amounts of capital can be borrowed from hundreds or even thousands of investors through a single, uniform instrument.

■ HOW A NEGOTIATED CORPORATE UNDERWRITING WORKS

Once the corporation's board of directors decides to offer a bond issue, it almost always employs the services of an *investment banker,* that is, a securities dealer acting as an underwriter in a primary offering of corporate securities.

Corporate underwritings are similar to municipal offerings in that an underwriter acts as the intermediary between the issuer and the investing public, but there are several important differences. For one thing, corporations are not under a mandate, as many municipalities are, to obtain competitive bids. So almost all corporate offerings are negotiated. Also, unlike municipal debt securities, corporate bonds are subject to the requirements of the Securities Act of 1933. So the underwriting process is different enough from a negotiated municipal offering to merit further description.

The Securities Act is simple in this respect: Unless the law classifies a security as "exempt," any security sold interstate must be registered with the SEC before it may be offered publicly. (Figures 7.1 and 7.2 list exempted securities and transactions.) Although the word "security" calls to mind stocks and bonds, the Act defines a security as *any* note, stock, bond, evidence of debt, interest or participation in a profit-sharing agreement; investment contract; voting trust certificate; fractional undivided interest in oil, gas, or other mineral rights; or any warrant to subscribe to or to purchase any of the foregoing. Thus, the 1933 Act, sometimes referred to as the "Full Disclosure Act," protects investors in any public offering by threatening those who willfully violate the law with fines of up to $10,000 and jail sentences of up to five years.

1. U.S. Government, including ones it guarantees

2. States their political subdivisions, and their political instruments, including ones they guarantee

3. Domestic banks or trust companies (but not bankholding companies)

4. Commercial paper or bankers acceptances maturing within 9 months

5. Building and loan associations

6. Farmers' cooperative associations

7. Equipment trust or similar, issued by common carriers, such as railroads

8. Court-approved receivers' or trustees' certificates

9. Small business investment companies (SBIC)

10. Intrastate (see SEC Rule 147 in "Private Placement" section)

11. Religious, educational, charitable, or nonprofit

12. Insurance policies or mixed annuity contracts (but not variable annuities or variable life insurance policies)

13. Offerings that qualify under Regulation A of the Securities Act of 1933. A less costly way to accomplish a distribution, Regulation A permits a qualified registration exemption for small yearly offerings of not over $5,000,000 by a corporation. It does require distribution of an informative offering circular.

14. Offerings that qualify under Regulation D of the Securities Act of 1933. SEC Rules 501-506, under Regulation D, set forth the terms and conditions under which issuers can offer unregistered securities for sale in limited dollar amounts to a limited number of investors and/or to defined "accredited persons." For the most part these unregistered offerings are called private placements.

15. Generally, securities issued in exchange for other securities.

16. Securities offered and sold only to residents of a single state by an issuer resident and doing business in the state, or a corporation incorporated by and doing business within the state.

FIGURE 7-1. SECURITIES EXEMPTED FROM REGISTRATION UNDER THE SECURITIES ACT OF 1933

1.	Those by anyone other than the issuer, a dealer, or an underwriter
2.	Broker's transactions that are not solicited from the customer (in other words, the customer takes the initiative)
3.	Private placements (as opposed to public offerings)
4.	Transactions by securities dealers (*except* when the dealers are still handling an unsold allotment of a registered new issue, or handling trades within ninety days of an initial public offering or forty days of subsequent public offerings of that registered new issue)

FIGURE 7-2. TRANSACTIONS EXEMPTED FROM REGISTRATION UNDER THE SECURITIES ACT OF 1933

THE COOLING-OFF PERIOD

Unless either the security or the transaction is classified as exempt, all new issues of securities must be registered with the SEC. To do so, a registration statement must be filed which must contain the information and documents relevant to the affairs of that company and to the offering in question. If the issuer omits or misrepresents any material fact, the purchasers of the offering may sue to recover part or all of their investments from the issuer, the underwriter, or both.

The date on which the public offering is to commence is usually set for twenty days after the statement is filed with the SEC. During this 20-day *cooling-off* period, as it is frequently called, the SEC examines the statement to determine whether it contains any obvious omissions or misrepresentations. If it finds any, it sends the issuer a *deficiency* (or *bedbug*) *letter*, and the effective date is postponed until the deficiency is corrected. Sometimes a longer period may be required, especially for complicated offerings or during especially active periods.

In some cases, the issuer may request an earlier effective date. If it has a record of compliance with previous issues, if it is up-to-date in its SEC reporting requirements, or if it promises to deliver a preliminary prospectus (covered later in this chapter) at least 48 hours prior to the effective date, the public offering may begin as soon as 48 hours after filing the registration statement with the SEC. After receiving either a regular registration statement or an application for an earlier effective date, the SEC notifies the issuer only if the date is not approved for any reason.

Whatever the effective date turns out to be, it must be strictly observed. In no case may a distribution take place before this date. Even an offer to sell before that date violates the law. On the other hand, if the issuer/underwriter does not make the offering within three days after the effective date, the SEC must be notified immediately.

Whether an all-or-none offering is going to be offered may be unclear for weeks or months. In such a case, the registration statement may remain effective for up to nine months, and in the case of bond or stock issues by large publicly held corporations, for up to two years, as long as no material changes occur in the affairs of the corporation.

Only the issuer—that is, a corporation, trust, or association that issues securities in return for funds—may register the security with the SEC.

When the statement becomes effective, it assures would-be investors *only* that the prospectus contains all the information required by law. By accepting the statement, the SEC neither guarantees the issue nor approves the security as an investment. It does not even state that the information is accurate.

Thus, investors have to make their own investment decisions based on what they see in the prospectus. The law does stipulate, however, that the prospectus is the only written offering for a new issue that may be used and that the prospectus must be delivered to purchasers with the confirmation of purchase—at the very latest. The prospectus, therefore, is the basis for any suit by investors against the issuers or underwriters whose names appear in the statement. Misrepresentation by a salesperson may also give rise to suits.

The Trust Indenture Act of 1939 picks up where the 1933 Act leaves off on bond issues. For SEC-registered debt securities, issuers are obliged to make the same relevant facts available to the SEC in a formal registration statement.

United States Government and municipal securities are exempt from the Trust Indenture Act. However, corporate issuers of bonds with a principal amount of $1 million or more must give the SEC an *indenture qualification statement* that specifies the obligations of the issuers and the duties of the trustee(s). The law also requires that one or more trustees be appointed to see to it that the terms of the indenture are carried out. Trustees, who must not have conflicting interests, qualify themselves with the SEC annually, and act as a fiduciary for the bond issue.

The indenture qualification statement registers only the indenture with the SEC. In general, it is part of the registration statement for a bond issue. If a bond is not required to be registered, the statement will be filed separately.

The corporate issuer may distribute securities without meeting the requirements of this Act, in what is known as a *private placement.* Subject to numerous restrictions and requirements, a *private placement* is an offering of securities that has not been registered with the SEC. Since it does not require registration and a prospectus because the investors do not intend to resell the securities in the immediate future, a private placement is less costly than a public offering. Such investors, however, must give the issuers "investment letters," which state the investors' intention not to resell the securities. If they should resell the unregistered securities, they may be regarded as "statutory" underwriters under the terms of the Securities Act of 1933. Each subsequent transfer of unregistered securities must be accompanied by an investment letter, which transfers title to the new private owner, who likewise intends to hold the securities for a portfolio and not for resale. Each unregistered certificate must be imprinted with a legend that warns the holder about distribution restrictions under the law. Because a private placement represents an exemption from the Securities Act of 1933, however, it is laden with numerous restrictions and requirements. It is not an option that is practical for every issuer.

Many corporate issuers opt instead for a public offering, in which the new issue is distributed directly to investors at large. (The process is described later in this chapter.) In a private placement, the issue is offered to a limited number of purchasers, who are often institutional investors. The offering is sold directly by the issuer to the purchaser, often without the help of the investment banker, at lower overall cost because such a placement avoids the expenses of a public offering.

THE INVESTMENT BANKER

Once the corporation has selected a securities dealer to act as underwriter, the investment banker may act as either principal or agent. As *principal*, it purchases the issue from the firm, assumes the financial responsibility for selling it, and resells it to the public. Regardless of its success—or the lack of it—in selling the issue to the public, the underwriter must pay the full contracted price to the issuer. Generally, only the more reputable corporations whose securities have a proven history of success can get such an arrangement. For making this commitment, investment bankers receive a higher fee than they would if they acted as agents. In fact, sometimes the commitment is so risky that underwriters ask for a *market-out* clause—an "escape hatch" provision that relieves them of their obligations under certain conditions. When underwriters make such a guarantee to the issuer, it is called a *firm commitment*; that is, they agree to sell all of the offering or retain any securities that they cannot distribute, at the same time guaranteeing the full proceeds to the issuer. In effect, they absorb a loss for any undistributed securities. Note that this is somewhat similar to a competitive bid for municipal securities, in which the successful underwriter owns the securities whether or not he or she can sell them at the original offering prices.

When acting as agent, an investment banking firm is committed to selling only as much of the issue as possible. It has no financial responsibility to the issuer for any part of the offering not distributed. Naturally, the fees are lower for this kind of service, known as a *best efforts* commitment. Small corporations with little or no track record must content themselves with this arrangement. In some cases, if a concern cannot get a firm commitment, it may decide on an *all-or-none offering*, that is, if *all* of the offering is not sold, then *none* of it will be. The entire offering is then canceled.

Investment bankers may also act as "standbys" in the issuance of new securities by a *subscription privilege*. This right or privilege enables present holders to purchase portions of the new issue within a fixed period (usually thirty to sixty days) before the issue may be offered to the public. In such a case, the issuer may ask an underwriter to guarantee the distribution of any leftover shares or bonds not sold through the rights offering. The underwriter, acting as a principal, agrees to "stand by" until the rights period expires. Such an arrangement is called a *standby agreement*, or a *standby underwriting*.

After registering the security with the SEC, the issuer and underwriters have a number of additional obligations:

■ The preliminary prospectus must be issued.
■ The due-diligence meeting must be held.
■ The issue must be "blue-skyed."
■ The agreement among underwriters must be signed.
■ The agreement between the underwriters and the issuer must be signed.

After these matters are attended to and the registration statement is scrutinized by the SEC, a final prospectus is issued for the public offering.

Let's take these steps one by one.

THE PRELIMINARY PROSPECTUS

Solicitation of orders for new issues may not take place until the effective date, and the only offer in writing that may be made is by the prospectus. Yet the law allows underwriters to obtain *indications of interest* ("circle") from investors by sending them a preliminary prospectus. This prospectus, the *red herring*, alerts prospective buyers that the document is not final and that it is not a solicitation for an order. Although the red herring contains most of the pertinent information, often including the "maximum" offering price to give investors a general idea of the issue's value, that information is incomplete and possibly even inaccurate. Customers who indicate an interest in the new issue simply contact their broker/dealer, who often uses this indication of interest to decide whether or not to participate in the underwriting group.

DUE-DILIGENCE MEETING

All syndicate participants and corporation officials must hold a "due-diligence" meeting sometime before the effective date. The purpose of this meeting is to review the items to be included in the formal agreement between them, such as what is to go into the registration statement, what is to go into the final prospectus (used to solicit orders), and points of negotiation for the underwriting agreement between the issuer and the investment bankers. Price may also be discussed, but it is not set until the night before or the morning of the effective date to allow for accommodation to prevailing market conditions.

In a competitive bidding situation, the competing groups do not discuss price with the corporation, only within their own group so that no group gains an unfair advantage. In this case, the due-diligence meeting is usually called an *information meeting*.

BLUE-SKYING THE ISSUE

To be sure that the offering complies with state laws, attorneys for the underwriters check out the laws of each state where an offering will be made. This process is called *blue-skying the issue*. (When the Kansas state legislature passed the nation's first state securities law in the early 1900s, one of the lawmakers quipped, "Now Kansas citizens will have more of a basis for making investment decisions than merely by the shade of the blue sky.") If the legal maze makes the underwriters' involvement impractical, they will often cancel out of the deal.

AGREEMENT AMONG UNDERWRITERS

Soon after the due-diligence meeting, the underwriters participating in the distribution draw up an agreement among themselves, which specifies, among other things, the responsibilities of the manager, including the following:

1. *Forming the Syndicate.* Once part of a syndicate, an investment banking firm may safely assume that its association with the group will continue for all future underwritings in which any one of them acts as manager. In fact, once established as a significant distributor of securities in such offerings, an investment banker becomes recognized as a "major-bracket" participant, and its name is publicized near the top of the group's tombstone ad. The percentage of its underwriting commitment ranks equally with other major-bracket firms. Other investment bankers in those syndicates may be classified as submajor-, middle-major-, and minor-bracket underwriters, depending on their percentages of participation.

Once an underwriter has taken indications of interest and decides to participate in a group, it becomes subject to Rule 10b-6 of the SEC. This rule prohibits an underwriter from either buying a security in the marketplace for its own account or from inducing someone else to buy it while the distribution is pending.

2. *Appointing a Selling Group.* The manager also appoints other broker/dealer firms who agree to act as agents for the underwriters and to offer some of these securities to their customers. These firms make up what is known as the *selling group*. Each selling group member is allocated a portion of the issue to sell. Though selling group members abide by the terms and restrictions of the underwriting agreement, they do not receive the full underwriters' spread, because they assume no individual responsibility or financial liability to the issuing corporation. Their *selling concession* may range from 25% to 75% of the spread, depending on how difficult it is to sell the issue.

It is not unusual to see firms wearing two hats, acting as both underwriters and as members of the selling group. With a commitment as underwriters and an allocation as selling group appointees, their "double duty" enables them not only to enjoy greater participation in the offering, when the issue is popular, but also to better satisfy their clients. Even when the issue isn't that popular, underwriters use selling groups because members of today's selling group may be tomorrow's managing underwriters in other offerings.

3. *Establishing the Underwriters' Retention ("the Pot").* The manager holds back a part of the issue (often about 25%) for allocation to the selling group and to institutional purchases, who deal in substantial quantities. This reserved allocation is called *the pot.* Since, in effect, each group member gets only 75% of its commitment, the manager's juggling of percentages is a touchy responsibility. Keeping everyone happy is the name of the game. Participants or customers want what they want, and the underwriters' rationale is easily understood: "If we must assume financial responsibility for the deal, we should enjoy the benefits of popular distributions and be able to satisfy our own customers first."

4. *Conducting Group Sales. Group sales* are not sales made by the selling group. Rather, they are sales made out of the pot. If an institutional investor wants, say, $1,000,000 worth of bonds, the manager fills the order out of the pot, rather than taking the securities from each of, say, ten underwriters. Unless the purchaser designates otherwise, all syndicate members benefit pro rata according to their participations. In this respect, group sales are similar to those from a municipal bond syndicate. Group sales are good sales stimulators. When the manager announces, "The pot is clean!" sellers find that orders come in more quickly because investors realize that institutions consider the offering a good investment.

5. *Stabilizing the Market.* Either on the effective date or within a couple of days thereafter, the underwriters begin making their public offering. At about the same time, the security begins to trade openly in the marketplace. This trading activity is called the *aftermarket.* Since the underwriters are bound to the terms of their agreement with the company, they cannot allow the market price to go much below the public offering price. So unless the offering is an immediate

sellout, the managing underwriter is empowered to maintain a bid in the aftermarket at or perhaps slightly below the public offering price, on behalf of the syndicate. This *syndicate bid* may be continued for as long as necessary, but it typically lasts no more than two weeks.

This is the one time when manipulating a market price is legal. Ordinarily, anyone found manipulating the market price of securities is subject to prosecution by the SEC under the terms of the Securities and Exchange Act of 1934. But stabilization to facilitate a bona fide distribution of securities is exempt from this restriction. Prompt notice, however, must be filed with the SEC and with the appropriate exchange.

When stabilizing aftermarket prices, the syndicate manager has no intention of repurchasing the entire issue. Often the manager notifies participating firms that the stabilizing bid is made with a penalty attached. In this case, their customers should not enter the aftermarket to sell this new security at the price of the stabilizing bid. Otherwise, the member firms either lose their spread or concession, are penalized so much per bond, or are not allowed to participate in future offerings.

A "penalty syndicate bid" is written into agreements between the underwriters and selling groups to ensure that participants strive to distribute the issue to investment portfolios and not to traders and speculators intent upon quick profits.

Although syndicate managers must make every attempt to maintain the public offering price, they have the authority to release members from that obligation if they see that the task has become hopeless. The security then fluctuates to its true level, as determined by market forces, even though the underwriters are still financially responsible to the issuer.

6. *Allocating Hot Issues.* Syndicate managers need not worry about maintaining the public offering prices of "hot issues," which are securities that trade at an immediate premium in the aftermarket. This situation is a happy but delicate one. Using their business judgment, managers can legally oversell issues by up to 15% of the offering, because they will probably get that many cancellations.

Even if they do not, they can cover their short positions in one of two other ways: Managers can go into the aftermarket and purchase the securities. This alternative is not considered a stabilization effort because the syndicate pays the offering price or more. Any loss sustained in this process, like the losses sustained in stabilization, is apportioned pro rata to each member. That's one way.

Another way is for the corporation to grant the underwriters an option or warrant to purchase additional securities of the offering at a price below that of the public offering. This arrangement, called a *green shoe privilege*, is usually exercisable within thirty days after the effective date at the underwriter's guaranteed price. This right, considered a new security, is registered with the SEC via an amendment to the original registration statement. The manager exercises the option, closes out the short position, and distributes the profit to each member pro rata.

AGREEMENT BETWEEN UNDERWRITERS AND THE CORPORATION

This formal contract, called the underwriting agreement or the purchase agreement, establishes firm prices. Signed the evening before or on the morning of the effective date, the contract is immediately filed with the SEC and becomes part of the registration statement via amendment. The agreement also reflects the nature of the syndicate's responsibility to the issuer.

THE PUBLIC OFFERING

Once the public offering is permitted to begin, underwriters start to solicit orders from investors, whether those investors saw the red herring or not. The only way that the underwriters may legally solicit orders is by means of a *final prospectus*, which is a condensation of the information in the updated, amended registration statement. At the very latest, the final prospectus must be sent to purchasers with their confirmation statements. This requirement is so strict that investors who make a purchase without having seen the final prospectus may cancel their orders, even after receiving their confirmation orders, without any penalty or loss.

No margin may be extended by a participating distributor to purchasers of a new issue during the distribution and for up to thirty days thereafter. A tombstone advertisement is also published about this time.

Once the bonds have been fully distributed through the efforts of the underwriters' salespeople, the security starts trading in the secondary market along with the debt issues of the United States Government, federal agencies, municipalities, and other corporations.

■ TYPES OF CORPORATE BONDS

The lower interest rate is particularly important to a corporate issuer because the corporation's purpose is different from that of the United States Government or municipalities. Governments at any level must raise money to provide public services, but business corporations exist to make a profit. When they borrow money, the interest becomes part of the cost of doing business. They must earn a profit at a greater rate than they incur expenses—including interest expense. Using borrowed money to generate a greater return than the rate of interest paid out on the loan is called *leverage*, and this is a characteristic of corporate debt offerings, but not of Treasury or municipal issues.

Corporate bonds also differ from government issues in that the ability of the issuer to pay must be more closely scrutinized. Whereas Treasury and many municipal securities are backed by taxing power, corporate debt needs to be secured in other ways. As a result, corporate bonds are usually categorized according to how they are collateralized. Corporate bonds vary widely in this respect. If a company is financially strong and if the amount of money needed is reasonable, a company may be able to issue a bond that is secured only by its general credit. On the other hand, if the issuer is not financially sound, investors will probably be interested only in bonds secured by tangible assets.

Mortgage bonds are secured (or collateralized) by a legal claim to specific tangible assets of the issuer, such as real property like an office building or factory. If the company defaults on payments due the bondholders, the bondholders have direct claims on the assets pledged.

If the bond indenture states that the agreement is *open-end*, the company can also use the property so pledged as collateral for *additional* borrowing. Open-end mortgage bonds are normally issued in a series. All issues in the series give the holders the same claim to the common collateral, or equal "seniority," that is, no holder has a "senior" claim over the holder of another bond in the series.

Issues in a series can differ by having varying interest rates and other distinguishing features. One way in which issues differ is that their maturities are usually staggered according to a schedule set forth in the indenture. The issuing company's total long-term capital needs are met with the capital borrowed only as needed, and the debt is paid off in stages instead of in a lump sum.

If the bond is *closed-end*, the first lender has "senior status," that is, first claim on the mortgaged property. Other loans can still be secured by the same property, but they are junior to the claims of the prior bondholders.

Sometimes, if a company undergoes reorganization or faces bankruptcy, it might ask senior bondholders to surrender their status to a new class of creditors willing to lend capital; these new creditors, in turn, become senior bondholders. This new issue, called a *prior lien bond*, is then regarded as a first mortgage, and the former issues become second mortgages.

Any investor in corporate bonds should note that just because a bond is secured by a mortgage does not mean that the foreclosure process is a quick and smooth one. In fact, usually even mortgage bonds must accept new securities in a reorganization. In addition, the property pledged frequently has rather restricted uses; it may have been used for the purposes of a particular business, and may be useful only in that business. The business that actually used the property may have had difficulties; that is why the bonds are being restructured. For example, property used to secure railroad bonds is likely to be railroad property, useful only to a railroad that is already having trouble.

A *debenture* is a bond that is backed only by the general credit of the issuer. Investors who purchase debentures become *general* creditors of the company. They are protected by the overall assets of the issuer, not by a particular asset, as are mortgage bondholders. Usually, only strong corporations with excellent credit are able to sell debentures, whereas financially weak corporations typically must resort to pledging specific assets as collateral.

Debentures can be senior or subordinated. A *senior* issue has first claim on company assets; a *subordinated* debenture by the same company has second claim.

An *equipment trust certificate* is a specialized type of security that is backed by specific types of equipment. Frequently this is railroad rolling stock (railroad locomotives, cars, and the like), but trucks, airplanes, and other similar equipment have also been financed by equipment trust certificates. These securities tend to be very safe because the owner is protected by the value of the equipment if the company defaults. Holders have an extra measure of protection in that the payback on equipment trust certificates is generally arranged to stay ahead of the depreciation on the equipment. Also, the equipment generally is easily transferable and standardized. For example, almost all railroads can use rolling stock from another railroad. This gives the trustee of the security (who has the actual title to the equipment) the practical advantage of being able to sell the collateral easily and quickly, to a large number of possible buyers, and is what makes the equipment trust certificate more advantageous than a mortgage bond to investors in cases of difficulty.

The typical equipment trust certificate (ETC) is arranged somewhat as follows. The buyer of the equipment:

- Pays a 20% down payment on the purchase price of the equipment.

- Gives the equipment's title to an independent trustee (a bank), which collects payments from the company and makes payments to the security owners. In case of default, the trustee has the actual title to the property, and can easily sell it to pay the security holders. This ability of the trustee to take prompt, practical action to protect the security holders, as much as any legal rights, actually protects the value of the investment.

After the entire issue is retired, title to the equipment passes from the trustee to the railroad, airline, or transportation company that has been using the equipment. In effect, the user of the equipment pays for it on the installment plan.

This type of issue is structured as a serial issue because it is self-liquidating. That is, it requires partial repayments of principal by means of a series of annual maturities. Smaller amounts often come due for redemption in the first few years, allowing time for the user to build up revenues by making use of the new equipment. Over time, the size of the repayments increases. This progressive increase in the size of payments is called a "balloon effect."

Income bonds are different in that they are not usually issued, but given in exchange for other bonds, usually in the case of impending bankruptcy. The company makes the promised interest payments only if it can afford to do so. If the company is losing money, it may omit making its interest payments. However, if the company is operating profitably, as defined in the bond indenture, it may not take this action.

If the company can't make the interest payments on its income bonds, the missed payments may accrue at a predetermined interest rate and perhaps must be paid off before any dividends can be paid to the common or preferred shareholders. If a company misses an interest payment on any type of bond other than an income bond, the bondholders have the right to force the company into bankruptcy so as to protect their interests. Holders of income bonds, however, cannot force a company into bankruptcy for missing interest payments. In exchange for forfeiting this right, investors earn a higher rate of return on an income bond *when and if* the company makes interest payments. The bond indenture determines the exact contractual requirements for the income bonds. Sometimes interest must be paid to the extent earned, sometimes not. Sometimes interest accumulates if unpaid, sometimes not. Analysts of income bonds examine the indenture very carefully to determine the value of the proposed investment.

■ PRICING CORPORATE BONDS

Like Treasuries, municipals, and most other fixed-income instruments, corporate bond prices react to interest rate fluctuations and to changes in the inflation rate. However, the creditworthiness of the corporate issuer—its ability to pay—is a much more important factor in pricing. The ability to make interest payments and ultimately to repay the loan is indicated by a bond's rating. A highly rated bond, being less risky, commands a lower interest rate than a bond with a low rating.

A bond rating is an opinion on the relative investment merit of a bond. Bonds are rated by bond-rating agencies. The two largest and best known are Moody's Investors Service and Standard & Poor's (owned by McGraw-Hill, Inc.). A smaller but well-regarded rating agency is Fitch Investors Service. A former rating agency, Duff & Phelps, has been absorbed by Fitch. The ratings represent their current opinions on the quality of most large corporate and municipal bond issues, as well as notes, commercial paper, and some other securities. Bond investors watch ratings very closely in order to reduce their exposure to adverse developments.

In evaluating a bond, the rating agencies are most interested in the issuer's financial health, as evidenced by its financial statements. Of course, because ratings are updated periodically, a bond's rating will change with the financial fortunes of the issuer. The rating agencies also consider the business and economic circumstances of the issuer in assigning ratings. For example, is the issuer's economic situation improving, staying stable, or is it possibly declining?

Until the late 1960s, the rating agencies did not charge issuers a fee for their rating services. Instead, they published information services to investors, and earned their profits from these services. In the 1960s, however, rating agencies started charging issuers a fee, and now virtually all issuers, corporate and municipal, must pay. If a rating is not requested, the agency will usually not rate the bonds. Sometimes both an issuer and the investment banker will select one particular rating agency to rate the issuer's bonds because they think that that particular agency has special experience with that particular kind of issuer and will rate it higher. This could result in considerable savings in interest expense.

Figure 7-3 shows the ratings published by the three rating agencies, together with a brief description of each rating. The rating notations of all the services are similar. Moody's ratings range from Aaa, Aa, A, and so on down to C, its lowest. S&P goes from AAA down to D, its lowest. Fitch follows the S&P rating system. Moody's sometimes adds a "1" to indicate the strongest bonds in the groups Aa, A, Baa, Ba, and B. The other agencies sometimes add a "+" or "−" to indicate relative rankings within their assigned rating.

Bond Ratings

Moody's	S&P	Fitch	Meaning of rating
Aaa	AAA	AAA	Highest rating
Aa	AA	AA	Very strong
A	A	A	Strong
Baa	BBB	BBB	Adequate
Ba	BB	BB	Uncertain
B	B	B	Vulnerable
Caa	CCC	CCC	High risk
Ca	CC	CC	
C	C	C	
	D	DDD,DD	Default or
		D	liquidation

Adjustments can be made within a rating category by adding a + or −. For example, AA+, AA, and AA− are all within the AA category. Moody's adds a 1, 2, or 3 to its corporate Aa, A, Baa, and Ba ratings to indicate a rating within the generic category: 1 indicates the higher range; 2, the middle range; and 3, the lower range within the rating category. Moody's sometimes adds a 1 to its municipal Aa, A, Baa, and Ba categories to indicate a somewhat higher municipal rating.

Sources: *Moody's Investors Service; Standard & Poor's, a division of McGraw-Hill, Inc.; Fitch.*

FIGURE 7-3. BOND RATINGS

The one- or two-word description of the meaning of each rating does not do full justice to the one-paragraph description of each rating provided by each bond rating agency. However, it is a reasonable approximation of the meaning. For example, S&P and Fitch consider an A rating "Strong," while Moody's considers it "Adequate." Refer to the full descriptions in the publications of each rating agency for a more complete description of the meaning of each rating from each rating agency.

The bond industry generally considers equivalent ratings as roughly equivalent in meaning. When an issuer has ratings from more than one rating agency, the ratings are usually the same. Different ratings from different rating agencies for the same issuer are rare, and are called *split ratings*. They usually differ by only one level; differences of more than one level are extremely rare.

The first four categories, Aaa (AAA) through Baa (BBB), are called *investment grade*. Many trust investment managers are restricted to investing only in bonds of investment grade; they can own only bonds with these ratings. Bonds with Aaa or AAA ratings reflect the highest capability of the issuer to meet all obligations, whereas Baa-rated bonds indicate below average, but still investment grade quality. Institutional investors, even if not formally restricted, usually confine their bond purchases to the top four categories of bonds.

Bonds with lower than investment grade ratings (Ba, B, Caa, Ca, C, and D) are considered to be *speculative*, which means that the issuer's ability to meet obligations is less certain. These bonds are sometimes called *junk bonds* due to their high yield and high risk.

Some bonds are not rated by a particular agency, so that agency will assign it an NR, meaning "not rated." Frequently, these bonds will be rated by another rating agency. An NR does not necessarily mean that the bond is of inferior quality; it only means that the particular rating agency did not assign a rating. Many fine bonds are NR. However, an issuer that would receive a high rating will generally ask to be rated because the interest savings from the high rating will more than offset the cost of the rating. Investors should particularly scrutinize nonrated bonds for this reason.

To improve the attractiveness of its bonds, an issuer may institute several features that enhance either its creditworthiness or the appeal of the security itself.

One enhancement, especially for municipal issuers, is *bond insurance*. (This was discussed more fully in Chapter 6.) However, sometimes corporations can also buy bond insurance, and sometimes they have other credit enhancement possibilities, such as the use of a letter of credit (LOC). A letter of credit guarantees that the issuer of the LOC will lend money to the company to guarantee that the bond payments will be made. Of course, the company must still repay the LOC issuer if it borrows from it.

Another enhancement is the *sinking fund*. In a sinking fund, the issuing company sets aside a portion of current earnings for the sole purpose of retiring an issue of bonds. Sinking funds offer great protection to the bondholder. To reflect the additional security, the prices of bonds secured by sinking funds are often higher than those of bonds without such funds, and the yields are lower. One reason for the lower yields, of course, is that the bonds with sinking funds will have a shorter average life than bonds without sinking funds, so that the effects of a normal yield curve will result in lower applicable interest rates. This, as well as the greater security, will lead to a lower yield on the bonds.

■ CONVERTIBLE BONDS

Another enhancement is convertibility. A *convertible bond* may be exchanged for a specified number of shares of common stock in the issuing corporation at a predetermined price. Such a bond offers holders not only income, but also the chance to share, through conversion, in the company's fortunes as owners of common stock. Convertible bonds usually yield less than equivalent bonds that are not convertible; this is what the bondholders give up to gain the conversion feature.

The issuing corporation states the conversion price of a convertible bond in the indenture. The *conversion price* is the common stock price at which the bond may be converted. The price is set at such a level that the bondholders do not benefit financially if they convert before the stock reaches the conversion price. For example, suppose a bond's indenture specifies that each $1,000 bond may be converted into stock at $40 per share. That means that each such bond may be converted into 25 shares of common stock ($1,000 face value divided by $40). Bondholders do not benefit financially by conversion, however, until the common stock price exceeds $40 per share, assuming the bonds were originally issued at 100. If the bonds were originally issued at a price less than 100, they would benefit financially at share prices under $40.

Generally, by the time the stock reaches the conversion price, the price of the bond has increased as well.

The number of shares that the holder of a convertible bond receives at conversion is determined by the *conversion ratio*, which is calculated by dividing the face amount of the bond by the conversion price. In the preceding example, the conversion ratio is $1,000 divided by $40, or 25 shares of stock.

The conversion price must be adjusted downward in cases of stock dividends and splits. For instance, suppose the bond has a conversion price of $40, and the stock has a two-for-one stock split. The $40 conversion price is adjusted to $20, and the number of shares to be received (the conversion ratio) is doubled ($1,000 divided by $20) to 50 shares.

These adjustments protect bondholders against "dilution" of their prospective equity in the company. Dilution of equity occurs when additional common stock is issued, resulting in a reduction of the percentage of the company owned by a present shareholder.

Conversion parity is the point at which the market prices of the convertible bond and the corresponding common stock are equal. Conversion parity is calculated using the following formula:

$$\frac{\text{Par value of bond}}{\text{Conversion price}} = \frac{\text{Market price of bond}}{\text{Market price of stock}}$$

Here is an example: A bond is convertible at $20 per share, and the common stock is selling at $35. The formula is then:

$$\frac{\text{Par value of bond}}{\text{Conversion price}} = \frac{\text{Market price of bond}}{\text{Market price of stock}}$$

$$\frac{\$1,000}{\$20} = \frac{\text{Market price of bond}}{\$35}$$

$$\$1,750 = \text{Market price of bond}$$

When the bond is trading at 175, or $1,750 per $1,000 bond, it is worth the same as (that is, it is at "parity" with) the underlying common stock at $35 per share.

If a discrepancy arises between the value of the stock and the value of a convertible bond, an investor could make a profit by simultaneously buying one security and selling the other on the bond and stock markets. This activity is called *arbitrage*, and it is usually practiced only by professional traders called *arbitrageurs*.

■ UNDERSTANDING BOND QUOTATIONS

The investor who wants to enter orders to buy or sell stock needs to know only the issuer's name and current price of the stock. Bond investors need additional information: the bond's coupon rate and its maturity date. Figure 7-4 shows an example of how corporate bond trades are reported if the bonds are traded on an organized exchange. Not all newspapers carry these reports, but many of the major daily newspapers carry them.

Let's look at the first bond, the ATT 6s due in 2009. The description (ATT 6s 09) means that the issuer is AT&T, the bond has a 6% coupon, and the bond matures in the year 2009. Bond investors would refer to this as "sixes of oh-nine." This information tells you two things: First, that the bond will pay $60.00 per year, in two equal semiannual payments of $30.00 each; second, that the bond will mature in the year 2009.

Skip the next column, labeled "Cur Yld," for now.

The column headed "Vol" tells you the number of these AT&T bonds that traded yesterday. In this case, 175 bonds ($175,000 par value) traded.

The column headed "Price" shows the closing (last) price at which the bond traded yesterday. In this case, the bond closed at

94¼, or $942.50 for each $1,000 par value bond. This particular report does not show the highest and lowest prices identified as such; it only shows the closing price.

Remember that bond quotations are not read the same as stock quotations. In stock trading, "94¼" means a stock price of $94.25 for each share. In bond trading, "94¼" means 94.25% of par value, so that a bond with par value of $1,000 would trade at $942.50. In other words, a "point" in a stock price is $1, but a "point" in a bond price is 1% of par, or $10 in a $1,000 par value bond.

Company	Cur. Yld.	Vol.	Price	Chg
ATT 6s 09	6.4	175	94¼	+ 1/2
AMR 9s 16	8.3	25	108⅜	. . .

FIGURE 7-4. A TYPICAL REPORT OF CORPORATE BOND TRADES

The "Chg" (net change) column marks the change in the closing price from the last day's closing price. The AT&T 6s 09 closed up ½ in price from the previous close. This is equivalent to $5.00 per $1,000 of par value.

Now let's go back to the "Cur Yld" (current yield) column. Because the price of the bond is below its face value, it is said to be trading at a *discount*. Because the buyer needs to pay less than par to own the bond, the yield on the investment is increased. So if you apply the current yield formula to this bond, you will find that the current yield is 6.4%—just the figure shown in the column.

A bond that is selling for more than the face amount, such as the second bond shown, the AMR 9s of 2016, is said to be trading at a *premium*. Because the premium in the price represents an increase in the price paid to buy the bond, the buyer is getting a lower percentage return on his investment than if he had paid par. In this case, if you apply the current yield formula, you get a current yield of 8.3%—the amount shown in the column.

New issues of corporate bonds are brought to market almost always through a negotiated underwriting. When the issue is sold out and the syndicate disbanded, most corporate bonds, along with the debt securities of the United States Government, federal agencies, and municipalities, are traded in the over-the-counter market. This part of the so-called "secondary market" is the subject of Chapter 9.

International Bonds

Hanging on the wall of my home office is a defaulted Czarist Russian bond, a gift from a friend. The bond was issued in late 1894, with the first payment, coupon number 1, due March 1/14, 1895. The bond's annual interest rate was 4 percent, and interest was paid quarterly, in rubles. Coupon number 97, due March 1/14, 1919, and subsequent coupons are attached. Coupon number 96, due December 1/14, 1918, was detached for payment. Whether it was actually paid is another matter.

Since 1918, Russian governments have made virtually no payments on defaulted Czarist Russian debt. The loss on Czarist Russian bonds was total, and in the case of the bond displayed on my wall, occurred only about 24 years after its original issuance in 1894.

Yet in 1894, and even up to 1914, it would have been hard to find a country that had better prospects for debt repayment than Imperial Czarist Russia. The government had been in power about 300 years, since Michael Romanov founded the Romanov dynasty in 1613. In 1914, few countries anywhere in the world could have claimed such a long period of governmental continuity; certainly Great Britain, France, Germany, Italy, China, Japan, and even the United States of America could have made no such claim. Russia had the largest land mass empire in the world. The government appeared to be progressing and its competence level appeared to be improving. Russia had repelled the Swedish invasion of the early 18th century and the French invasion of the early 19th century with losses to both invading armies. Napoleon's invading French Imperial Army was almost wiped out in one of the world's most famous retreats (admittedly the weather helped). The Russian economy was growing and living standards were on the rise. And the country's currency was, reportedly, backed almost 100 percent by gold.

What could possibly go wrong with an investment in Russian bonds?

A lot, as it turned out. The Czarist Government helped start a war, which led to its fall in the Revolution of March 1917. The new Provisional Government in turn fell in the Bolshevik Revolution of November 1917. The new Bolshevik Government defaulted on both internal and external debt. Some recoveries were made from Russian government assets in other countries, to make payments on some Russian debts, but the loss on these bonds was almost total.

On the back of my certificate are translations from the Russian into French and German. This is due to the existence of both French and German investors in this debt. Russian external bonds were underwritten by German (Berlin) bankers in the 1870s, and sold mostly to German investors. In the mid-1880s French (Parisian) bankers took over some of this underwriting, and sold the bonds mostly to French investors, in line with the development of the Franco-Russian Alliance. Although both the French and German currencies lost a great deal of value during the First World War and its aftermath, the loss on these currencies, even in the famous German inflation of 1923 and 1924, could not have been any larger than the loss on the Russian bonds (in 1917 or 1918). Perhaps these investors wanted to diversify internationally into what were, for them, foreign bonds. The results could not have been worse for them.

Keep these events in mind as you read this chapter, and whenever you hear about the virtues of investing in foreign securities (of any sort) and of international diversification.

Note also, that with modifications, the third paragraph of this scenario could apply to the United States. Our government has existed for more than 200 years, making it among the oldest and most stable in the world. We have won almost all our wars. Our standard of living is among the world's highest, and our money is accepted worldwide, in some countries as actual legal tender, and in others as a medium of exchange. But who knows what the future will bring?

■ THE DISTINGUISHING CHARACTERISTICS OF A FOREIGN BOND

A domestic, or internal, bond is issued, underwritten, and traded in a country, with the borrower domiciled in the country, in the denomination of the country's currency, and under the laws and regulation of the country. For example, when the United States Treasury, the General Electric Company, or New York City issues a bond in the United States of America, denominated in American dollars, registered with the SEC (if required), and sold by a syndicate of Wall Street (American) investment bankers (or directly, as in the case of Treasuries), and generally bought by Americans, that is a domestic bond for American buyers. These bonds are discussed in other chapters of this book.

You will frequently hear the term *sovereign* bond. Sovereign bonds are issued, and/or guaranteed, by an independent nation. United States Treasuries are sovereign bonds of the United States. The Czarist Russian bonds were sovereign bonds of Russia. Suppose Germany issues some bonds, guaranteed by Germany. These would be sovereign bonds. If an American or German state or city, such as New York State, or Chicago or Bonn, for example, issued bonds, these would not be sovereign bonds.

■ TYPES OF INTERNATIONAL BONDS

Many types of foreign bonds, now called *international bonds*, exist. This section describes the main types and their features. The usual general features of bonds, such as call features and sinking funds, may also apply, depending on the features of each individual bond. These features are also discussed in other chapters of this book.

For most American investors, the important feature of foreign bonds is whether they are denominated in United States dollars (and make payments in U.S. dollars), or in some other (foreign) currency, and make payments in that currency. The former bonds are called *U.S.-Pay International bonds*, the latter bonds are called *Foreign-Pay International bonds*. The complete description of an international bond depends on the issuer's domicile, the domicile of the primary (intended) buyers, the nature of the underwriting syndicate, and the currency denomination of the bonds.

U.S.-Pay International Bonds

There are two main types of U.S.-Pay bonds: Eurodollar bonds and Yankee bonds; however, most are Eurodollar bonds. *Eurodollar bonds* are denominated in U.S. dollars, issued and traded outside of the jurisdiction of any one country, and underwritten by an international syndicate. They are issued in bearer form and pay interest annually. For example, if the City of London issues a bond denominated in U.S. dollars, but underwritten by British underwriters, and traded in several countries, this is a Eurodollar bond.

Yankee bonds are registered with the SEC, underwritten by a United States syndicate, traded primarily in the United States, are in registered form, and pay interest semiannually. For example, if a Japanese firm issues some bonds, registers them with the SEC, has them underwritten by an American underwriter, and they are traded in the United States and payable in United States dollars, with primarily American buyers, this is a Yankee bond.

U.S.-Pay International bonds can be added to a U.S. portfolio without concerns about currency risk. Provided the credit risks are acceptable, they can become part of a portfolio, just like any domestic American bond. The main portfolio concerns are the interest rate and capital gain (or loss) possibilities, just like any domestic bond. With the higher quality credits, the analysis is similar to any domestic bond.

	Eurodollar bonds	**Yankee bonds**
Denomination	U.S. dollars	U.S. dollars
Traded	Outside any one jurisdiction	United States
Underwritten	International syndicate	American syndicate
Form	Bearer	Registered
Pays interest	Annually*	Semiannually

(*Recently, some Eurodollar bonds pay interest semiannually.)

FIGURE 8-1. COMPARISON OF EURODOLLAR AND YANKEE BONDS

Recently an increasing number of global bonds have been issued. *Global bonds* have the characteristics of both Eurodollar and Yankee bonds, and are designed to operate in both markets. The United States tranche (part) of these bonds are registered with the SEC, and are offered and traded in the United States. Another part would not be so registered.

For example, in August 2001, the United Mexican States (Mexico) sold some 8.30% bonds, due August 15, 2031. These were registered, interest and principal payable in United States dollars, and sold in the United States, as part of a global issue. These are Yankee sovereign bonds.

For another example, at about the same time, the Transcontinental Gas Pipeline Corp. sold some 7.00% bonds due August 15, 2011. These were not registered with the SEC, and were not to be sold in the United States, but had interest and principal payable in United States dollars. These were Eurodollar bonds. They were not sovereign bonds, because they were issued by a private corporation, and not by a government.

Another important group of U.S.-Pay International bonds are *Brady bonds*. These are designed for emerging markets and have special features, and are discussed later in the chapter.

FOREIGN-PAY INTERNATIONAL BONDS

For U.S. investors, foreign-pay international bonds are bonds denominated in any currency other than the U.S. dollar. A wide variety of bonds are available to the U.S. investor, but almost all of them are traded outside of the United States. All of them are paid in a foreign currency, which introduces another investment management factor.

NON-U.S. DOMESTIC BONDS

A non-U.S. domestic bond is issued in a country other than the United States, in that country's currency, by a borrower within that country, and meant for purchase by that country's investors. For example, suppose France issues some bonds, denominated in French francs, and meant for purchase by French investors. That would be a non-U.S. domestic bond.

FOREIGN BONDS

Foreign bonds, as a descriptive term, means a bond sold by one country primarily in another country, denominated in the other country's currency. For example, a yen-denominated bond, sold in Japan, by an American corporation such as IBM, would be such a bond; these are called *Samurai bonds*. *Bulldog bonds* are denominated in pound sterling and sold in the United Kingdom by issuers in another country. These bonds allow borrowers to borrow directly from another country's source of funds.

INTERNATIONAL FOREIGN-PAY BONDS

Eurobonds are issued directly into offshore (or international) markets, in a wide variety of currencies. Eurodollar bonds, covered earlier in this chapter, are the U.S.-Pay variety of this bond. However, Eurobonds are denominated in a wide variety of currencies, including pound sterling, Japanese yen, German Deutsche mark, Italian lira, and many other currencies. Previously, Eurobond meant a bond issued by a European country. Now the term means a bond issued in international markets.

▪ SOURCES OF INCOME (AND LOSS) FOR AMERICAN HOLDERS OF INTERNATIONAL BONDS

A typical bond investment for Americans produces income (or loss) from two sources: interest (coupon) income, and capital gain or loss on sale or redemption. The purchase of a foreign-pay bond introduces a third source of gain or loss: currency fluctuation. The investor must decide whether or not to hedge against currency fluctuations. If the investor decides to hedge against currency fluctuations, he or she has protected against them, but at a cost of reduced return. If the investor decides not to hedge, he or she will run the currency fluctuation risk. This may increase the investor's return, if the currencies fluctuate in a favorable way, but could be costly if currencies fluctuate differently. One study showed that income was the most important component over a long (ten-year) time frame, but currency fluctuations can be very important over shorter periods of time. Most individual investors may be unwilling to undertake this additional management concern. The investor will also need access to foreign bond markets to make his trades in these bonds; his own broker may be able to give him this access.

▪ THE SIZE OF THE INTERNATIONAL BOND MARKET

The Bank for International Settlements (BIS) reports on the size of the international bond market. Reporting is somewhat delayed, and also probably subject to variances by country, due to different reporting standards and other factors. In late 2000, the BIS issued a report showing outstanding amounts of international debt securities, by currency of issue, by net issues, and by year.

For 1998, the latest year with full reporting, the BIS showed a total of $4,297.7 billion outstanding, about 80% of the size of the total United States public debt at that time, including nonmarketable issues. About 46% of this, $1,966 billion, was in U.S.

dollars. The next largest currency of issue was the Japanese yen, amounting to about 11% of the total. The Deutsche mark was next, with about 10% of the total. The BIS reported on issues in thirteen currencies, with an "All Other" category for the remaining currencies.

For 1999, the BIS reported on only eight currencies, including the "All Other" category, with a total of $5,365.5 billion. The outstanding amounts in ECU/euro increased from $158.8 billion in 1998 to $1,561.2 billion in 1999, and all the unreported currencies were European, so probably the ECU/euro category replaced most or all of the European currencies. Net new issue in 1998 totaled $681.5 billion, and for 1999 totaled $1,225.1 billion, once more with a big increase in the ECU/euro category.

The United States dollar continues as the currency with the largest use in issuance. The ECU/euro has replaced the Japanese yen as the next largest, amounting to about 29% of total issuance. Yen usage continued relatively steadily, as a percentage, at about 10% of total in 1999. Also, as international issuance continues to increase, and if the Treasury pays down the United States public debt, the ratio of international bonds to Treasuries outstanding may continue to increase.

■ RATING BONDS

Many international bonds are rated, using the same general rating systems as for domestic bonds. Here are some statistics, compiled from several sources, that will give you some idea of the portion of this market that is rated, as of year-end, 1998.

Moody's rated corporate debt	$ 3,190
Other corporate debt	1,100
Government debt	1,060
Total	$ 5,350

Sources: *Moody's Investors Service, Bank for International Settlements*

You can see that about three-quarters of the corporate debt has a Moody's rating. This provides investment guidance, as well as information, about these bonds.

Moody's offers extensive reporting on foreign debt, and publishes an annual four-volume manual on international securities.

Standard & Poor's has an extensive rating system for international securities. S&P publications show a wide range of rated securities, including both sovereign and local debts, providing worldwide coverage. A brief description of the issuer and the issuer's financial status is provided in their rating reports.

Fitch has offices in many major cities around the world, and offers a wide variety of ratings and publications on international bonds, providing worldwide coverage.

Analysis of the better quality international bonds by these rating services is similar to analysis of bonds issued in the United States, with an additional focus on the status of the individual country, and the state or local government within that country. Investing in bonds of emerging markets requires careful scrutiny, and ratings for these bonds can be an invaluable resource. Remember also, when investing in bonds payable in a foreign currency (foreign-pay bonds), the currency risk should be carefully examined because it adds volatility to this instrument. This may require hedging to protect against the risk.

■ REGULATING INTERNATIONAL BONDS

Yankee bonds, which are registered with the SEC, will also be under SEC regulation in the United States, and to the extent that the regulation can be enforced, in foreign countries. However, regulation for other international bonds is more problematic.

International regulation of bonds can take many forms. One important contributor, and information source, in the regulation of international bonds is the *Basel Committee*, part of the BIS. The main interest of the Basel Committee, and of most other international regulatory organizations, is financial stability, including monetary stability, stability in the financial markets, and banking stability. The regulation of the actual securities markets is done with these objectives in mind. For them, the pursuit of full disclosure, and fair, honest, and efficient markets, is only part of a much larger overall picture. In the United States, securities markets regulation is performed by the SEC, the Federal Reserve System, and similar organizations, and is considered an important regulatory goal by itself. However, some international regulatory interest in the securities does exist. Most of the actual regulation must, of necessity, reside in the individual nations.

The *International Organization of Securities Commissions* (IOSCO), an independent organization, is also active in regulating international securities. In late 1999, IOSCO released a report on hedge funds and other highly leveraged institutions (HLIs). The report made recommendations on strengthening risk management processes at security firms, guidance to security regulators on the scrutiny they should apply to these firms' dealings with HLIs, and improving information flows about HLIs. In this case, the IOSCO tried to improve regulation in the management of security firms, improve securities regulation, and improve full disclosure to help provide fair, honest, and efficient markets.

■ BRADY BONDS

Brady bonds—named after former United States Secretary of the Treasury Nicholas Brady—are among the most important of international securities for emerging markets, and have special features that give them special sources of security.

Brady bonds are issued by sovereigns in exchange for bank loans that are being rescheduled. They do this under a program that gives debt service relief if the debtor country has complied with structural reforms mandated by the International Monetary Fund and the World Bank.

Par and discount bonds account for more than half of total outstanding Brady debt. Pars are issued in exchange for rescheduled debt, at equivalent face value, and have an interest rate that is below market. Discounts usually have a floating rate, and are issued for less than the face amount of the rescheduled loans. Both usually have United States Treasury zero coupon bonds as collateral for the principal, and some interest is secured by deposits at the New York Fed. Default on interest can occur when these reserves are paid out and the issuer no longer makes additional interest payments. These two types form the central part of the Brady deals done. The investor will receive his principal at maturity for the collateralized bonds, so the bonds have at least this security.

Other types of Brady bonds exist, varying according to the individual arrangements worked out for each issue. Their quality is generally about the same as the other debt of the issuer. Considering the quality of most Brady issuers, few, if any, Brady bonds have investment grade ratings. In April 2001, S&P (the source for this data, along with Bloomberg) rated just four of the twenty Brady bond issuers (Croatia, Poland, Slovenia, and Uruguay) as investment grade.

In early 1996, thirteen countries had taken advantage of this debt relief program, but four Latin American countries— Argentina, Brazil, Mexico, and Venezuela—accounted for over 80% of the total. A total of about $135.3 billion of Brady bonds was then outstanding.

By March 2001, twenty countries had issued Brady bonds, and a total of about $119.9 billion of Brady bonds was outstanding. Thus, in five years, the total Brady bond debt outstanding had declined about 11%, while general international debt was increasing.

Latin American debt accounted for only about 62.4% of total Brady bond issuance in March 2001, with Argentina, Brazil, Mexico, and Venezuela accounting for about 54% of the total. At that time, Russia had the largest issuance of any country, accounting for $26.6 billion outstanding, slightly ahead of Brazil, with $23.5 billion, and Mexico, with $23.1 billion, outstanding. These three countries had the largest individual country amounts outstanding. The next largest was Argentina, with $10.2 billion outstanding, and Venezuela, with $8.4 billion outstanding. You can see that, although twenty countries have issued Brady bonds, just five of them accounted for about 77% of the total amount outstanding.

Although fewer Brady bonds are outstanding than five years ago, they are still an important asset class for emerging markets.

■ THE RISKS OF BUYING INTERNATIONAL (FOREIGN) SECURITIES

Whenever you buy, sell, trade, invest in, or simply look up information about an American business or government, you take advantage of a governmental system that ensures that business and governmental information is accurately and fully disclosed, and that trading markets are fair, honest, and efficient. Individual exceptions exist, of course, and are usually promptly stopped, with the participants prosecuted if appropriate. The American securities marketplace is the best in the world, by a wide margin, and is a major reason for the American business success.

The same can't always be said of foreign securities markets. Their regulation is frequently less thorough, honest, and competent than American securities regulation. Their reporting is likely to be inferior to American reporting, and the markets much more problematic. For example, many European corporations rarely disclose detailed quarterly information. For an investor in foreign securities markets, it can be costly to assume that reporting is fully accurate, that information is fully disclosed, and that foreign securities markets are as fair, honest, and efficient as American markets.

But less-than-thorough reporting isn't the only problem. The United States has a body of applicable law for securities and for bankruptcy. Admittedly, the United States' laws on municipal bankruptcy are murky and unexplored, but most bankruptcy procedures are reasonably well known. No such laws exist in many foreign countries, and when they do, they are rarely as extensive as American law. Frequently, in foreign countries, if a business (or a person) cannot (or will not) pay its bills (or declares bankruptcy), it is not clear what happens. In any case, a foreign creditor of that person or business is likely to wait a long time for a claim to be paid, no matter how well founded that claim may be.

Investors in government (sovereign) securities can rely only on the general good faith and resources of the national government. This is especially important, because many foreign bonds have some kind of sovereign guaranty. In the case of foreign countries, such guarantees have sometimes not been enough to ensure payment. Many times, the holders of foreign bonds have had to await the actions of a bondholder protective organization, or some other group, for some kind of eventual settlement. These settlements have almost always been for much less than the face value of the claim, even without considering compounded interest. For example, during the 1920s many Latin American countries sold bonds in the United States. During the 1930s most of these defaulted. The Latin American countries made huge amounts of money during World War II, but the investors in those bonds received hardly any recoveries.

Foreign laws and regulations that govern the issuance and trading of securities, and the disclosure of corporate information, are also generally much inferior to those of the United States. Even if they exist, they are likely to be difficult for a foreign investor to enforce.

In his well-known book, *The Intelligent Investor*, first published in 1949, Benjamin Graham advises against the purchase of any foreign securities whatever. Fifty-one years later, in November 2000, the chief global investment strategist of Merrill Lynch, as reported in a leading daily newspaper, apparently came to much the same conclusion. According to the newspaper report, he recommended that the firm's clients limit their foreign stocks to 5% of their total portfolio, down from 35% previously. He couldn't go much lower and still be in the business. At about the same time, J. P. Morgan, now part of J. P. Morgan Chase, lowered its allocation guideline for foreign stocks to 10 to 15 percent.

Note the large amount of Latin American Brady bonds issued. Yet, in the last half of the 19th century, some Latin American countries were among the richest in the world; "As rich as an Argentine" was a common phrase at that time. Now Argentina is sometimes considered a third-world country, and has been a major Brady bond issuer. In late 2001, Argentina verged (again) on default on its foreign debt, and actually defaulted on $132 billion shortly thereafter.

When you invest in foreign bonds, you don't have adequate legal protection, you don't have adequate government regulatory protection, and you don't have adequate markets. You are far from home, and without any friends. Thus, investing in international (foreign) bonds is probably a task best left to the experts.

The Secondary Market

Once a bond—corporate, municipal, Treasury, or agency—is brought to market, it begins to trade in the *secondary market*. The syndicate, now disbanded, or the primary dealer, no longer plays a role in offering the securities. Instead, the bonds are bought and sold among investors, both individual and institutional.

Generally, buying and selling bonds in this market is easy and convenient. Most bonds, especially those issued by highly rated corporations, the United States Government, and highly rated municipalities, are readily marketable and are usually traded over the counter, although a few are listed. They are therefore considered liquid investments—that is, readily convertible to cash.

The secondary market includes both exchange and over-the-counter (OTC) trading and, in fact, a few bonds are traded on the New York Stock Exchange. However, the great preponderance of bond trading takes place in the OTC market. All United States Government securities, all federal agency issues, all municipal bonds, and almost all corporate debt instruments are traded OTC. So when we talk about bond trading, we are really talking about the over-the-counter market.

■ THE BROKER/DEALERS

The over-the-counter market is not located in any one place. Rather, it consists of thousands of broker/dealers located

169

throughout the country who transact business by telephone. Of the great variety of over-the-counter firms, some engage only in OTC business and some specialize in particular types of securities, such as Treasuries or municipal bonds. Some firms deal both on the exchanges and in the over-the-counter market.

These firms are called broker/dealers because they can buy or sell securities either as customers' brokers (agents) or as dealers (principals). When acting as agents, they buy and sell on behalf of their customers, who assume the responsibility for losses and who benefit by profits. The broker receives only a commission for executing the customer's orders. When acting as principals, they buy and sell securities for their own inventories, not for their customers. They assume the risk of ownership. When they sell the securities to customers or to other broker/dealers, they make a profit, or lose money, depending on market action and the success of their selling efforts. They do not receive a commission; instead, they charge a markup on sales and a markdown on purchases.

On any one trade, broker/dealers may act as brokers or as dealers, never as both. They must also tell their customers whether they are acting as agents or as principals. When they act as agents, they must disclose the amount of commission charged.

Broker/dealers conduct all their over-the-counter business by telephone. When a customer calls the brokerage firm with an order, the broker/dealer can sell the bond to or buy it from the customer, if the firm is a market maker in the security. If the firm doesn't have the security in its inventory, it can go short the security to the customer, as long as its price is competitive with the best market in the street. Or it can negotiate a transaction with another firm that is a market maker on behalf of the customer.

Many broker/dealers *make markets* in securities; that is, they specialize in buying and selling certain securities. These "market makers" are willing at all times to buy or sell the security at the quoted price and in multiples of the security's basic trading unit. For many corporate bonds, the basic trading unit is ten bonds. For institutional trades, the trading unit may be $250,000 or even higher.

Because transactions are effected in this way, the OTC market is called a *negotiated market*. This contrasts with the way business is transacted on a stock exchange, which is an *auction market*. On an exchange, the shares are actually auctioned—the price of the stock is set by the highest bid or the lowest offer.

Broker/dealers acting as market makers may deal with many kinds of customers. Some are wholesalers and deal only with other dealers in what is often called the *inside market*. Some deal only with large institutions, such as pension funds or insurance companies. Some smaller firms buy from wholesalers and sell to individual investors.

■ HOW AN OTC TRADE IS EXECUTED

Whether acting as agents or as principals, the traders in the trading department are supposed to make the firm's inventory of debt securities as profitable as possible. Like many businesses, brokerage firms finance their inventories; bonds in the firm's own account cost the company interest expense every day. Furthermore, just holding the inventory exposes the company to market risk. Sometimes, to hedge that risk on a large inventory, two or more dealers will hold the securities in a joint account. The traders' job is to turn inventory—that is, to buy and sell it—quickly and profitably.

A broker/dealer, whether receiving an order from a customer or trading for the brokerage firm's investors, locates the market makers in the security and the current price ranges of all over-the-counter securities by means of several information sources:

- The National Association of Securities Dealers Automated Quotations (NASDAQ)
- The National Quotations Bureau (NQB) sheets

For municipal bonds, the trader can get information from:

- *The Bond Buyer*
- Wires and offering services of other vendors and broker/dealers

Created in 1971, the NASDAQ system is an electronic communications network with hookups for market makers, investors, and regulators. Market makers can enter their quotations for display on terminals throughout the system.

Three levels of service are available on NASDAQ. The *Query only* level is used by registered representatives; the terminal screens reflect the highest bids and the lowest offers available for NASD securities. The *Order entry service* level not only provides current quotations, but also allows order entry. The *Market maker* level is used by market makers. For each security, the system provides current quotes and identifies all market makers. This level also allows users to enter, delete, or update quotations for securities in which they are making a market. To be an authorized subscriber to level three, a NASD member must meet certain net capital and other qualifications.

Broker/dealers may also use the National Quotation Bureau (NQB) sheets, or "yellow sheets," which contain information on corporate bond offerings.

The Bond Buyer, in addition to important news, contains news of upcoming municipal offerings, official notices of sale, and such statistical information as:

- *20-Bond Index*—an index ranging from high quality (Aaa) to medium quality (Baa), with 20-year maturities, indicating a hypothetical composite "bid" by a municipal bond dealer. This is known in the municipal business as "The Bond Buyer Index."

- *11-Bond Index*—an index containing only issues rated Aa and higher, which thus has a higher rating and a lower yield than the 20-bond index.

- *Placement Ratio (Acceptance Ratio)*—the percentage of bonds sold of those offered for sale as new issues during the previous week. A high placement ratio (90% or more) indicates the public's ready acceptance of the new offerings and gives an insight into the underwriter's risk and the current state of the market.

- *30-Day Visible Supply*—new offerings announced for sale within the next thirty calendar days. This gives an idea of the supply "overhanging" the market at a given time. The visible supply does not include short-term offerings, such as municipal notes.

■ The Municipal Index and its related futures are traded on the Chicago Board of Trade, but they are extensively reported in *The Bond Buyer,* along with options on the municipal index.

■ A huge amount and variety of bond market trading information, including trading prices of recently issued bonds, market indices of Treasuries and other bonds, and other valuable information for investors and traders.

The Bond Wire is a subscription wire service provided by *The Bond Buyer,* similar to other news services, such as Dow-Jones, Reuters, Telerate, and Bloomberg, except that it is aimed particularly at the municipal bond industry and the municipal securities professional.

During the mid-1990s other wire services actively expanded their coverage of the municipal bond industry as individual ownership of municipals increased. These services increase the information available to both municipal professionals and municipal investors.

For all bond traders, however, the best source of information consists of their contacts in the business. Who among other firms' traders has a certain type of bond in inventory? Which of them owes a favor, and to whom? Who quoted a favorable price on a certain bond just this morning? Who is trying to sell off a weak issue? And so on. Information like this is so specialized and often so fleeting that not even a highly automated quotation system like NASDAQ can capture it. This is the kind of information that is gathered during the course of countless phone calls and used at the precise time of its greatest effectiveness.

■ HOW BONDS ARE QUOTED

CORPORATE BONDS

When dealing in corporate bonds, traders for broker/dealers must specify:

■ The name of the issuer

■ The months and days when interest is paid

■ The bond's coupon rate (its stated interest rate)

■ The bond's maturity month and year

For example, a corporate bond might be described as follows:

"IBM-JJ15-7% of '010."

This shorthand description indicates that the bond is issued by IBM Corporation, pays its interest on January 15 and July 15 of each year, offers a 7% annual coupon rate, and matures in the year 2010.

Let's look more closely at this description. Almost all corporate bonds pay interest on either the first or the fifteenth of two months that are six months apart; that is, interest payments are semiannual. Thus, there are only twelve possibilities:

MONTHS INTEREST IS PAID	ON THE 1st*	ON THE 15th
January-July	JJ	JJ-15
February-August	FA	FA-15
March-September	MS	MS-15
April-October	AO	AO-15
May-November	MN	MN-15
June-December	JD	JD-15

*By convention, if interest is paid on the first of the month, the date is omitted.

Interest rate is always expressed as a percentage of the bond's face value. The final component, the year the bond matures, is usually expressed without the first two digits. Thus, 2008 is expressed as '08, and 2018 as '18.

In corporate bond trading, price is expressed as percent of par, in (percentage) points and eighths of a point. Thus, for a $1,000 bond, each point equals $10. For example, a price of 86⅜ for a $1,000 bond means:

$$\$1,000 \times .86375 = \$863.75$$

And a price of 123⅛ means:

$$\$1,000 \times 1.23125 = \$1,231.25$$

The quotation itself in bond trading consists of a *bid* and an *ask price*, which is characteristic of OTC trading. For example, if the bid is 9.40% and the ask is 9.25%, the quoting dealer is willing to buy the bonds at 9.40% yield and sell them at 9.25% yield.

In the secondary market, the *spread* is not the difference between the underwriter's purchase and sales prices; it is the difference between the quoted bid and asked prices.

As such, the spread is based on issuer quality, time to maturity, supply and demand, call features and other bond features, coupon rate, and other market factors.

The spread is also called the *dealer's markup* or *markdown*. In the OTC market, when a dealer buys a security from a market maker and sells it to a customer at a higher price, the difference in prices is called a *markup*. When the dealer buys from the customer and sells to a market maker at a higher price, the difference is a *markdown*. Either way, the markup or markdown determines the spread. Neither need be itemized on the customer's trade confirmation in principal transactions.

(When quoting bond prices, traders often repeat themselves to assure accurate communication. Often they even call back after a trade if they have any doubt about the terms.)

MUNICIPAL BONDS

Municipal bonds are similarly quoted, although there is no specific unit of trading. However, when professional municipal traders say "one bond," they mean "$1,000 face value." They use this term even though most municipal bonds have been issued in denominations of $5,000 or higher since the early 1960s. Why? Old habits die hard. To the municipal professional, "a bond" is still a $1,000 certificate.

Otherwise, the language used to describe a municipal bond is pretty straightforward. Take the following example: A "$20,000 State of New York, 3.40% of June 1, 2007, at a 4.60% yield." This is a municipal bond (or, more likely, bonds) with a face value of $20,000, issued by the State of New York, with a coupon rate of 3.40%, maturing on June 1, 2007, and trading at a price to yield 4.60% to maturity.

Serial bonds are usually quoted on a yield-to-maturity basis, with the equivalent dollar price added as a convenience. Term bonds are usually quoted only as a dollar price, or percentage of par value. For example, the quotation of 92⅛ is a percentage. It would mean a dollar price of $921.25 for a $1,000 par value bond, but $4,606.25 for a $5,000 bond.

Larger purchases tend to have a "better price" than smaller purchases. Odd lots, usually par amounts under $25,000, will trade for much higher yields. Occasionally, secondary market trades are quoted all-or-none (AON); in this case, the quote is firm only for the number of bonds given.

Spreads on municipal bonds vary widely; for a typical bond, they might be from ¼ point to 2 points or even more on issues that are difficult to sell. Municipal notes may have spreads from ⅛ point to ½ point.

■ SHOPPING THE STREET

Once a broker/dealer identifies the market makers in a security, the next step is to call all the market makers to get the best price. The broker/dealer is said to be "shopping the street." While on the phone with the market maker, the broker/dealer may obtain one of several types of quotes:

1. Firm bids or offers are prices at which the quoting broker/dealer is committed to buy or sell at least a round lot of bonds, even though the broker/dealer requesting the quote is not obliged to do business. A firm bid or offer can be good for the moment that the quote is given or for a longer period. Sometimes the quote is good for the entire day; other times, it is good only for the duration of the telephone call (called "on the wire"). Also, unless otherwise stated, it is good for one unit of trading, or for the block of bonds being considered. In other words, the broker/dealer's com-

mitment to buy or sell at the quoted price is limited to ten bonds at the quoted price (for corporate bonds) or the block of bonds being discussed.

How does the second dealer know whether the quote—firm or not—is the best available? Generally, a dealer giving a quote allows the inquiring dealer up to one hour to make a transaction. If, during that hour, a third dealer wishes to take advantage of the quote, the original inquirer usually has five minutes to make a sale or forego the quote.

Let's look at an example. Dealer A calls Dealer B, who is a market maker in Belliup Corporation bonds, for a quote. Dealer B says, "Firm at 97½ for an hour, with five." This accommodation is sometimes referred to as an "option." Dealer A hangs up and continues inquiring with other dealers, knowing that he or she has one hour to take advantage of that quote. The Belliup bonds are said to be "out firm."

Occasionally, the option has a recall privilege attached to it. For example, Dealer C calls Dealer B, hears the quote, and wants to do business right away. In that case, Dealer B advises Dealer A that he or she has five minutes to make a deal; otherwise, Dealer C will be given the bonds.

The prices quoted in the yellow sheets and on NASDAQ are not firm quotes. The NASDAQ and the yellow sheets only make it easier for buyers and sellers to find each other and provide a good indication of price. Firm quotes, sometimes referred to as the "actual market," must be obtained verbally from the market maker, and all transactions are executed verbally by telephone.

2. If the broker/dealer gives a quote and says that it is "subject," then the quote is subject to confirmation. Generally, the broker/dealer has to have more information before making the quote firm.

Subject quotes can be expressed in several ways:

■ "It is quoted (that is, I'm not quoting it) 85"
■ "Last I saw, it was 85"
■ "It is 85, subject"

3. Sometimes the broker/dealer gives a quote with a very wide spread and follows it by the word "workout." A workout quote is not firm. Instead, it provides a range in which the dealer believes a price can be worked out. These quotes are typically used for infrequently traded securities.

BID OR OFFER WANTED

Occasionally, a broker/dealer wants to buy or sell, but receives no bids or offers. In these cases, the broker/dealer hangs something like a "for sale" sign on the security by advertising the would-be transaction in the National Quotation Bureau sheets or in one of the electronic market systems. The phrase "bid wanted (BW)" tells other broker/dealers that the bond is for sale and that the advertising broker/dealer is looking for bids. "Offering wanted (OW)" means that the broker/dealer wants to buy the bond and is soliciting offerings.

The bid-wanted business is a typical job for the broker's broker. When dealers cannot sell a bond, they frequently turn to a broker's broker, who then seeks bids for them. The broker's broker will report the highest bid to the offering broker/dealer, who will then decide whether to accept or reject the bid.

Sometimes broker/dealers use broker's brokers to hide the actual owner of the bonds, although frequently this information leaks out to the Street anyway. Brokers do not reveal the names of their clients without permission. Sometimes broker/dealers use broker's brokers to keep the sale confidential.

Perhaps the bond brokers' greatest service is their continuous contact with major dealers. They closely track who owns and who's buying or selling bonds. This view is known as a "picture" of the market. The dealers' anonymity often makes them more willing to give out information. Often, the bond broker has access to more information than a dealer. When brokers make a trade, they earn up to ⅛ point per bond, or $1.25. Usually, the commission is considerably lower.

EXECUTING OTC ORDERS

The most common types of order entered by customers in the over-the-counter market are *market orders* and *limit orders*. A market order must be executed as soon as possible and at the best possible price. A limit order specifies the price at which the security must be bought or sold. Limit orders may be entered for the day, in which case they become invalid if not executed by the close of trading. They can also be market "good 'till canceled (GTC)," which means that the order remains valid until it is executed by the broker or canceled by the customer.

Other types of orders are available. *All-or-none* (AON) orders must be executed in full or not at all. Frequently blocks of municipal bonds are offered AON, especially if the block is of such a size that selling a part would result in a less salable remainder. For example, a municipal bond dealer with a block of twenty-five bonds would probably offer them AON; a sale of part of the block would leave an odd lot of bonds, which would be much more difficult to sell. A variation of the all-or-none order is the *fill-or-kill* (FOK) order, which is canceled if it cannot be filled immediately.

Regardless of the type of order entered, the broker must always get the best possible price for the customer.

How a broker/dealer is compensated for transactions in the secondary market depends on whether the firm acted as agent or as principal. As the customer's agent, it may charge a commission. As a market maker, it may charge a markup or markdown. Most OTC transactions are principal transactions, with the broker/dealer's compensation coming in the form of a markup or markdown.

When acting as a broker or agent, the NASD member must disclose to the customer the amount of the commission charged. The actual dollar amount charged must be printed on the confirmation.

Sometimes a broker may receive orders from different customers for both the buy and the sell sides of a transaction. This is called a *riskless transaction*, because the broker/dealer is not subject to any risk but has only to cross the two orders. In such a case, each customer sees only his or her part of the commission, if it is an agency transaction.

The amount of the commission charged by broker/dealers must be fair, reasonable, and in accordance with the NASD's 5% markup policy (which is explained shortly).

When trading from the firm's own account as a market maker, a broker/dealer makes a profit on either a markup or markdown. Unlike commissions, markups and markdowns do not need to be disclosed to customers. The only requirement is that the broker/dealer must tell the customer that the firm is acting as a principal in the trade.

The NASD's 5% guideline governs markups and markdowns. Its purpose is to assure that NASD members earn profits that are fair, equitable, and proportionate to current market prices. The 5%, however, is intended to be used as a guide, not as a rule. The key message is that markups and markdowns must not be unfair, regardless of the percentage. For example, a markup of over 5% would not be unfair if the dealer had owned the security for a long time and computed the markup on the basis of current market prices rather than on cost. On the other hand, a 5% markup could be unfair if a broker/dealer buys a security for a customer by using the proceeds from the sale of another one of the customer's securities; in other words, he is doing a swap for a customer.

How does a broker/dealer know what is fair? The NASD board believes that, in determining fairness, NASD members and committees should consider the type of security, the availability of the security, its prices, the size of the transaction, the pattern of markup, and the nature of the member's business. For example, markups would be very much lower on large trades of newly issued Treasuries than on relatively small trades of odd lots of municipals.

■ THE NATIONAL ASSOCIATON OF SECURITY DEALERS (NASD)

The National Association of Security Dealers (NASD) was organized under the Maloney Act, an amendment to the Securities Exchange Act of 1934. Although established by Congress and supervised by the SEC, the NASD operates, not as a government agency, but as an independent membership association.

The NASD's power to regulate lies in its ability to deny membership to any broker/dealer operating in an unethical or improper manner. Because only NASD members have the advantage of price concessions, discounts, and similar allowances, the loss of membership privileges all but prevents a firm from competing in the marketplace. In addition, NASD members are permitted to do business only with other members. Nonmembers are therefore severely restricted in the business they can do.

The NASD imposes its requirements on members through two sets of regulations: the Rules of Fair Practice and the Uniform Practice Code. These regulations spell out the terms and conditions of everyday operations, as well as the classification, qualification, and responsibilities of its members.

Membership in the NASD is open to all properly qualified "brokers" and "dealers" whose regular course of business is transacting in any part of the investment banking or securities business in the United States. A *broker* is defined as a legal entity (individual, partnership, or corporation) that effects transactions for the accounts of others. A *dealer* is a legal entity that engages in the buying or selling of securities for its own account. By definition, banks are not broker/dealers and are therefore not eligible for NASD membership.

■ MUNICIPAL SECURITIES RULEMAKING BOARD (MSRB)

The Securities Acts of 1933 and 1934 did not cover municipal securities, so they were left unregulated for more than forty years. However, certain regulations to the municipal market and its participants did apply. The antifraud provision, Section 10b-5, applied to municipal bonds as well as to any other security; cheating people with municipal bonds (or any other secruity) is illegal. In addition, under the Glass-Steagall Act, banks could work in the municipal bond industry, but could no longer underwrite and trade municipal revenue bonds; they could only underwrite and trade general obligation bonds. Those banks that act as municipal bond dealers are called *dealer banks*. The dealer operation is set up as a separate department in the bank or as a separate subsidiary of the bank. Dealer banks are not members of the NASD, and the NASD rules do not apply to their municipal bond dealer operations. Instead, special rules for municipal bonds apply to dealer banks, and to the municipal bond dealings of broker/dealers.

In the early 1970s several events occurred that highlighted apparent inadequacies in the municipal bond market. New York City defaulted on four issues of notes, and at the same time concerns arose about the extent of disclosure of information on new issues of municipal bonds. These concerns were compounded by the apparent lack of full information on the New York City notes when they were sold. At about the same time, the SEC brought fraud actions against several municipal securities professionals alleging dishonest trading and selling activities.

These concerns led Congress to pass the Securities Act Amendments of 1975, which brought self-regulation to the municipal bond industry. It set up the Municipal Securities Rulemaking Board (MSRB) as part of the regulatory mechanism. The MSRB is funded by annual fees from broker/dealers and dealer banks, assessments on underwritings of new securities with final maturities of two years or more from issue date, together with an initial fee for new entrants into the municipal bond business.

Actual regulation of the municipal bond industry is somewhat complex. The MSRB proposes regulations and invites the industry, and others, to comment on them. Based on the comments received, the MSRB may revise the proposed regulations. However, the MSRB does not have power to approve the regulations, which are actually approved by the SEC.

Neither the MSRB nor the SEC enforces the regulations. That is the job of the NASD or one of the bank regulatory agencies. For broker/dealers, who will be members of the NASD, enforcement of the MSRB regulations is the job of the NASD. For dealer banks, the enforcement is done by their normal regulatory authority.

Although the MSRB does not have a rule like the NASD's 5% rule, it does require that municipal bond dealers deal fairly with all persons and that they shall not engage in any deceptive, dishonest, or unfair practice. MSRB members must also give and abide by fair quotations that reflect current market prices, are fair and reasonable, and are bona fide bids and offers. "Nominal" or information quotations may be given if they are clearly identified as such. MSRB members also may not give or receive gratuities in excess of $100 per year.

More recently, the MSRB has been interested in the reporting of recent municipal trades (called *transparency*); contributions by municipal professionals to political campaigns; and continued reporting by municipal security issuers. Recent municipal trades are now reported by the MSRB on its website, under a subscription service. The Bond Market Association also reports municipal bond trades. This is part of a continuing SEC effort to provide better disclosure in dealer markets, to pursue the important SEC objective of fair, honest, and efficient markets.

Within the last few years, the MSRB has set limits on the contributions allowed by municipal professionals to candidates in political campaigns. This followed a long train of perceived abuses in which municipal investment bankers, and their employers, made campaign contributions to candidates in which they had no immediately obvious interest as voters or constituents. In general terms, municipal professionals may only contribute limited amounts to candidates for elective office, and only to those candidates for whom they may vote. Most individuals reasonably active in municipal bond work would be considered municipal professionals. If you are at all active in political activities, and if you are in any way involved in the municipal business, you should check to find out whether or not this rule (MSRB Rule G-37) applies to you. If it does apply, you should take it very seriously; determine to whom you may give and how much is allowed. In late 1997, the amount was $250 to a candidate for whom the donor is eligible to vote, but this amount can be changed.

Another area of recent interest is continuing reporting by issuers. This includes financial reporting. Many large issuers, such as The Port Authority of New York and New Jersey, who sell new issues several times each year, have always issued informative annual reports. But other issuers, who may come to market much less frequently, have issued reports either much less frequently (if at all), or with much less information. The SEC is concerned with full disclosure by all issuers. The Tower amendment does not permit direct SEC regulation of issuers of municipal securities, so the SEC has required the underwriters of the issuer's securities to pledge that the issuer will publish full reports on a frequent, regular basis.

■ BOND TRADING AND SETTLEMENT

CORPORATE BONDS

When two investors want to enter into a secondary market transaction, they have to agree not only on the price at which the transaction will occur, but also on when the actual exchange of bond certificates and cash will occur. Thus, if on a Monday two parties (in separate parts of the country) agree to enter into a bond transaction, they have to agree not only on the price at which the transaction will occur, but also on which day the bonds and the cash will actually change hands. Tuesday? Wednesday? The following Monday? Perhaps the seller has to get the bonds out of a safe deposit box. Or the buyer may need to liquidate some money market investments before making payment.

By convention, the transaction may take place, or settle, in one of five common ways, each involving a different day. These dates are called the *settlement options.*

1. A *regular-way trade* settles on the third business day after the trade date. (Note that Treasuries generally settle on the next business day.) Only business days are counted—no weekends or holidays. Regular-way settlement is assumed for all corporate and municipal bond trades unless the parties specify a different settlement option at the time they enter into the trade. This means that most corporate and municipal bond trades settle regular way.

2. A *cash settlement trade* settles on the same day on which the trade is made. Obviously, both parties have to agree to, and be prepared for, a cash settlement. By convention, any cash trade that occurs at or before 2:00 P.M. settles at 2:30 P.M. EST

in Federal Funds. Any trade that occurs after 2:00 P.M. settles one half-hour later.

3. A *next-day settlement* settles on the first business day after the trade date.

4. A *seller's option trade* settles up to sixty days after the trade date. This kind of settlement is usually chosen if the seller is not able to deliver the bonds within the time required by the other settlement options. For example, a seller may be on vacation when she wants to sell some bonds. If the bonds are in her safe deposit box at home, she has to opt for a seller's option settlement (a "seller's 60.") When she returns home, she can deliver the bonds to the buyer at any time up to the 60-day limit, providing that she gives the buyer a one-day written notice of when the bonds will be delivered. Sellers who need to settle via this option usually get a slightly lower price from buyers than they would if they were able to use one of the other settlement options. Seller's option cannot be earlier than the fourth day.

5. A *buyer's option delivery* gives the buyer the option to receive securities on a specific date.

Usually, the seller can negotiate any reasonable settlement day.

Three-day, regular-way delivery applies to most trades in over-the-counter securities and securities listed on an exchange, except Treasuries. All corporate, municipal, and most federal agency securities trade the regular way. United States Treasury securities are delivered for cash, regular way, on the day following the trade, and the seller's option of not less than two nor more than sixty days.

After a trade, each broker/dealer sends the other a notice to confirm the details of the trade. If both parties recognize and acknowledge the trade, it is "confirmed" or "compared." Sometimes, however, the contrabroker (the broker/dealer with whom the trade was made) sends back a signed "DK," a "don't know," notice telling the confirming broker that the contrabroker does not "know"—or recognize—the trade.

Suppose the contrabroker has not responded to a confirmation at all by two days after trade date. In that case, not later than the fifteenth calendar day after the trade date, the confirming member sends a DK notice to the contrabroker. The contrabroker then has two business days after receiving the notice either to confirm or DK the transaction. Failure to receive a response from the contrabroker by the close of two business days constitutes a DK, and the confirming member has no further liability.

Transfer of Ownership

Bonds are negotiable in that they can be readily transferred from one owner to another. The method of transfer depends on the form of ownership, of which there are three: *registered, bearer,* and *book entry.* Bonds in registered form have the owner's name and address printed on the bond certificate and registered on the issuer's books. Interest payments are sent directly to the bondholder. If a registered bond is sold, the broker sends the bond to a transfer agent who reissues it in the name of the new owner.

Book entry bonds do not have certificates. Instead, a depository keeps records of ownership on its books for its members. The members are brokerage houses, banks, and other institutions. These members, in turn, keep records of the bond owners on their own books. Transferring bonds means simply changing the records on the books of the depository and its members to reflect the bond trade. Usually no certificates are issued, and sometimes, in the case of "pure book entry," no certificates will ever exist, except for global certificates for the entire issue, or for each maturity within the issue. The depository will hold the global certificates.

Bearer bonds are rarely issued now in this hi-tech time when registering bonds is not the time-consuming, labor-intensive task it was in the past. New issues of municipals must be in registered or book-entry form for their interest to be exempt from federal income taxes. However, there are still a few bearer bonds in circulation. Because these bonds were issued and distributed without registration, they are assumed to belong to the bearer. Consequently, they are fully negotiable, like cash. To be paid the interest amount, the bearer must cut (or "clip") coupons from the bond certificate and present them for payment when they become due. Each coupon represents one payment.

To assure clear ownership, the NASD requires "good delivery" in all transactions; that is, the security must be in proper form so that the record of ownership can be transferred. To facilitate transfer of ownership, the NASD defines the requirement of good delivery.

MUNICIPAL BONDS

The requirements for the settlement of municipal bond trades are very similar to those for corporate bond trades. While most munis settle the regular way, some trade on a cash basis. Buyer's and seller's options also occur. In addition, "when, as and if" trades for new issues may settle anywhere from three business days to the time stated in the confirmation.

Municipal bond settlement differs from corporate settlement, however, in that the legal opinion must be part of the transaction. For bonds issued since the mid-1960s, the legal opinion is printed on the certificate; for older issues, it is a separate document. Very rarely, these older issues are offered without their legal opinion; these are called "illegals" or "exlegals." If the buyer accepts this condition, delivery is legal, but otherwise they are not acceptable.

If the bond is mutilated (that is, if any part is unreadable), the broker/dealer must have the certificate validated by the trustee, registrar, transfer agent, paying agent, issuer, or an authorized agent of the issuer. A brokerage firm or one of its sales representatives *cannot* validate a mutilated certificate. Mutilated coupons must be endorsed or guaranteed by the issuer or a commercial bank. Canceled coupons must be endorsed or guaranteed by the issuer, the issuer's agent, or by the trustee or paying agent. Also, for a bond to be good delivery, all unpaid coupons must be attached, although a check for a coupon payment due within thirty days may replace that particular coupon.

Upon delivery to the buying broker/dealer by the selling broker/dealer, the buyer has the *right of rejection*. That is, the buyer may refuse to accept delivery should the certificate not be in good delivery form. If, after the securities have been delivered, *either dealer* realizes that the certificate does not constitute a good delivery, either party has the *right of reclamation* (returning or demanding the return of the securities). Note that rejection takes place *before* acceptance of delivery, whereas reclamation takes place *after* acceptance of delivery.

The purchaser does not have to accept partial delivery. The seller pays the shipping costs. The confirmation should be delivered to the contrabroker/dealer the next business day with all pertinent information.

■ ACCRUED INTEREST

Sellers of bonds are entitled to any interest accrued on a bond up to the day before the settlement date. So if a bond is sold anytime between interest payment dates, some interest is due to the seller and the rest to the buyer. Yet the issuer's paying agent is going to issue only one check for the full interest amount to the holder of record on the payment date, or to the person presenting bearer coupons for payment. How, then, do sellers get the accrued interest to which they are entitled? The answer is that the buyer of the bond pays to the seller the interest that the seller is entitled to, and then takes the full interest amount on the next payment date.

The only thing remaining is to calculate the actual accrued amount. The regular-way settlement date is the third business day after the transaction, but if the trade is for "cash," it is the same day as the transaction. In the event of same-day settlement, accrued interest is computed up through the *previous* business day.

Let's look at an example. An Awac bond has a coupon rate of 10¾%. The price of the bond is 98¾—that is, $987.50 for a $1,000 face value bond. A buyer of this bond would have to pay the seller $987.50, plus any interest accrued since the last payment. Assume that the bond is purchased midway between payment dates (actually, this would be on the 91st day of the 180-day period between interest payment dates). Since each six-month interest payment is $53.75 (10¾% times $1,000 divided by two payments), the accrued interest for three months is $26.88. The buyer would pay the seller $987.50 plus about $26.88 for a total payment of $1,014.38. On the next interest payment date, the entire coupon payment of $53.75 is paid to the buyer.

Naturally, not all bonds are sold conveniently at the midway point between payments. To calculate the exact amount of accrued interest, regardless of when the bond is sold, use the following formula:

$$\frac{\text{Accrued}}{\text{Interest}} = \frac{\text{Annual}}{\text{Interest}} \times \frac{\text{Days in holding period}}{360 \text{ days}}$$

For corporate and municipal bonds and some municipal notes, all whole months are assumed to have 30 days, and the year is figured on the basis of 360 days; this is called a "30-day month, 360-day year basis." For example, bondholder Mathers received her last interest payment on a municipal bond of $53.75 on April 1. Her next check is due on October 1. In June, she sells the bond to buyer Ridgemount for 97½ (or $975) for settlement on June 28. Disregarding commissions and fees, Ridgemount has to pay Mathers $975, plus an amount for accrued interest:

$$\frac{\text{Accrued}}{\text{Interest}} = \frac{\text{Annual}}{\text{Interest}} \times \frac{\text{Days in holding period}}{360 \text{ days}}$$

$$= (2 \times \$53.750) \times \frac{(30 \text{ days} + 30 \text{ days} + 27 \text{ days})}{360 \text{ days}}$$

$$= \$107.50 \times \frac{87 \text{ days}}{360 \text{ days}}$$

$$= \$25.98$$

Note that April and May count for 30 days each and June for 27 days.

The check that goes to Mathers is for $1,000.98, equal to $975 purchase price plus $25.98 accrued interest.

Some bonds, such as some income bonds, and bonds in default, trade without any accrued interest. Such bonds are said to trade "flat."

This method for calculating accrued interest is valid for municipal and corporate bonds and for some municipal notes. *Treasury* securities, and some municipal notes, however, are figured on an "exact days over exact days" basis. In this case, the exact number of days in the semiannual interest payment period is calculated, and divided into the exact number of days from the latest interest payment date to the settlement date. Thus, a month is figured at 28, 29, 30, or 31 days, depending on its exact day count. The semiannual payment period may be anything from 181 days to 184 days, depending on the exact day count.

Heavy volumes of corporate, municipal, and United States Treasury and agency securities trade every day in the secondary market. Yet, as large and active as the bond market is in the United States, it is only a part of the worldwide fixed-income trading arena, which includes the issues of overseas companies and governments. But that is a subject requiring another whole book.

E-Trading and the
Bond Market

Electronic techniques have been used in the financial world for more than forty years. The first use was in stock price reporting, which came to be heavily used in the early 1960s. Among the earliest vendors of electronic stock price reporting systems were Bunker Ramo, Quotron, and Ultronic Systems. At first, these systems furnished only stock quotations, usually the stock price at the latest trade. But as time went on and the services were further developed, they became capable of providing more expanded information, such as daily and yearly high and low prices, stock market indices, and interest rate data. The systems could compute data such as price/earnings ratios, yields, and possible earnings and dividend projections. Yet the earliest use—electronic access to database information—is still one of the most important uses (arguably the most important use) of electronic techniques in the financial markets. For example, America Online (AOL), by far the largest online service provider, offers a free service showing three important market indices, along with stock quotations. Many brokers also offer online stock quotations and market indices.

Expansion from accessing databases to trading electronically was natural and, in principle, not terribly difficult. The hardware and software for managing databases, and changes to these databases, already existed. The database for trading simply became a database of bids and offerings of securities. Each security would have its own database of bids and offerings. Of course, actual implementation, as usual, was much more difficult than originally thought.

■ ELECTRONIC TRADING AND THE BOND MARKET

Expansion of electronic trading techniques to bonds lagged behind stock electronic trading. However, in the last several years (as of March, 2001), electronic trading of bonds expanded, with new systems being added almost weekly. The Bond Market Association (TBMA) maintains a periodic report on electronic bond trading systems, which can be accessed on their website (www.bondmarkets.com). It reports on systems meant to serve dealers, brokers, and institutional investors, but not retail investors. In March 2001, TBMA's report contained seventy-four electronic trading systems. The five kinds of bond trading systems are *auction systems, cross-matching systems, interdealer systems, multi-dealer systems,* and *single-dealer systems.* Because almost all bond trades are in a dealer market, many systems show both bids and offerings. Some systems show the identities of prospective buyers, but in others the identity is kept secret. This is important because often dealers wish to make trades without anyone in the market knowing they are trading, knowing who has made the actual trades, and even knowing the actual seller of the securities. They may have a particular lot of bonds to sell, or they may be executing some customer portfolio transactions to implement portfolio management changes, and neither they nor the customer wishes anyone else to know who is making the trades. During 2001, the number of electronic trading systems (platforms) contracted to forty-nine, according to The Bond Market Association.

Auction Systems

Auction systems conduct actual auctions of individual offerings of bonds. Individual systems may have a particular specialty, such as primary issues or secondary issues. The seller shows the features of the security, and sets the time that the auction will be open. In some cases, the identities of the prospective buyers are shown, but in other cases they are kept unknown. The offering is awarded to the highest bid price (or lowest yield). In March, 2001, TBMA reported on fifteen auction systems.

CROSS-MATCHING SYSTEMS

Cross-matching systems bring both dealers and institutional investors together in a network to offer cross-matching opportunities. When opposite orders match in price, or posted bids or offers are accepted, the trades are executed. Some systems offer negotiating features, and may allow users to follow complicated portfolio management strategies, usually involving multiple orders in different securities. Buy and sell orders are anonymous in this system. In March 2001, TBMA reported twenty-three cross-matching systems, making this the most common type of electronic trading system in the bond market.

INTERDEALER SYSTEMS

Interdealer systems offer dealers the execution of transactions with other dealers, using broker's brokers. Full anonymity is kept in this system. All the major Treasury interdealer brokers either offer such a system, or expect to soon. In March 2001, TBMA reported on ten such systems.

MULTI-DEALER SYSTEMS

Multi-dealer systems allow customers to consolidate orders from several dealers, using availability of multiple quotations from many dealers. Sometimes the system will select and show the best price posted in a security by the dealers in the system. These systems can offer a selection of security types. In March 2001, TBMA reported on ten such systems.

SINGLE-DEALER SYSTEMS

Single-dealer systems give institutional investors the chance to execute transactions directly with their choice of individual dealer. Recently, these systems have increasingly used the Internet for access, but some still use proprietary systems. In March 2001, TBMA reported on seventeen such systems. A major broker/dealer explains its own single-dealer system as follows: Customers can execute transactions in Treasury bills, notes, and bonds, agency discount notes, municipal securities, commercial paper, and repurchase agreements. A foreign branch allows transactions in European sovereign debt. Transactions in institutional money funds and variable-rate preferred securities are also allowed.

This broker/dealer also has a system offering content, markets, and services for its clients in a wide variety of securities. The firm provides research services, analytical tools, and trade processing services for its clients, with new products and services added periodically. Further, clients can access markets in a truly wide variety of securities, options, and derivatives.

■ RETAIL BOND TRADING

In addition to the electronic bond trading systems for institutional investors, many brokers also offer systems for individual, or retail, investors. Here is a description of a system offered by a major brokerage firm for its retail clients in early 2001.

Clients access the system via the Internet and sign on using either a sign-on code or their Social Security number along with a password, all of which is standard database access procedure. Clients then may review their accounts, the firm's research reports, market data, and may even execute trades. To do that, they must look at the bonds the brokerage firm has for sale.

Most bond trades take place in a dealer market, meaning that the client can only buy what a dealer has offered for sale. And while most U.S. Treasury securities will be offered by somebody, of the possibly more than two million different municipal securities that exist (nobody knows for sure exactly how many), most will probably not be available for purchase from a dealer. A few, however, are widely traded, especially from recent large new municipal issues. The client will make a choice from the relatively few current municipal offerings available. This situation also holds for many corporate bonds, especially equipment trust securities.

Sometimes you will want to buy a particular bond. Suppose, for example, you already own $20,000 par value of the Treasury 5¼s due 05/15/04, and you have just received a $10,000 inheritance. You could easily want to purchase another

$10,000 par value of these particular securities, and, considering that they are Treasuries, you will almost certainly be able to buy some more.

But suppose you own $25,000 par value of the Schenectady, NY, 4.75% bonds due 10/01/2019, AMBAC insured (yes, there are such bonds), and you wish to buy more. You would probably not be able to buy them because only $325,000 exist (at least, of that particular issue), you already own $25,000 of them, and it is not likely that any will be offered for sale at the time you want to buy them. You might buy a similar type of bond, such as some Schenectady, NY, 4.75% bonds due 10/01/2018, AMBAC insured (yes, they exist too, and were part of the same issue), but you would have the greatest success if you were to simply look for "New York insured paper in the 20-year range." With these requirements, your broker could look for a wide variety of offerings that might meet your needs.

For most retail bond trades, the retail bond buyer client really only wants a bond that meets certain requirements of quality, maturity, issuer, and, particularly in the case of municipal issuers, issuer location. For example, the client may be looking for Treasuries in the 3- to 5-year maturity range, or for high-grade Florida municipals in the 10- to 15-year range. This restricts the number of offerings available to a particular client, but also identifies the offerings that the client may reasonably consider. It also requires that the client either know roughly what he or she wants, or have an advisor, such as a salesperson or financial advisor, to provide assistance.

The electronic trade execution system we are looking at offers the client a choice of issuer, face amount, credit rating, and maturity range. For municipal securities, a choice of state or territory is also offered. Of course, the client may look at every single offering, but most clients will want to select only a few for inspection.

The system offers the following five choices for type of bond:

1. Treasuries
2. Corporates
3. Treasury zeros (STRIPS)

4. Federal agencies
5. Municipals

Clients may then enter choices of:

■ Face amount (minimum face, or your desired face)

■ Minimum credit rating (choice of best, high, good, medium) (Note that the broker used in this description does not offer bonds with lower than a medium rating. It does not offer junk bonds to its clients.)

■ Time to maturity (choice of ten maturity ranges)

■ For municipals, it also offers a choice of state or territory

The system makes a default selection in some cases if the client does not enter a choice. Once the choices are entered, the system produces a list of eligible bonds, showing security name, description, offering price, and yield to maturity for each. The client can select one, and make the trade.

The client must first agree to the terms of the system use. The system also advises clients that the bonds offered are the ones in the broker's inventory. Some bonds might not be available because many clients might be accessing the same bonds at the same time, and some bonds might be sold before the client can accept the offer. Offering prices are also subject to change without notice.

Some brokerage firms offer discounts if the trade is made automatically, using only the computer trading system. However, there may be benefits to paying the full commission and doing business directly with someone on the broker's bond desk, because this could lead to a better offering and a better execution of the order.

In any case, the client receives an offering price, which he or she may either accept or reject. If the client accepts the price, the trade will be done, if the bonds are still available at that price. However, it still may not be done at the agreed-upon price if a lower price can be obtained—through further broker inquiries or a fast-changing market. If the bonds are no longer available, the client must obtain another offering.

You can see that even for individual retail clients, it is possible to trade bonds electronically. Well-known and active securities, such as many U.S. Treasury obligations, can be traded electronically easily, cheaply, and conveniently. However, in many cases, especially if the client has special requirements such as special tax-exempt features, special maturity requirements, or special needs for a retirement account, it may still be more advantageous to trade using the broker's bond desk.

■ ONLINE BOND INFORMATION SOURCES

A variety of organizations offer online information on bond-related issues. For example, The Bond Market Association has a website offering a wide variety of bond-related information, such as descriptions of the various electronic trading systems. Rating agencies, trade associations, government agencies, newspapers and other publications, as well as many issuers, all have websites providing a broad range of information on bonds. The content for each website depends on its sponsor. Further, some websites may be available only by subscription, others may be free, and still others may have a free area and another part available only by subscription. For example, the rating agencies have websites that are part free and part available only by subscription. These websites contain research information, as well as the actual ratings assigned by the rating agency.

The SEC and other regulatory authorities use electronic techniques to capture and report security transactions, thereby maintaining their "transparency." The Municipal Securities Rulemaking Board (MSRB) reports municipal bond trades as a subscription service. The Bond Market Association reports recent trades on its website.

Meanwhile, electronic information services continue to establish themselves in the marketplace. In 2001, a paper-based information service, *The Blue List*, a daily publication showing municipal bond offerings, suspended publication. *The Blue List* had been in business since (if memory serves) 1938. Many persons on the muncipal bond industry believe that this business was taken up by online offerings, such as Bloomberg. Other services, such as the Bond Buyer Worksheets and Multifacts, are now offered online.

No book can hope to present fully the resources available to bond investors. Organizations are constantly creating new websites, and updating existing ones. The investor in bonds should be aware of the available sites, and make some effort to become acquainted with relevant ones as well as maintain awareness of developments in the field.

Portfolio Management

If you own even one bond or one share in a bond mutual fund or unit investment trust, you have what professionals call a "portfolio." This portfolio will be managed either actively by you or inactively. Even if you don't do anything at all, you are still making a portfolio management decision, indirectly. By your inactivity, you are deciding not to do anything. This chapter gives you some ideas on how best to manage a bond portfolio, some practical things you can do to manage your own portfolio better, and things to think about as you manage your bonds and other investments. The three main areas covered are *diversification*, *portfolio structure*, and *bond swapping*.

There aren't many introductory-level books on fixed-income portfolio management investment for average investors. This chapter is an effort to overcome this shortage.

■ DEFINING DIVERSIFICATION

Diversification of investments consists of investing in a variety of different securities. The purpose is to avoid a large loss. You do this by investing in a variety of securities, so that a loss in one security will have only a small overall effect on the portfolio, and may even be offset by gains in other securities.

You pay a price to avoid a large loss; you also avoid the chance for a large gain. The best way to make large investment gains is simply to pick the single best performing security and put all your investment funds into that security. Few people can do this, so most people diversify to protect themselves against overall large loss.

■ WHY DIVERSIFICATION IS IMPORTANT

Diversification actually should include all aspects of your life, including your job, home, other investments, such as real estate, and other possible items, such as jewelry. If a person works for a company, owns his home in a town where many other employees of his company also live, and invests heavily in his employer's stock, how diversified is he? If his employer has bad times, the stock price will be affected, he may take a pay cut or even lose his job, and the price of his home may also be affected.

For example, a large, world-famous manufacturing company, well-known for its excellent treatment of its employees, eventually fell upon less prosperous times. Over a period of a few years, the stock price fell from about $175 to about $40, although it eventually recovered to over $100. For the first time in its history, the company laid off employees, many of whom lived in areas in which the company was by far the largest employer and which were also somewhat removed from other employment centers. These laid-off employees had no real employment opportunities in their immediate geographic area; their savings, represented by years of investment in company stock, were depleted by the stock decline; and the value of their homes plummeted, with many prospective sellers and few prospective buyers. The diminished home value made a move difficult even if their skills made it possible for them to find a job elsewhere; for many employees of large corporations, their skills are quite closely related to the employer's requirements, and are not easily transferable. Their situation was tragic in human terms; from the diversification point of view, they were not diversified. Their jobs, homes, and savings were all wrapped up in their employer. What could they have done? They could at least have owned as little as possible of their employer's stock, so that the substantial market decline in that stock would not have affected them as much.

There are other examples as well. Reports on the bank disasters in the last few years told of bank employees who had invested most or all of their retirement funds in their bank employer's stock. The banks were frequently taken over, or liquidated, with resulting substantial losses, and virtual elimination of the employees' retirement savings. There are similar stories of employees of stock brokerage firms who had invested their retirement funds in their employer's stock; the broker went out of business, with resulting total loss of the employees' retirement savings. In late 2001, the decline in Enron stock seriously hurt the retirement accounts of many Enron employees.

Diversification is a desirable investment objective, as these examples show. It is important to avoid large losses. Giving up the chance for a large gain (and being content with a moderate investment return) is a worthwhile price to pay to avoid a large loss.

■ INVESTMENT DIVERSIFICATION

Investment diversification starts first with a decision on allocation of investments between bonds and common stocks. Other investments, such as real estate, are not usually considered, except in the original decision on how much to allocate to financial investments.

This is very much an individual decision for the investor. It includes an emotional component as well as a rational component. Some individuals simply don't like to own much common stock; others simply don't like to own much fixed-income investment. There are no standard rules on how to do this, but certain considerations and guidelines have developed.

Over the years most suggestions have been for a split of about 50% bonds and 50% stocks, with a range from 75% in bonds and 25% in stocks to vice versa. Many advisors suggest that the percent in bonds increase as the investor approaches retirement age, but others think that the threat of inflation, combined with reduced earnings capability, should move the aging investor to increase the proportion in stocks. As this writer grows older, he tends to agree that investment in common stocks probably should not be reduced. Pensions generally don't increase with inflation, although Social Security is adjusted for inflation. (Note, however, that Social Security has its own set of problems.) For most investors, only common stocks offer some protection against inflation. However, in 2001, common stocks didn't come close to offering the rate of return of good fixed-income investments. For example, in early February 2001, the long-term Treasury bond offered a return of about 5.55%, while the Standard and Poor's 500 Index, a widely known common stock index, offered a return of about 1.2%, or less than one-quarter of the return available on the long-term Treasury bond. This means that stock prices must increase more than 4% each year just to equal the return from T-Bonds. Stock prices didn't exactly do that in 2001. Perhaps fixed-income investments, with savings to allow for inflation, are a suitable substitute.

Opinions also differ on whether a change in the market should cause an adjustment of the portfolio. Suppose you start with a 50-50 split between bonds and stocks, and a roaring bull stock market causes the split to be 65% in stocks and 35% in bonds. Should you sell some stocks to bring the ratio back to 50-50? Opinions of experts differ on this matter as well. Most investors probably will not sell, and if stocks go down again, the ratio may return to 50-50.

■ INCREASED BOND MARKET VOLATILITY

The bond market has also increased enormously in volatility during the last several decades. This development has attracted considerable comment.

No one knows for sure why bond market volatility has increased. Some think that fear of inflation has caused it. One leading analyst thinks that increased borrowing on "projections rather than on assets and performance" has contributed to increased volatility, according to a leading daily newspaper in late 2001. Perhaps increased yields themselves have contributed to the volatility. Perhaps increased investor interest in and trading in bonds has caused it. Perhaps all of these have contributed something to increased volatility. However, there is little doubt that bond market volatility, and therefore bond market risk, has increased.

This increased risk can offer trading opportunities for enterprising (aggressive) and knowledgeable investors. But for most investors, volatility is something to be guarded against. In a later section, we will discuss the choice investors make in becoming an enterprising or defensive investor, and the ladder approach in constructing a bond portfolio. Most investors will be defensive investors. The ladder portfolio protects against bond market volatility, to some extent.

■ ASSET ALLOCATION MODELS

Many brokerage firms offer suggestions on how to allocate funds between the different kinds of investments. These are called *asset allocation models*. They usually offer suggestions on the breakdown of total financial assets among cash, bonds, and stocks. For example, an asset allocation model might suggest 10% in cash, 40% in bonds, and 50% in stocks. The broker also usually offers specific suggestions for actual individual investments in these areas.

Asset allocation models offer the investor a look at his suggested portfolio, and allow him to answer "What if?" questions, such as, "What if interest rates rise?" or "What if stock prices fall?" These can be useful for the investor's planning purposes.

■ ARE YOU AN ENTERPRISING OR A DEFENSIVE INVESTOR?

For many years, advisors have suggested that the investor first decide whether he will be an enterprising (or aggressive) or a defensive investor. This suggestion was first made by Benjamin Graham, in his book *The Intelligent Investor*, first published in 1949 and still one of the best books around on investment policy for individual investors. The enterprising investor is willing to spend time and effort managing his investments; the defensive investor is willing to make only the minimal required effort to manage his investments and is content with a lower return. The size of the investment doesn't matter much; the important question is the amount of effort the investor is willing to make to manage his investments. Most investors have many demands on their time; they may also lack the special training required, as well as the interest, for active investment management. Therefore, most investors will be defensive investors.

■ HOW TO STRUCTURE A BOND PORTFOLIO

Structuring a portfolio means setting objectives for the portfolio and then selecting the bonds in the portfolio to meet these objectives. The objectives include the time to maturity of the portfolio, the type of bonds the investor wishes to hold in the portfolio, income-tax considerations, and other matters.

There are three main types of portfolio structure: the *ladder portfolio*, the *bullet portfolio*, and the *barbell portfolio*. We'll consider each of these. The most important is the ladder approach, which many defensive fixed-income investors will choose.

Fixed-income investors can also invest in bond mutual funds and unit investment trusts to achieve their portfolio objectives. We'll consider these later in the chapter.

■ HOW A LADDER PORTFOLIO WORKS

Suppose you just received an inheritance of $100,000, and you decide to invest it in a ladder portfolio. In February 2001, here is how you might have done it. You decide to invest in ten maturities, of $10,000 par value each, starting next year (2002) with a final maturity in 2011. You also decide to invest in Treasury securities, with a maturity month of February for all ten investments. Your portfolio might look like this:

MATURITY DATE	VALUE	ANNUAL INCOME
02/2002	10,137.50	625.00
02/2003	10,134.38	550.00
02/2004	9,962.50	475.00
11/2004	10,312.50	587.50
02/2006	10,278.13	562.50
02/2007	10,590.63	625.00
02/2008	10,209.38	550.00
05/2009	10,193.75	550.00
08/2010	10,406.00	575.00
08/2010	10,406.00	575.00
Total	102,630.77	5,675.00

Note that only six of the maturities have the same maturity month, February. The other months were selected because some maturity years had no February maturity at a price close to par. The 11/2004 maturity is within three months of the 02/2005 maturity, and the 05/2009 maturity is within three months of the 02/2009 maturity. The two different lots of the 08/2010 maturity indicate that they substitute for the 02/2010 and the 02/2011 maturities.

The values are a little above par, because the bond market had been moving up when this table was created in mid-February 2001. If you set up this portfolio, you must have to save and put aside about $2,630 from your income to maintain your total investment of $102,630, because the principal repayments will total only $100,000. This type of operation is called *amortizing principal*. Tax regulations would probably allow you to deduct this amount from your income stream over the life of the bonds for tax purposes. (Always consult with your tax accountant on matters like this.) Special Internal Revenue Service regulations cover this accounting and tax-reporting procedure.

In this case, we could not construct a portfolio with strict annual maturities for ten years. The recent (in February 2001) large Federal Government surpluses have reduced the need for governmental borrowing, so the Treasury has made fewer borrowings in the market. However, even with this reduced availability, we could still construct a good ladder portfolio in Treasuries. Portfolios of corporate or municipal bonds could have more choice, depending on the investment features desired for these portfolios.

In February 2002, your first securities will mature. You use the proceeds to buy $10,000 par amount of ten-year notes, maturing in February 2012; probably the Treasury will auction these off at that time, and you will be able to buy them noncompetitively at the auction. If no such securities are available, you will be able to purchase securities with a maturity date of close to February 2012.

Now let's look at what you have done after this purchase in February 2002. You still have a ten-year ladder portfolio, only now the maturities go from February 2003 to February 2012. You haven't changed the life of the portfolio to any great extent. You have kept the ladder concept, and bought some new securities to replace the maturing securities at low transaction cost. You still own Treasury securities, so you haven't lowered the portfolio quality. Your portfolio looks much like it did before the maturity and new purchase. As long as you continue to use each annual maturity to buy ten-year Treasuries, you will continue to have a portfolio with these same characteristics that you originally chose.

Let's see what happens to your portfolio value and income if the bond market changes drastically, up or down. Suppose, first of all, that bond yields fall between February 2001 and February 2002, and the ten-year note yields only 3.7%. This is a huge decline in yields, about 200 basis points, and would represent a large rise in the bond market, especially for such a short time. What will happen to the income from the portfolio? Your new note will pay you $370 annually, replacing the old security that paid you $625 annually. Your annual income will decline by $255, a relatively small amount compared to the total annual portfolio income of $5,675 before the maturity, or $5,420 after the change.

Your diversification of maturities has protected you against a large income decline due to the fall in interest rates. Your income has fallen a little, and if interest rates continue low, it will continue to fall as you roll over maturing investments into new ones. However, you have had protection for a few years. Note also that the value of your portfolio would increase as money rates fell.

In the early 1990s, as interest rates fell, many retired people saw their incomes from fixed-income investments decline sharply. The reason was that they had invested in money market funds. Money market funds respond almost immediately to changes in short-term interest rates, and the income paid from money market funds fell sharply. Persons who held only these funds suffered, and in some cases even had trouble paying everyday expenses. They were not diversified; had they been diversified, their problems would have been fewer, although still existent. During 2001, the same thing happened. Money market yields fell, and resulting income fell, in some cases by more than 70%.

Now suppose that the bond market falls, with interest rates on ten-year Treasuries rising 200 basis points instead of falling. This would be an enormous decline in bonds, especially in such a short time. How would your portfolio respond to this?

The longest bonds would decline about 15% in market value; the income, of course, would continue at the previous levels. The five-year securities would decline about 8% in market value. The shorter-term securities would decline relatively little, and you would still have them available as a ready source of emergency funds. Your diversification by maturity has protected you against a decline in the bond market. Your new ten-year investment, made in February 2002, will yield about $725 in annual income, so your total annual income from the portfolio will increase by $100 to a total of $5,775.

Note also that, with a ladder portfolio, each new investment of the proceeds of the maturing security is invested at the rate for ten-year securities. With a normal yield curve, this will be the highest of the rates available during the ladder period. The ladder technique guarantees that all your investments will be made at the highest, long-term rate normally available to them, within the constraints you originally chose for the portfolio.

Summarizing, what have you accomplished with the ladder approach to portfolio management? You have diversified by maturity so that changes in interest rates will not affect you much; you have protected yourself against changes in interest rates, both upward and downward. Your portfolio will roughly maintain its value in widely fluctuating markets, and your income stream won't change much, either, over a short period of time. The management effort involves only one investment once each year (in February) and you can probably buy these securities at the auction. They will probably have the highest yield of all the securities in the ladder period. You have given yourself this diversification protection at relatively little management cost, and relatively low transaction cost, especially since the maturing bonds will provide cash at no transaction cost whatever.

THE DECISIONS YOU MADE TO CONSTRUCT THIS PORTFOLIO

When you first constructed this portfolio, you made two decisions: You decided on the time period of the ladder, and you decided on the issuer of the bonds.

For the issuer, you decided on Treasuries. If your portfolio is composed solely of Treasuries, no further diversification by issuer is needed, because Treasuries have no credit risk. However, if you had decided to buy other securities, such as corporate or municipal bonds, you would have had to diversify further as to issuer and other factors. We'll talk more about these later on.

You also picked the ten-year time period of the ladder. You could have picked other periods instead. For example, you could have had $10,000 par amount maturing every two years for twenty years; you would then have bought a new twenty-year bond every two years as the earliest maturity matured. You could have picked a five-year period, with $20,000 maturing every year for five years. In fact, you could have picked almost any desired period, as long as Treasuries were available to make up your portfolio.

This choice of ladder period is really a choice of how much market risk you are willing to take. A longer ladder would be riskier, because long-term bond prices fluctuate more than short-term bond prices for the same change in yield.

HOW TO MEASURE MARKET RISK

When you chose the amount of risk you were willing to accept by choosing the length of the ladder, you measured the risk by a time period; in other words, the length of time of the ladder was a measure of the amount of risk of the portfolio. Almost all professional portfolio managers use some time measure to measure the market risk of their portfolio; this is also called a *measure of bond volatility.*

A well-known time measure is the average life of the portfolio. This is computed in the following way:

1. For each individual maturity, multiply the maturity amount by the time to the maturity date.
2. Add the products computed in 1.
3. Divide the total by the total maturity amount.

For example, suppose you have a portfolio of $3,000 total par amount, with $1,000 maturing in 2, 3, and 4 years. What is the average life?

We have: ($1,000 × 2 years) + ($1,000 × 3) + ($1,000 × 4)
= ($2,000 + $3,000 + $4,000)
= ($9,000)

Average life = ($9,000 years) divided by ($3,000), the total par amount of the portfolio.

Therefore, the average life equals three years, in this case.

In the case of the ten-year ladder portfolio, the average life, after you have just bought the new ten-year securities, is 5½ years.

Many sophisticated portfolio managers use a variation of this concept, called the *modified duration.* Modified duration includes the coupon income along with the maturity amounts, and evaluates the present value of these, using a present value equation. However, for most individual defensive investors, average life is much easier to compute and to understand, and is a perfectly adequate risk measure for their purposes.

■ HOW THE BULLET AND BARBELL APPROACHES WORK

Is there some other way to structure your portfolio so that it would have the same risk as the ladder portfolio, and might have other advantages as well? Two ways to do this are the *bullet approach* and the *barbell approach.*

The bullet approach is simply to buy one security with the chosen life, and manage that security. In this case, the investor would buy $100,000 market value of a security with maturity day 5½ years from February 2002; that is, the security would mature in August 2007. As time passes, and the time to maturity shortens, the investor sells the old security and buys another security, once more with a time to maturity of 5½ years.

You can see that this requires a higher volume of trading, and a closer attention to management. However, the need to do more frequent swapping can offer trading possibilities that don't exist in the ladder portfolio. Also, depending on the shape of the yield curve, the income might be somewhat higher using this approach. However, changes in the yield curve can also make this approach, and the barbell approach, less attractive than a simple ladder approach.

Another way to manage a bullet approach is simply to select a maturity, such as a five-year maturity, which has relatively little risk. Hold the security for a while, say for three years. After three years, you now have a two-year security. Sell this security and buy another five-year security. With a normal yield curve, this will result in an increase in yield from the two-year yield, and increased earnings for the next two-year period. This method can also give good results.

A second approach is to buy two maturities, which together have an average life equal to that desired. This might consist of equal amounts of one-year and ten-year securities. Depending on the shape of the yield curve, this also can give you a somewhat better return. However, it too requires more active management.

■ THE IMPORTANCE OF DIVERSIFICATION BY ISSUER

So far, we have considered portfolios consisting only of United States Treasury obligations. We showed how diversification by maturity was important, even for portfolios composed of Treasuries.

Diversification by issuer is unnecessary for Treasuries because they have no credit risk, but portfolios of other securities, such as corporate or municipal bonds, will require issuer diversification. Here are several examples showing why this consideration is important.

Orange County, California, used to have an Aa Moody's rating. This is the second best rating that is possible for a bond to have. Very few municipal issuers, except for advance refunded bonds, have an Aaa rating, and so Orange County had one of the country's best. Its residents are generally well off; it is one of the world's richest counties. If you were buying municipal securities, you could easily have considered and bought those of Orange County.

Yet Orange County ran into financial trouble in 1994, and in 1995 was forced to declare a moratorium, delaying payment on several of its obligations, and even considered entering bankruptcy. The reason? Orange County had lost approximately $1.6 billion in financial futures; much of this was owed to other governments and governing bodies in the area. These other governments pressed claims against Orange County for the full amounts owed to them. The Orange County voters refused to approve tax increases to pay this debt, but eventually the security holders were paid with new issues of debt. The County reduced government expenses, and even considered the sale of county-owned property, including their airport. It would have been hard to find a better rated bond than one issued by Orange County, yet that issuer ran into serious financial trouble.

This episode indicates the importance of diversification by issuer in any bond portfolio—except one composed of Treasuries. (In early 2001, Orange County's Moody's rating was Aa3. This is the lowest category in the Aa range, but still a very good rating.)

Corporate bonds are subject to similar events. For example, RJR Nabisco (a successor firm to the old National Biscuit Company) had been a well-regarded investment, and its bonds sold at relatively low yields. Then, in the fall of 1988, it was the subject of a leveraged buyout. The yields of its bonds promptly increased, compared to what they had been, as the increase over comparable Treasury yields rose from 100 basis points to 350 basis points. Owners of what had been a highly rated investment suddenly owned bonds with much lower ratings. This, too, illustrates the importance of diversification in bond investment.

This type of situation is called *event risk* in corporate and municipal bonds. "Events" in event risk occur all too frequently, and require diversification by issuer in corporate and municipal bond investments.

How much diversification by issuer is enough? Opinions vary, and the individual investor will have her own ideas on this subject. But if you had equal diversification among twenty different issuers, and if the investment in one issuer were wiped out, you would have a decline of only 5% in your portfolio. The individual investor would decide whether this was adequate.

Diversification among twenty different issuers, with additional differences between them as discussed later in this chapter, could provide enough issuer diversification for most needs of most defensive investors. Of course, this requires enough investment capital to invest in this many different issuers. Mutual funds and unit investment trusts can also provide issuer diversification for relatively small investments.

■ OTHER DIVERSIFICATION CONSIDERATIONS

Other considerations include diversification by the issuer's type of business (for corporate bonds), by the source of revenues (for municipal bonds), and by the issuer's geographic location.

Suppose you invested in twenty different bonds (either municipal or corporate) from twenty different issuers, but they all were in the electric utility (or public power) business. You would not be really diversified; if anything happened to the electric utility business, you could suffer severe loss. Your diversification should be by type of industry if you are investing in corporate bonds, and by type of revenue if you are investing in municipal revenue bonds. Investment in municipal general obligation bonds should be diversified by issuer's geographic location. Investment in municipal revenue bonds should also be diversified by issuer's geographic location, while investment in corporate bonds should be diversified by the geographic location of the business.

■ DIVERSIFICATION AND MANAGEMENT BY INVESTING IN BOND MUTUAL FUNDS AND UNIT INVESTMENT TRUSTS

Diversification can also be accomplished by investment in bond mutual funds and unit investment trusts (UITs). (These are beyond the scope of this book; there are many fine books on these investment possibilities, including one in this New York Institute of Finance series.) We will look at ways in which you might use these to diversify.

Each mutual fund or UIT has investment objectives, which are stated in the fund's prospectus and its reports. These objectives include the type of bonds it owns, maturity range it will own, and investment objectives. These should be the same as the investor's own objectives for fixed-income investment.

Funds will also offer portfolio management to the investor; this is the management of the fund's own portfolio. UITs have no management, since they do not trade the bonds they own, but may only sell them if they wish, without replacement. Also, with UITs, bonds that mature or are called are not replaced. This gives UITs a fixed, limited life, which is stated in the original prospectus.

Most funds and UITs will offer diversification by issuer. Diversification by maturity is somewhat harder, but can be accomplished by choosing investments in several funds, each of which has a maturity objective.

■ BOND SWAPPING AND WHY INVESTORS SWAP BONDS

A bond swap is a simultaneous sale and purchase of bonds. The sale and the purchase are separate transactions, but the objective is that the amounts of the sale and the purchase should be roughly similar, and usually the par amounts of the trades are roughly equal as well.

Swaps can be done for four major reasons, but not all of them apply equally to portfolio management. Some apply to the investor's personal situation, and some apply to market levels.

The four reasons for swapping a bond are:

1. Change in market levels
2. Change in the investor's personal situation
3. Change in the bond's characteristics
4. Portfolio improvement

In considering a swap, always remember that the swap should be made within the overall context of managing your portfolio; never make a swap simply for the purpose of making a swap, or for any purpose not related to your portfolio. Your portfolio objectives and plans should drive your swaps, not the other way around.

For example, in the ladder portfolio example given earlier, you swap once each year, as securities mature and you replace them with new ten-year securities. This is the only swap planned for your portfolio. Any others should be considered within that planning framework. For example, you would not swap your five-year maturity for a twenty-year maturity because that is outside the range of your portfolio's maturity schedule.

Large bond price changes, by themselves, may not be a reason for a swap. If you have made the decision to allocate a portion of your portfolio to bonds, then market changes may cause you to reevaluate this decision, but if you don't change your mind on your asset allocation, then you may not wish to swap.

CHANGES IN MARKET LEVELS (TAX SWAPS)

If the bond market has moved down, you may wish to consider what is called a *tax swap*. A tax swap is the sale of bonds at a loss with replacement by similar bonds that are different enough to comply with Internal Revenue Service requirements for the loss to be deductible for income-tax purposes. Compliance ensures tax deductibility, and if you have replaced the bonds sold with similar bonds, you remain within your portfolio's original planning ideas. With tax swaps especially, you should consult with your tax advisor in advance.

CHANGES IN PERSONAL SITUATION

A change in your personal situation could be a reason for swapping, but first you should reexamine your original portfolio management ideas. For example, personal situation changes might include retirement; a move to another location, especially another state; a sudden change in financial status, such as a large bonus or an inheritance; or some other personal change, such as a divorce or death in the family. Retirement might cause a change in asset allocation, resulting in possible bond portfolio changes, with resulting possible swaps. If the investor has a portfolio of municipal bonds, a move to another state might mean swapping into bonds issued within the new state to avoid state income taxes in the new location.

CHANGES IN BOND CHARACTERISTICS

A change in bond characteristics might require a swap. In the case of the ladder portfolio, each year a bond changes its characteristics by maturing; the proceeds are then reinvested ("swapped") into a new bond. But suppose the investor had a ladder portfolio with maturities from six to fifteen years. Each year, the investor would sell the shortest bond, which would then be a five-year bond, and buy a new fifteen-year bond, the longest term in the ladder portfolio. This swap is done for the purpose of maintaining the original portfolio characteristics. Other changes in bond characteristics include advance refundings and large changes in ratings. An advance refunded bond will usually be refunded to the call date and price, which may not be within the investor's portfolio plan. This bond would be a possible swap.

PORTFOLIO IMPROVEMENT SWAPS

Portfolio improvement swaps can sometimes be done, but these require continual attention to opportunities in the market. Most defensive investors probably won't have the time or the inclination to do that and, in any case, for most individual investors, the expense of making the swap uses up the possible advantages. Sometimes, however, investors have the opportunity to swap one bond for another, remain within the range of the portfolio's plan, and pick up an improvement in yield (called a *yield pickup swap*) or an improvement in quality. Usually, however, most proposed swaps that give a yield improvement also require an extension in maturity. If the new bonds are within the plan, that may be acceptable. In fact, this is what is done with the ladder portfolio concept with bonds that mature or move outside the ladder period, but in most cases the extension of maturity will take the proposed new bonds outside the maturity range of the portfolio.

Bond swaps of any kind will probably create a capital event for federal and state income-tax purposes, so you should always consult with your tax advisor before making the swap. But first, you should make sure that the swap conforms to your portfolio plan.

■ THE LADDER PORTFOLIO TEN MONTHS LATER—AN UPDATE

The section on the ladder portfolio was written in February 2001. The review of the copyedited proofs in December 2001, gave the author a chance to look at what happened since last February, and its effects on the portfolio.

During 2001, the Fed reduced interest rates eleven times, from 6.5% at the start of the year to 1.75% in mid-December, with a resulting huge decline in short term interest rates generally. However, long-term rates didn't decline so much. As a result, the yield curve became much steeper. This resulted in an increase in most bond prices, especially in the shorter term bonds. This effect is shown in the following table of the value of the portfolio in December 2001.

MATURITY DATE	VALUE FEB. 2001	VALUE DEC. 2001	ANNUAL INCOME
02/2002	10,137.50	10,100.00	625.00
02/2003	10,134.38	10,393.75	550.00
02/2004	9,962.50	10,356.25	475.00
11/2004	10,312.50	10,634.38	587.50
02/2006	10,278.13	10,584.38	562.50
02/2007	10,590.63	10,846.88	625.00
02/2008	10,209.38	10,481.25	550.00
05/2009	10,193.75	10,412.50	550.00
08/2010	10,406.00	10,550.00	575.00
08/2010	10,406.00	10,550.00	575.00
Total	102,630.77	104,909.39	5,675.00

In mid-December, the ten-year bond was yielding about 4.9%. If yields stay unchanged until February, the first maturity on the ladder will mature, and be replaced with a bond yielding about $487.50 in income. This will result in a decline of about $137.50 in annual income, about 2%. The ladder has protected you against an income decline in a time of sharply declining short-term rates, while the value has increased a little over 2%. During this time, some money market funds reduced income by about 70%, and were the subject of at least one TV news report.

Glossary

ACCRUED INTEREST. (1) The amount of interest due the seller from the buyer, upon settlement of a bond trade. (2) Prorated interest due since the preceding interest payment.

ACTIVE BONDS (THE "FREE CROWD"). A category of debt securities that the New York Stock Exchange Floor Department expects will trade frequently. Consequently, they are handled freely on the trading floor in much the same manner as stocks. *See* Inactive Bonds.

ACTIVE BOX. A physical location where securities are held awaiting action on them.

ADJUSTMENT BONDS. *See* Income Bonds.

ADVANCE REFUNDING. (1) Sale of new "refunding" municipal bonds in advance of the first call date of old bonds to lower interest costs, change the bond indenture, or for other reasons. Proceeds from the refunding issue are usually invested in Treasury securities until the older, higher-rate bonds become callable. (2) Exchange of maturing U.S. Government securities prior to their due date for new securities with a later maturity for the purpose of extending the national debt.

AFTERMARKET. A market for a security either over the counter or on an exchange after an initial public offering has been made of the security.

AFTER-TAX BASIS. An investor's yield to maturity calculated to take into account federal and state income taxes. This basis is used to compare returns of taxable bonds and tax-exempt municipal bonds. For example, a corporate bond paying 10% would have an after-tax basis of 5% for an investor in the 50% tax bracket. By contrast, a fully tax-exempt municipal bond paying 5% would have an after-tax basis of 5%.

AGREEMENT AMONG UNDERWRITERS. An agreement among members of an underwriting syndicate specifying the syndicate manager, the duties, and the privileges, among other things. Also called a *syndicate letter. See* Underwriting Agreement.

ALL-OR-NONE (AON) OFFERING. A "best-efforts" offering of new securities in which the issuer instructs the investment banker to cancel the entire offering (sold and unsold) if all of it cannot be distributed. In the secondary market, an indication that a particular lot of bonds will not be split up, but is offered only as a block.

ALTERNATIVE MINIMUM TAX. An income tax levied to make certain that taxpayers with a large number of deductions, credit, and exemptions do not escape all tax liabilities.

AMORTIZATION. The process of gradually reducing a debt through installment payments of principal and interest. Also applies to reducing the premium paid for a bond by applying part of the interest payments to premium reduction.

AND INTEREST. A bond transaction in which the buyer pays the seller a contract price plus interest accrued since the issuer's preceding interest payment.

ARBITRAGE. The simultaneous purchase and sale of the same or equal securities in such a way as to take advantage of price differences in separate markets. *See* Bona Fide Arbitrage; Risk Arbitrage.

ARBITRAGE CERTIFICATE. A document showing compliance with the limitations on arbitrage imposed by the Internal Revenue Code.

ARBITRAGER. One who engages in arbitrage. Although "arbitrager" is the preferred form of the word for general usage, the financial community frequently uses "arbitrageur."

ARREARAGE. The amount by which interest on bonds is due and unpaid.

AS AGENT. The role of a broker/dealer firm when it acts as the intermediary, or broker, between its customer and another customer, a market maker, or a contrabroker. For this service the firm receives a stated commission or fee. The trade is called an *agency transaction. See* As Principal.

AS PRINCIPAL. The role of a broker/dealer firm when it buys or sells for its own account. In a typical transaction, the firm buys from a market maker or contrabroker and sells to a customer at a fair and reasonable markup. If the firm buys from a customer and sells to the market maker at a higher price, the trade is called a *markdown*. *See* As Agent.

ASCENDING OR POSITIVE YIELD CURVE. The condition in the bond market when long-term interest rates are higher than short-term interest rates on debt securities of the same investment quality.

ASK-BID SYSTEM. A system used to place a market order for securities. A market order is one the investor wants executed immediately at the best prevailing price. The market order to buy requires a purchase at the lowest offering (asked) price, and a market order to sell requires a sale at the highest (bid) price. The bid price is what a dealer is willing to pay for a security, while the asked price is the price at which a dealer will sell. The difference between the bid and ask prices is called the *spread*. *See* Bid-and-Asked Quote.

AT-THE-CLOSE-ORDER. An order to be executed at the market at the close of trading, or as near as practicable to the close.

AT-THE-MARKET. (1) A price representing what a buyer would pay and what a seller would take in an arm's-length transaction. (2) An order to buy or sell immediately at the currently available price.

AT-THE-MONEY. A term used to describe a security option where the strike price and market price are the same.

AT-THE-OPENING (OPENING ONLY) ORDER. An order to buy or sell at a limited price on the initial transaction of the day for a given security; if unsuccessful, the order is automatically canceled.

AUCTION MARKETPLACE. A term used to describe an organized securities exchange where transactions are made in the open and any exchange member may join in. Most bond trades are not done in an auction market but are done in over-the-counter trading. *See* Over-the-Counter Market.

AUTHORITY BOND. A bond issued by a government agency such as the Port Authority of New York and New Jersey or the Los Angeles Department of Water and Power. The bonds are usually payable from revenues of the agency and not from the general revenues of the state or city establishing the agency.

AWAY FROM ME.   When a market maker does not initiate a quotation, transaction, or market in a security, he says it is *away from me.*

AWAY FROM THE MARKET.   An order where the limit bid is below the market quote for the security or where the limit offer is above the market quote.

BABY BOND.   A bond with a face value of less than $1,000, usually in $100 denominations. Baby bonds are issued chiefly by local governments to give moderate-income savers a way to purchase small-denomination tax-exempt bonds.

BACK OFFICE.   A securities industry phrase to describe a firm's cashier and clearing operations along with its accounting and compliance departments.

BACKING AWAY.   A refusal by an over-the-counter market maker to honor the quoted bid or asked price for a minimum lot of bonds. This practice is outlawed under the National Association of Securities Dealers Rules of Fair Practice.

BALLOON.   A larger principal repayment in the later years of some serial bond issues. *See* Serial Bonds.

BAN.   *See* Bond Anticipation Note.

BANKERS ACCEPTANCES.   Bills of exchange guaranteed (accepted) by a bank for payment within one to six months. They are used to provide manufacturers or exporters with short-term funds to operate between the time of manufacturing or exporting goods and receiving payment from purchasers.

BANKS FOR COOPERATIVES.   A farmer-owned agency operating under supervision from the Federal Farm Credit Bank System that makes loans to farm cooperatives.

BASIS POINT.   One one-hundredth of a percentage point. The most common measure of changes in bond yields. For example, if a Treasury bond yielding 8.17% changes in price so that it now yields 8.10%, it is said to have declined seven basis points in yield.

BEAR MARKET.   A prolonged period of falling securities prices. The greatest bear market for bonds lasted from 1946 until 1981.

BEARER BOND.   A bond that does not have the owner's name registered on the books of the issuing corporation or government and one that is payable to the bearer. Since July 1, 1983, municipal bonds have not been permitted to be sold as bearer bonds for their interest to be tax-exempt. Treasuries and most corporates are no longer issued in bearer form.

BEARER FORM. Securities issued in such a form as not to permit the owner's name to be imprinted on the certificate. The holder of the security is presumed to be the owner or the owner's agent.

BELLWETHER. In the bond market, the most recently issued long-term Treasury bond, widely followed as a measure of the direction and magnitude of price changes in the bond market. In 2001, the ten-year Treasury is often considered a bellwether.

BENEFICIAL OWNER. The owner of securities who receives interest and repayment of principal even though they are registered in the name of a brokerage firm or nominee bank.

BEST-EFFORTS OFFERING. An offering of newly issued securities in which an investment banker acts merely as agent, promising only to make the best effort to sell the securities but not guaranteeing to sell them. Such offerings usually involve common stocks and not bonds.

BID-AND-ASKED QUOTE. The bid price is the highest price that anyone has declared willingness to pay for a security at a given time. The asked price is the lowest price anyone will accept at the same time.

BIDDING SYNDICATE. Two or more investment banking firms working together to submit a proposal to underwrite a new issue of securities.

BLOWOUT. A securities offering that sells out almost immediately.

BLUE-SKY LAWS. State antifraud securities laws pertaining to registration requirements and procedures. "Blue sky" is used to mean *lacking substance or fanciful*, and the regulations are designed to halt the sale of securities having "no more value than a patch of blue sky."

BLUE-SKYING THE ISSUE. The efforts of the underwriters' lawyers to investigate and analyze state laws regulating the distribution of securities and to qualify specific issues of securities under those laws.

BONA FIDE ARBITRAGE. Arbitrage transactions by professional traders to take advantage of different prices for the same securities in different markets. The risk is usually minimal and the profit, correspondingly small. *See* Risk Arbitrage.

BOND. A security representing long-term debt issued by governments or corporations. The security may be in bearer, book-entry, or registered form, and the issuer pays interest on the bonds at specified dates and redeems them when the loan is scheduled to be repaid, called the *maturity date or call date.*

BOND AMORTIZATION FUND. An account in a sinking fund. An issuer makes periodic deposits of money eventually to be used to purchase bonds on the open market or to pay the cost of redeeming the bonds.

BOND ANTICIPATION NOTE (BAN). A short-term debt instrument issued by states, cities, and other local governments, usually offered on a discount basis. Proceeds from a forthcoming bond issue are pledged to pay off the notes at maturity.

BOND BANK. An agency created by a state to purchase entire issues of bonds of municipalities. The purchases are financed by the issuance of bonds by the bond bank and are made to provide better access to capital for smaller, less well-known issuers.

BOND BROKER. A person who acts as an intermediary between buyers and sellers of securities for commissions. Bond brokers work on securities exchanges and in the over-the-counter market, handling Treasury, corporate, municipal, and other types of bonds.

BOND COUNSEL. A lawyer or law firm with expertise in bond law who can deliver an opinion as to the legality of issuance, and in the case of municipal bonds, deliver an opinion as to the tax-exempt status of the securities.

BOND EQUIVALENT YIELD. *See* Equivalent Bond Yield.

BOND FUND. An investment company or mutual fund that invests chiefly in long-term bonds. The most important are Treasury bond funds, corporate bond funds, convertible bond funds, municipal bond funds, and foreign bond funds.

BOND INSURANCE. Insurance as to timely payment of interest and principal, chiefly on municipal bonds. The cost of insurance is usually paid by the issuer to reduce the cost of borrowing.

BOND INTEREST DISTRIBUTION. In a bond trade, the payment of interest accrued since the preceding interest payment by the issuer. The bond interest distribution payment is made by the bond purchaser to the bond seller, thereby making the purchaser entitled to all the next payment of interest by the issuer. The interest due the seller is calculated by multiplying Principal × Rate × Time.

BOND ISSUE. Bonds sold under one indenture or resolution and having one settlement date. The bonds of a single issue may have different maturity dates, however.

BOND MARKET ASSOCIATION (THE). The national trade association for securities firms underwriting, trading, and dealing in U.S. Treasury, federal agency, municipal, mortgage, corporate, and money market issues.

BOND PURCHASE AGREEMENT. The contract between bond issuer and underwriter setting down final terms (most importantly, price and yield) and conditions governing the purchase of the securities.

BOND RATING. A measure of the quality, safety, and potential performance of a bond issue. Moody's Investors Service, Standard & Poor's, and Fitch are the largest rating agencies.

BOND YEAR. $1,000 of debt outstanding for one year; an element used in calculating average life of a bond issue and net interest cost, chiefly on municipal serial bonds maturing annually over a span of years and bond sinking funds.

BONDED DEBT. The portion of an issuer's total indebtedness represented by outstanding long-term bonds.

BOOK-ENTRY BOND. A bond for which no certificate exists, but records of the beneficial owner are kept by a depository and its members (banks and brokerage firms).

BOUGHT DEAL. In securities underwriting, a firm commitment to purchase securities from an issuer. It differs from a *stand-by* commitment in which underwriters agree to purchase part of an issue if it is not fully subscribed, and it differs from a *best-efforts* deal in which underwriters strive to sell the securities but do not guarantee doing so. In a bought deal, investment bankers buy the securities with their own and borrowed capital and then seek to sell them at a higher price.

BROKER. A person who acts as an intermediary between a buyer and a seller, usually charging a commission.

BROKER'S BROKER. A bond broker who acts as intermediary only with municipal bond dealers and not with the general public.

BULL MARKET. A period of rising securities prices. In the bond market, it is a period of declining bond yields.

CALL. Action taken to pay principal of bonds before their stated maturity date, in accordance with the indenture.

CALL PREMIUM. A dollar amount, usually stated as a percentage of principal, paid as a penalty or premium when an issuer exercises its right to redeem securities prior to maturity.

CALL PROTECTION. Assurance that bonds may not be called for part of the time, usually ten years, that they are scheduled to be outstanding. See Noncallable Bond.

CANADIAN INTEREST COST. *See* True Interest Cost.

CARRY. The net interest cost of financing an inventory of securities.

CASH CONTRACT. A securities contract that calls for delivery of securities to the purchaser on the same day they were traded.

CASHIER DEPARTMENT. A division of a securities firm responsible for the physical handling of securities and money, delivery and receipt, collateral loans, borrowing, lending, transfer of securities, and other financial transactions.

CATASTROPHE CALL. An issuer's call for redemption of a bond issue when certain unexpected events occur. Also called an *extraordinary call.*

CERTIFICATES OF ACCRUAL ON TREASURY SECURITIES (CATS). Receipts for interest on principal payments of U.S. Treasury issues. They are sold at deep discounts from face value, and pay no interest during their lifetime but pay full face value at maturity. *See* Zero Coupon Bonds.

CERTIFICATE OF DEPOSIT (CD). Short-term negotiable debt security issued by commercial banks with maturities ranging from a few weeks to several years. Interest rates are determined by the money market. Also nonnegotiable bank savings deposits with specified maturities.

CLEARING HOUSE FUNDS. Funds represented by checks that are transferred between banks through the Federal Reserve System and that require three days to clear. *See* Federal Funds.

CLOSE-OUT. The procedure that enables dealers who have bought securities but have not yet received them to take action to complete the transaction.

CLOSING DATE.   The date on which a new issuance of bonds is delivered to the purchaser upon payment of the purchase price.

CLOSING QUOTATION.   A market maker's final bid and asked prices for an issue at the end of a business day.

COLLATERAL.   Securities and other property pledged by a borrower until a loan is repaid.

COLLATERAL TRUST BOND.   A corporate bond issue that is protected by a portfolio of securities held in trust by a commercial bank or other trustee. It is usually issued by parent corporations that are borrowing against the securities of wholly owned subsidiaries.

COMMISSION.   The fee paid to a dealer when the dealer acts as agent in a securities transaction, as opposed to when the dealer acts as a principal in a transaction. See Net Price.

COMPETITIVE UNDERWRITING.   A sale of securities by an issuer in which underwriters submit competitive sealed bids or, rarely, oral auction bids to purchase the securities. The issuer awards the bonds to the highest bid (lowest net interest cost). *See* Negotiated Underwriting.

CONCESSION.   The allowance (or profit) that an underwriter may offer to a dealer who is not a member of the underwriting syndicate for helping to sell an offering of securities.

CONFIRMATION.   A written document certifying an oral transaction in securities that provides pertinent information to the buyer and seller.

CONTRABROKER.   A term used to describe the broker with whom a trade was made.

CONVERSION.   Exchange of one security for another, usually of corporate bonds or preferred stock for common stock.

CONVERSION PRICE.   The dollar value at which convertible bonds, debentures, or preferred stock can be converted into common stock under the terms of the indenture.

CONVERTIBLE BOND.   A bond that may be exchanged for another security, usually a specified number of common shares.

CORPORATE BOND.   A debt security issued by a corporation.

COUPON. (1) The detachable part of a bearer bond that denotes the amount of interest due, on what date, and where payment is to be made. Coupons generally are payable semiannually. They are presented to an issuer's paying agent or deposited in a commercial bank for collection. (2) The interest rate, expressed as a percent, paid on a bond.

COUPON BOND. A bond with detachable interest coupons, small ticket-like certificates denoting the amount to be paid. Prior to July 1983 most municipal bonds were issued in coupon form, but the law now requires most municipal bonds sold since then to be in registered or book-entry form for their interest to be exempt from federal income taxes. *See* Registered Bond.

COVER. The differential in basis points between first and second bids in a competitive bond sale. Also, the second-best bid.

COVERAGE. The margin of safety for payment of debt service on a revenue bond, stated as the number of times (e.g., 150% coverage) by which net annual earnings exceed annual debt service.

CURRENT YIELD. The rate of return on a bond based on the ratio of interest income to the purchase or market price. It is the actual rate of return, not the coupon rate. For example, a bond carrying a 6% coupon rate and trading at 95 is said to have a current yield of 6.32% ($60 coupon + $950 market price = 6.32%).

CUSHION BOND. A callable bond with a coupon rate higher than current market interest rates that is trading at a premium. If interest rates rise, the price of a cushion bond won't decline much.

CUSIP. An acronym standing for Committee on Uniform Securities Identification Procedures, which was established by the American Bankers Association to develop a standard method of distinguishing municipal, U.S. government, and corporate securities. Each security is given a CUSIP number, and each maturity of a municipal bond issue carries its own CUSIP number.

DATED DATE. The date of a bond issue from which the bond holder is entitled to receive interest, even though the bonds may actually be delivered at some other date.

DAY ORDER. A transaction order that remains valid only for the remainder of the trading day it was entered.

DAY TRADING. The act of buying or selling securities the same day.

DEALER. An individual or firm in the securities business acting as a principal rather than as a broker or agent.

DEALER BANK. A commercial bank that underwrites and trades municipal bonds.

DEBENTURE. A corporate debt security backed only by the financial strength of the issuer and not by any physical asset; an unsecured corporate bond.

DEBT INSTRUMENT. A written promise to repay an obligation.

DEBT LIMIT. Statutory restriction on the principal amount of borrowing that an issuer may incur or have outstanding at any one time.

DEBT SECURITY. Any security reflecting a loan; a bill, note, or bond.

DEBT SERVICE. Principal and interest required to make a periodic payment on the debt.

DEBT SERVICE REQUIREMENTS. Amount required to pay interest and current maturities of principal for a given period, usually one year.

DEBT SERVICE RESERVE FUND. An account into which is paid money required by a trust agreement or indenture as protection against interruption in the receipt of revenues pledged for payment of bonds, commonly one year's debt service on the bonds.

DEEP DISCOUNT BONDS. Bonds selling for far less than their face value, generally below 80% of par. Not a bond selling at an original issue discount, however.

DEFAULT. Failure to pay debt service when due, or failure to comply with other covenants in financing documents.

DEFEASANCE. A substitution of new debt for old debt, generally by structuring a portfolio of government securities sufficient to pay debt service on the outstanding, older securities. When a bond issue is defeased, the claim on the issuer is eliminated and the debt can be erased from the issuer's books.

DEFLATION. A contraction in the supply of money or credit that results in declining prices; the opposite of inflation.

DELIVERY. The time when payment is made to, and securities are received from, the issuer. New-issue delivery of bonds generally takes place several weeks after the sale.

DEMAND NOTES. Securities that can be sold by the holder back to the issuer on short notice, usually seven days. Demand notes can have maturities as long as thirty years, but their "resale on demand" attribute enables them to trade at yields of short-term instruments. Most demand notes carry variable rates.

DENOMINATION. The face amount or par value of a bond or note that an issuer promises to pay on the maturity date.

DEPOSITORY. A clearing agency that provides safe-keeping and book-entry settlement services to its customers.

DEPOSITORY TRUST COMPANY (DTC). The largest clearing agency, owned by broker/dealers and banks, and responsible for: (1) holding securities owned by broker/dealers and banks; (2) arranging receipt and delivery of securities among users by means of debiting and crediting their respective accounts, almost entirely electronically; (3) arranging for payments to users in the settlement of transactions.

DEPTH. (1) The amount of interest in the market, measured by comparing the number of issues traded with the number of issues outstanding: The more traded, the greater the market's "depth." (2) The ability of a security market to absorb large buy or sell orders without changing price greatly.

DESIGNATED ORDER. A large order from an institutional investor specifying preference for certain dealers in an underwriting syndicate and crediting them with the sale of specific amounts of bonds.

DIRECT DEBT. Borrowing by a state, city, or other local government in its own name and not through an authority or agency.

DISCOUNT. The amount, stated in dollars or as a percent, by which the market price of a bond is below its face amount. Also, the amount by which the total bid for an issue is less than the aggregate principal amount of that issue.

DISCOUNT BOND. A bond selling in the market at a price below its face value. *See* Deep Discount Bonds.

DISCOUNT NOTE. A noninterest-bearing, short-term security sold at a price lower than its maturity value that matures at par. The U.S.

Treasury sells three-month and six-month discount notes, known as Treasury bills.

DISCOUNT RATE (THE). The rate of interest that Federal Reserve Banks charge on loans to member banks.

DISTRICT BANK. *See* Federal Reserve Bank.

DISTRICT BUSINESS CONDUCT COMMITTEE. A National Association of Securities Dealers district group responsible for supervising rules of fair practice.

DOLLAR BOND. A bond that is quoted in terms of price rather than yield, usually long-term maturities of municipal revenue bond issues of substantial size.

DOUBLE-BARRELED BOND. A municipal bond with two distinct sources of revenue, usually the full faith and credit of the issuer plus some specific user charge.

DOUBLE-EXEMPTION BONDS. Securities that are exempt from state as well as federal income taxes.

DOWNGRADE. To lower the rating of a bond issue.

DUE DILIGENCE. Investigation of a bond issue by bond counsel for underwriters and issuers to insure that all material information has been included in the official statement informing potential investors about the securities and that there are no erroneous statements in the official statement or prospectus.

DURATION. A time measure of interest-rate risk exposure that takes into account the present value of coupon and maturity payments and the yield to maturity based on the price of the bond.

DUTCH AUCTION. A sale of securities in which the price is gradually lowered until it meets a responsive bid.

EASY MONEY. A state of the economy when interest rates are lower and ample funds are available in the banking system and credit markets. These conditions are governed largely by the Federal Reserve System.

EFFECTIVE DATE. The date on which a security may be offered for sale by underwriters if the Securities and Exchange Commission has not found the registration statement deficient. The date is generally no earlier than twenty calendar days after filing the registration statement.

EQUIPMENT TRUST CERTIFICATE.   A corporate serial bond collateralized with transportation equipment or machinery.

EQUIVALENT BOND YIELD.   The annualized return on a short-term discount security expressed on a comparable basis to yields on bonds with coupons. Also called *bond equivalent yield.*

EQUIVALENT TAXABLE YIELD.   The return that a taxable security must yield to give an investor the same after-tax return that he or she would earn on a tax-exempt bond.

EXECUTION.   Completion of a trade between a buyer and seller.

EXEMPT FACILITIES BONDS.   Tax-exempt securities authorized under the Internal Revenue Code that are sold to finance privately owned or privately used facilities. The Tax Reform Act of 1986 amended existing law and stated that convention centers, sports complexes, air and water pollution-control facilities, privately owned airports, docks, wharves, mass-transit facilities, and parking garages could no longer be financed with exempt facilities bonds.

EXLEGAL.   In municipal bond trading, the absence of a bond counsel's opinion.

FACE AMOUNT.   The value at maturity stated on a bond certificate. Also referred to as *par value.*

FAIR MARKET VALUE.   The price, based on supply and demand, at which buyers and sellers are willing to trade.

FANNIE MAE.   The Federal National Mortgage Association (FNMA).

FARMERS HOUSING ADMINISTRATION.   A federal agency established by the Department of Agriculture to make property loans to farmers. The FHA also makes loans to rural communities.

FEASIBILITY STUDY.   A report by an independent expert on the economic need and practicality of a proposed project, such as a toll road or airport.

FEDERAL FARM CREDIT BANK SYSTEM.   A system of banks established by the federal government to meet financial needs of farmers, ranchers, and fishermen.

FEDERAL FUNDS.   (1) Reserve deposits of commercial banks at Federal Reserve Banks in excess of reserves required by the Fed. Banks may lend these excess reserves to each other in overnight loans at rates of interest known as the *federal funds rate*. (2) Funds used to settle same-day transactions. (3) Funds used by the Federal Reserve to pay for its purchase of Treasury securities.

FEDERAL FUNDS RATE. The interest rate that commercial banks charge on overnight Federal Funds loans to other banks. The funds rate is a key measure of short-term interest rates because it is set daily by the market and is governed by the Federal Reserve through the addition or subtraction of reserves in the banking system.

FEDERAL HOME LOAN BANK SYSTEM (FHLBS). A government-sponsored agency that helps finance the housing industry.

FEDERAL NATIONAL MORTGAGE ASSOCIATION (FNMA, OR FANNIE MAE). A publicly owned, government-sponsored corporation that buys and sells mortgages insured by the Federal Housing Administration or guaranteed by the Veterans Administration. FNMA also issues mortgage pass-through securities.

FEDERAL OPEN MARKET COMMITTEE (FOMC). This important group comprises the seven Federal Reserve governors and presidents of six Federal Reserve Banks (New York permanently and five others on a rotating basis). The committee holds closed meetings to set short-term interest rates and determine the availability of credit.

FEDERAL RESERVE BANK. One of twelve central banks that make up the Federal Reserve System, established by the Federal Reserve Act of 1913 to regulate money, banking, and credit in the U.S. The twelve Federal Reserve Banks are located in Boston, New York, Philadelphia, Cleveland, Richmond, Atlanta, Chicago, St. Louis, Minneapolis, Kansas City, Dallas, and San Francisco.

FEDERAL RESERVE BOARD. The governing board of the Federal Reserve System, consisting of seven governors appointed by the President, subject to Senate approval, to serve 14-year terms. The board sets bank reserve requirements and discount rate, implements monetary policy, establishes regulations for national banks, and performs a variety of services for banks. The chairpersonship is considered one of the most powerful government positions to affect the economy.

FIDUCIARY. A person or institution entrusted to hold assets for a beneficiary.

FINANCIAL ADVISOR. A consultant to an issuer of municipal bonds who provides advice on structure, timing, and terms of new issues of securities.

FIRM PRICE. A price for a security in the over-the-counter market that a dealer says will not be changed for a specified period of time.

FIRST-CALL DATE. The earliest date specified in the indenture of a bond on which part or all of the issues may be redeemed at a set price.

FISCAL AGENT. A representative of a bond issuer who performs certain functions related to the sale and administration of a securities issue. The Federal Reserve acts as fiscal agent for the federal government.

FISCAL POLICY. Use of government taxation and spending policies to achieve economic growth and stable prices or other government objectives.

FISCAL YEAR. An accounting period covering twelve consecutive months and designated by its ending date. Most governments use fiscal years that do not correspond to the calendar year.

FITCH INVESTORS SERVICE. A credit-rating agency. Also publishes company, issuer, and industry reports.

FIXED-INCOME SECURITY. A security, such as a note or bond, that pays a guaranteed rate of interest.

FIXED-INTEREST-RATE PUT-OPTION BONDS. Bonds that pay a fixed rate of interest until some put option date, when the rate is then reset. See Put Bonds.

FLAT. In bond trading, without accrued interest.

FLIP. To sell securities quickly after purchasing them.

FLOATER. A bond sold with a variable, or floating, interest rate that changes at intervals ranging from one day to one year.

FLOATING-RATE PUT-OPTION BOND. A bond bearing a variable interest rate that the holder may sell back (or "put") to the issuer. Such bonds are backed by letters of credit to assure the issuer a source of funds to purchase the bonds. Usually called *Variable Rate Demand Obligation*.

FLOW OF FUNDS. The stream of revenues or money pledged to support certain municipal revenue bonds.

FLOWER BOND. A type of bond that is acceptable at par in payment of federal estate taxes.

FOURTH MARKET. Trading of securities between investors without the use of broker/dealers.

FULL FAITH AND CREDIT. The pledge of the general taxing power of a government to pay its debt obligations.

FULLY REGISTERED. A security that is registered, or recorded, for payment of both principal and interest.

FUNDED DEBT. Debt that is due after one year.

FUTURES. Contracts traded on exchanges for trades at future dates of delivery, at the trade prices of certain commodities or investments.

GENERAL OBLIGATION BOND (GO). A municipal bond secured by a pledge of the issuer's full faith and credit, and taxing power. The taxing power may be an unlimited *ad valorem* tax or a limited tax, usually on real estate or personal property, or other taxes, such as income or sales taxes.

GILT-EDGED. A bond that is high grade and meets its payments of principal and interest with no difficulty.

GLASS-STEAGALL ACT OF 1933. The federal banking law of 1933 that created the Federal Open Market Committee and the Federal Deposit Insurance Corporation and separated commercial banking from investment banking.

GLOBAL CERTIFICATE. A single document representing an entire issue of bonds or entire maturity of an issue, kept at a depository or book-entry agent.

GO-AROUND. The process used by the trading desk at the Federal Reserve Bank of New York, acting for the Federal Open Market Committee; contacts primary dealers for bid and offer prices of Treasury securities.

GOING AWAY. Bonds purchased by investors rather than by dealers for inventory.

GOOD DELIVERY. To send and turn over to a purchaser securities with all legal details in order.

GOOD FAITH DEPOSIT. A token amount of money, usually 2% of the face value of an issue of securities, given by bidders to issuers in competitive bond sales. The deposit, usually made as a cashier's check, is returned to a bidder if its bid is rejected.

GOOD-TILL-CANCELED (GTC OR OPEN) ORDER. An order to buy or sell that remains valid until executed or revoked by the customer.

GOVERNMENT ACCOUNTING STANDARDS BOARD. A body established by the Financial Accounting Foundation to write accounting rules for states, municipalities, and other local governments. After approval by the federal government, the rules become generally accepted accounting principles.

GOVERNMENT NATIONAL MORTGAGE ASSOCIATION (GNMA). A wholly owned government agency operated by the Department of Housing and Urban Development to purchase mortgages from private lenders, package them into pass-through securities known as "Ginnie Maes," and sell them to investors. The securities are backed by the full faith and credit of the U.S. and are fully taxable.

GROSS REVENUES. Income of an issuer before expenses.

GROUP. An underwriting account made up of investment banking firms, formed to buy new bond issues, either through negotiation or by competitive bidding.

GROUP SALES. Sales of bonds by an underwriting syndicate manager to institutional investors from the "pot," a portion of the issue set aside for such orders.

GUARANTEED INVESTMENT CONTRACT (GIC). An agreement between an insurance company and a pension fund or a municipal bond issuer assuring a specific rate of return on invested capital over the life of the accord.

HAIRCUT. A securities industry term referring to the formulas used to evaluate securities to calculate a broker/dealer's net capital. The haircut varies according to class of security.

HEDGE. Any combination of long and short positions in securities and options in which one position tends to reduce the risk of another; any strategy used to offset investment risk.

HIGH-GRADE BONDS. Top-rated bonds, usually triple-A, that carry relatively little risk.

HIT THE BID. A transaction in which a seller accepts a buyer's highest proffered price. For example, if the bid is 94, the seller "hits the bid" by accepting 94.

HOSPITAL REVENUE BONDS. Bonds issued by a municipal or state agency to finance construction, maintenance, or operation of hospitals or nursing homes.

HOUSING BONDS. Bonds issued by a municipal or state agency to finance construction of single-family or multifamily housing.

HOUSING PROJECT NOTES. Short-term securities sold by the Department of Housing and Urban Development for public housing agencies. Such note sales were suspended in August 1984.

HUMPHREY-HAWKINS ACT. A federal law enacted in 1978 that requires the Federal Reserve Board to report twice a year on monetary policy and the central bank's goals for economic growth, employment, and price stability.

INACTIVE BONDS. Corporate debt securities that are expected by the New York Stock Exchange to trade only infrequently. All bids and offers therefore are filed in a "cabinet" until they are canceled or executed.

INCOME BONDS. Debt securities on which payment of interest is contingent upon receipt of sufficient revenues or earnings. Frequently issued in cooperative reorganizations to previous bondholders, and called *adjustment bonds*.

INDENTURE. A written document, also called a *bond resolution or deed of trust*, describing the terms of a bond issue. It covers the form of the bond, amount of the issue, property pledged, protective covenants including any provision for a sinking fund, working capital and current ratio, and redemption rights or call privileges. The indenture also provides for the appointment of a trustee to act on behalf of bondholders in accordance with the Trust Indenture Act of 1939.

INDICATION OF INTEREST. An investor's early statement of interest in purchasing new securities soon to be offered for sale. It is not a binding commitment.

INDUSTRIAL DEVELOPMENT BONDS / INDUSTRIAL REVENUE BONDS. The two terms, which generally are interchangeable, describe revenue bonds sold by state or municipal authorities to finance facilities to be leased to corporations. If a distinction is made between IDBs and IRBs, it is that industrial development bonds are sold most often to build facilities to attract industry, while industrial revenue bonds are sold to finance pollution-control equipment or resource-recovery plants. The phraseology, however, depends chiefly on the issuer's preference.

INFLATION. A general rise in prices, measured by monthly indexes of wholesale prices (the Producer Price Index, or PPI) and retail prices (the Consumer Price Index, or CPI). Bond investors are vitally interested in inflation because most interest payments are fixed and do not vary over the time the bonds are outstanding. A high rate of inflation reduces the purchasing power of fixed-income investments and makes them less attractive.

INFRASTRUCTURE. The economic foundation of a country, including its transportation system, water and sewer facilities, electrical system, and other physical plant. Many general obligation bonds in the municipal bond market are sold to finance infrastructure capital spending.

INITIAL OFFERING PRICE. The charge to an investor for a new bond, generally stated as a percent of face value or yield to maturity. Members of the underwriting account may not offer the bonds for sale at any lower price during the initial offering period.

INSTITUTION. A bank, insurance company, investment company, pension fund, labor union fund, college endowment, or corporate profit-sharing plan, operating in the securities market. *See* Retail.

INTEREST. Compensation paid for the use of money, usually expressed as an annual percentage rate.

INTEREST RATE SWAP. An agreement between the two parties to exchange future flows of interest payments. One party agrees to pay the other at an adjustable rate; the other pays the first party at a fixed rate.

INTRADAY. Meaning "within the day," a term used most often to describe daily highs and lows of security prices.

INVERTED OR NEGATIVE YIELD CURVE. The interest-rate structure that exists when short-term interest rates exceed long-term interest rates.

INVESTMENT ADVISOR. A person, company, or institution registered with the Securities and Exchange Commission under the Investment Advisors Act of 1940 to manage the securities holdings of others.

INVESTMENT BANKER. A securities firm that serves as an intermediary between issuers of bonds (as well as stocks and other securities) and investors, usually risking its capital during the interval it holds the securities. Investment banking firms counsel their issuer clients and make markets in their issuer clients' securities.

INVESTMENT GRADE. Bonds that are appropriate for purchase by conservative investors because they represent moderate to low risk. Generally the top four grades of Moody's (Aaa, Aa, A, and Baa) and Standard & Poor's and Fitch (AAA, AA, A, and BBB).

JOINT BOND. A bond with more than one obligor or one guaranteed by a party other than the issuer, commonly used by parent and subsidiary corporations.

JOINT MANAGERS. Securities firms that share the leading role of investment banking groups underwriting offerings of securities.

JUNK BOND. Any bond with a Moody's rating lower than Baa or a Standard & Poor's or Fitch rating lower than BBB, i.e., lower than investment grade. Such bonds, usually issued by companies without well-established records of earnings, can produce high yields as long as they don't go into default.

L. The broadest measure of the money supply. It consists of money in circulation, demand deposits, savings deposits, credit union drafts, nonbank travelers checks, money market mutual fund shares, Treasury bills, savings bonds, commercial paper, and bankers acceptances. *See* M-1, M-2, and M-3.

LEAD MANAGER. The member of an underwriting syndicate charged with primary responsibility for conducting its affairs.

LEGAL LIST. A list of securities permissible for investment for regulated institutions.

LEGAL OPINION. Advice from bond counsel concerning the validity of a municipal securities issue, and the exemption of municipal bond interest from federal income taxes.

LEHMAN BROTHERS AGGREGATE BOND INDEX. A measure of the total return on about 6,500 bonds issued in the U.S.

LENDER OF LAST RESORT. A description of the Federal Reserve System for its role in helping banks faced with large withdrawals of funds.

LETTER OF CREDIT (LOC). A document usually issued by a bank that guarantees a loan to make payment of principal and interest of a bond.

LEVEL DEBT SERVICE. Provision in a bond issue to make annual debt service requirements approximately equal while the securities remain outstanding. The purpose is to make it easier for municipalities to estimate tax revenues needed to prepay debt.

LEVERAGE. Using borrowed money to invest. If a corporation earns a return on borrowed funds greater than the cost of its debt, it is successfully applying leverage.

LIMITED TAX BOND. A municipal bond secured by a pledge of a tax restricted as to rate or amount.

LIPPER GENERAL MUNICIPAL BOND FUND INDEX. An index that measures the net asset values of ten large municipal bond funds. The base of 100 was set on Dec. 31, 1980, when the Index was first published.

LIQUIDITY. The ease and speed with which an investment can be converted into cash.

LIST. In the municipal bond market, an inventory of bonds put out for bids.

LISTED BOND TABLE. Compendium of trades of bonds traded on the New York Stock Exchange or the American Stock Exchange, published daily in many newspapers.

LOCKED MARKET. A condition in the market when the bid and asked sides of a quote are the same.

LONG BOND. Generally the most recently issued 30-year Treasury bond, which is cited frequently as the benchmark for the movement of the long-term government securities market.

LONG MARKET VALUE. The market value of securities owned by a customer in his or her account.

LONG-TERM DEBT. Debt due in a year or more. Also, a bond with a maturity of ten years or more.

LOWER FLOATER. A variable-rate bond with a put option enabling the holder to put the security back to the issuer.

M. Abbreviation for 1,000, usually used to denote the face value of a bond, e.g., $25M for $25,000.

M-1. Symbol for the most basic measure of the nation's money supply, reported weekly by the Federal Reserve. M-1 consists of currency in circulation plus demand deposits at commercial banks.

M-2. A broader measure of the money supply consisting of money in circulation, demand deposits at commercial banks, and time deposits of less than $100,000 at commercial banks.

M-3. A still broader measure consisting of M-2 plus time deposits of $100,000 and term repurchase agreements.

MAJOR BRACKET PARTICIPANT. A member of an underwriting syndicate who takes down and reoffers to investors a relatively large number of bonds from the issue.

MANAGERS. The chief members of an underwriting syndicate. The lead, senior, or book-running manager runs the syndicate, making allotments of bonds. The joint or co-managers are the other top members of the group.

MANDATORY REDEMPTION ACCOUNT. An account in a sinking fund in which an issuer makes deposits to be used to retire bonds as they are called.

MANIPULATION. Making securities prices rise or fall artificially through aggressive buying or selling, often by several persons acting in concert. This practice is a violation of federal securities laws.

MARKDOWN. The amount subtracted from the dealer's selling price to another dealer when a customer sells securities to the first dealer in the over-the-counter market. See As Principal. Also, the difference between the cost of securities and their current price, when prices have fallen.

MARK-TO-MARKET. Recording actual market values of an inventory of securities.

MARKET MAKER. A person or firm actively making bids and offers in the over-the-counter market.

MARKET ORDER. An order to be executed immediately at the best available price.

MARKET TONE. The dominant feeling or atmosphere in a market at a particular time. The tone is good when dealers and market makers are actively trading on narrow spreads, and it is poor when trading drops off and spreads widen.

MARKET VALUE. The price at which buyers and sellers trade similar securities in an open market.

MARKETABILITY. A measure of the ease with which a security can be sold without causing its price to drop sharply.

MARKETABLE SECURITIES. Securities that can be traded.

MARKUP. The fee charged by a dealer acting as principal who buys a security from a market maker and sells it to a customer at a higher price. The fee, or markup, is included in the sale price and is not itemized separately in the confirmation.

MASTER RESOLUTION. A document stating the general terms under which an issuer may sell more than one issue of bonds.

MATCHED SALE/PURCHASE TRANSACTION. A Federal Open Market Committee sale of Treasury bills or other government securities for cash settlement with a provision that the securities be repurchased at the same price plus interest on a specific date in the future.

MATURITY. The date on which principal is due.

MATURITY SCHEDULE. A listing, with dates and amounts, of when principal becomes due.

MATURITY VALUE. The amount an investor receives when a security is repaid at maturity, not including any periodic interest payment. This amount usually equals par value, although on zero coupon bonds, compound interest bonds, and multiplier bonds, the principal amount of the bonds at issuance and accumulated investment return may both be included.

MEMBER BANK. A commercial bank that belongs to the Federal Reserve System.

MEMBER ORDER. An order for a new bond issue from a firm in an underwriting syndicate.

MEMBER TAKEDOWN. A purchase of bonds by a firm belonging to an underwriting syndicate, at the member's discount, which the firm then sells to a customer at the public offering price.

MISSING THE MARKET. A failure (sometimes due to negligence) of a securities dealer to execute an order.

MONETARY DEFAULT. Failure to pay principal or interest when due.

MONETARY POLICY. Management of money and credit to achieve economic growth and stable prices or other government objectives.

MONEY MARKET. The market for such short-term securities as Treasury bills, certificates of deposit, bankers acceptances, and commercial paper.

MONEY MARKET FUND. An open-end investment company whose portfolio consists of very safe, highly liquid short-term securities such as Treasury bills and commercial paper. Interest rates change daily, but the net asset value for one share generally stays at $1.

MONEY MARKET INSTRUMENTS. Relatively safe short-term debt of less than one year to maturity, usually issued at a discount.

MOODY'S INVESTORS SERVICE. A well-known bond rating agency. Moody's also rates commercial paper, short-term municipal notes and corporate stocks, and publishes reports on companies, issuers, industries, and security markets.

MORAL OBLIGATION BOND. A bond, issued by a state agency, that is not backed by the full faith and credit of the state. If necessary, the agency may request the state legislature to appropriate money to service its debt, but the legislature is not required to make the appropriation.

MORAL SUASION. The Federal Reserve's use of argument to influence member bank lending policies rather than taking such direct action as changing interest rates or reserve requirements.

MORNINGSTAR. A research company that rates the performance of mutual funds.

MORTGAGE. A loan secured by real property, usually with established repayment periods and interest rates.

MORTGAGE-BACKED SECURITY. A bond backed by mortgages on property, frequently issued by the Federal Home Loan Mortgage Corporation, the Federal National Mortgage Association, and the Government National Mortgage Association. Payments to investors are made from interest and principal payments from the underlying mortgages.

MORTGAGE BOND. A long-term debt secured by a lien on property.

MORTGAGE POOL. A bundle of mortgages with similar characteristics of class of property, interest rate, maturity date, and other features.

MORTGAGE REIT. A real estate investment trust that provides capital to real estate builders and buyers.

MORTGAGE REVENUE BOND. A security issued by agencies or authorities of state or local governments to make or purchase loans to finance single-family or multifamily housing.

MUNICIPAL BOND INSURANCE. Policies underwritten by private insurance companies guaranteeing payment on the insured bonds if the issuer fails to pay.

MUNICIPAL BONDS. Long-term debt securities issued by cities, states, and local governments, and their agencies and authorities. Interest on the bonds is generally exempt from federal income taxes.

MUNICIPAL SECURITIES PRINCIPAL. An employee of a municipal bond firm who has a supervisory responsibility for municipal securities activities of the firm.

MUNICIPAL SECURITIES REPRESENTATIVE. The broadest class of municipal securities professionals who are required to pass a qualifications examination under the rules of the MSRB. This group includes individuals who underwrite, trade, or sell municipal securities, conduct municipal research, offer municipal securities investment advice, or provide municipal financial advisory services.

MUNICIPAL SECURITIES RULEMAKING BOARD (MSRB). An independent self-regulatory body established by the Securities Acts Amendments of 1975 as part of the process of regulating municipal dealers, dealer banks, and brokers in municipal securities. The Board consists of fifteen members, five representing securities firms, five from banks, and five from the general public.

MUNIFACTS. An electronic news wire service associated with *The Bond Buyer* that transmits information on new municipal bond offerings, proposed issues, unsold balances of recently offered issues, market reports, and news for the municipal bond community.

MUTILATED. A term used to describe the physical condition of a security certificate when it is no longer considered negotiable.

NARROWING THE SPREAD. Action taken by a dealer to reduce the difference between bids and offers. Also called "closing the market."

NASD. *See* National Association of Securities Dealers.

NASD CODE OF ARBITRATION. A set of rules governing settling of controversies arising from over-the-counter securities transactions.

NASDAQ. *See* National Association of Securities Dealers Automated Quotation.

NATIONAL ASSOCIATION OF SECURITIES DEALERS (NASD). A nonprofit, self-regulatory organization of over-the-counter brokers and dealers. It enforces professional and ethical standards, and licenses securities professionals.

NATIONAL ASSOCIATION OF SECURITIES DEALERS AUTOMATED QUO-TATIONS (NASDAQ). A computerized quotations network by which NASD firms can communicate bids and offers for stocks and bonds traded over-the-counter, i.e., securities not listed on an exchange.

NATIONAL CLEARING CORPORATION (NCC). An NASD affiliate responsible for daily clearance of securities transactions of members.

NATIONAL INSTITUTIONAL DELIVERY SYSTEM (NIDS). Automated transmissions of confirmed orders from dealers to banks, mutual funds, trust funds, and other institutional investors, and the affirmation and book-entry settlement of such transactions. Also known as "institutional delivery," or ID.

NATIONAL QUOTATION BUREAU. A subsidiary of Commerce Clearing House, Inc. that collects bid and offer quotes for stocks and bonds traded over-the-counter. Stock quotes are distributed on pink paper called pink sheets and bond quotes are published on yellow sheets.

NATIONAL QUOTATIONS COMMITTEE. An NASD committee that sets minimum standards for the publication of quotations furnished to newspapers, radio, and television.

NEAR MONEY. A bond close to its redemption date.

NEGATIVE COVENANTS. A promise in a bond indenture not to do something.

NEGOTIABLE. Something that can be sold or transferred to another party in exchange for money.

NEGOTIATED MARKET. The over-the-counter market, in which transactions are arranged between two parties. *See* Auction Marketplace.

NEGOTIATED UNDERWRITING. A sale of new securities through bargaining with an investment banking syndicate rather than through competitive bidding.

NET INTEREST COST (NIC). The expense of a new bond issue, expressed in percent, computed by taking into account total coupon interest adjusted for any premium or discount and divided by total accumulated bond years of the issue. NIC does not consider time value of money.

NET PRICE. The amount paid for a bond by an investor.

NEW HOUSING AUTHORITY BONDS. *See* Public Housing Authority Bonds.

NEW ISSUE. Securities offered to the public for the first time.

NEW MONEY. Proceeds of a bond issue for capital, maintenance, or repair purposes, or the part of a refunding bond issue that exceeds the amount of outstanding bonds being refunded.

NOMINAL QUOTATION. An approximate price that could be expected on a purchase or sale and that is not considered firm in the event that a purchase or sale is effected.

NOMINAL YIELD. The annual interest rate payable on a bond, specified in the indenture and printed on the face of the certificate itself. Also called *coupon yield*.

NONCALLABLE BOND. A bond that cannot be redeemed at the option of the issuer before its specified maturity date.

NONLITIGATION CERTIFICATE. A written document stating that bonds, upon delivery, are free of legal questions.

NORMAL TRADING UNIT. The accepted minimum unit of trading in a given market. For NASDAQ-traded bonds, it is $10,000.

NORMAL YIELD CURVE. A graph that plots the yields of equivalent securities with different maturities at a given point in time. A *normal yield curve* shows short-term interest rates lower than long-term interest rates.

NOT RATED (NR). Indication used by Moody's, Standard & Poor's, Fitch, and other rating agencies to show that a security or company has not been rated. Lack of rating has neither negative nor positive implications; it means only that the security has not been rated by that agency.

NOTES.   Interest-bearing certificates of governments or corporations with shorter maturities than bonds. Treasury notes mature in ten years or less, while municipal notes generally mature in less than one year.

NOTICE OF REDEMPTION.   Announcement of a bond issuer that it will redeem outstanding bonds prior to their maturity.

NOTICE OF SALE.   Announcement of plans to sell municipal bonds at competitive bidding. It includes place, date and time of sale, principal amount, and other details of the issue.

ODD COUPON.   An interest payment period that is longer or shorter than the normal six months. It generally refers to the first payment of some new bond issues.

ODD LOT.   A securities trade made for less than the normal trading unit. *See* Round Lot.

OFF-BOARD.   A reference to transactions made over the counter in unlisted securities or to transactions involving listed securities away from a national securities exchange.

OFFER.   Notice of willingness to sell securities at a stated price or yield.

OFFERING CIRCULAR.   A publication prepared by underwriters to disclose basic information about an issue of securities to be offered in the primary market.

OFFERING DATE.   The day a security is first offered for public sale.

OFFERING PRICE.   The lowest price available for a round lot of securities; also the price at which members of an underwriting syndicate for a new issue will sell securities to investors.

OFFERING SCALE.   The price, expressed in eighths of a point, or yield, expressed in decimals, for each maturity of serial bonds. Most often used with municipal bonds.

OFFICIAL NOTICE OF SALE.   A municipality's paid announcement of an upcoming competitive bond sale.

OFFICIAL STATEMENT (OS).   A document prepared by an issuer that gives detailed financial and other information about the issuer and the securities. Usually applies to municipal securities.

OPEN-END FUND. An investment company or mutual fund that continually sells or redeems its own shares to meet investor orders to buy or sell. Many open-end funds invest in money market instruments or bonds.

OPEN-END LIEN. A security provision in a revenue bond indenture that permits an issuer to sell additional securities that have an equal claim on pledged revenues, if the issuer meets an additional-bonds test.

OPEN MARKET OPERATIONS. Purchases and sales of government securities by the Federal Open Market Committee of the Federal Reserve System to carry out monetary policy. These operations include outright purchase or sales of Treasury bills and other securities, matched sale/purchase agreements, and repurchase agreements.

OPERATIONS AND MAINTENANCE FUND. A fund set up in a municipal revenue bond indenture for money to be used to meet the cost of running the project financed with the bonds.

OPTIONAL REDEMPTION. The right to retire a bond issue or a portion of an issue prior to its stated maturity during a specified period of years. The right can be exercised at the option of the issuer, or, in pass-through securities, of the primary obligor. Optional redemption frequently requires the payment of a premium, called a *call premium*.

ORDER. A commitment made by a purchaser to buy a stated number of bonds at the offered price.

ORDER PERIOD. The period after a competitive municipal bond sale during which orders from account members are allocated without consideration of the time they are submitted.

ORIGINAL ISSUE DISCOUNT (OID). The amount below par at which new securities are priced when they are first offered for sale, provided the discount is large enough to qualify as OID. The most extreme version of an original issue discount is a zero coupon bond, which is originally sold at a price far below par. Tax treatment of the interest income and capital gain at sale or maturity of the bond is complex.

ORIGINAL PROCEEDS. The net amount received by a bond issuer after payment of all issuance expenses.

OVER-THE-COUNTER MARKET (OTC). A securities market conducted through negotiation over the telephone and not through the use of an auction system on any securities exchange. Most bond trading is done in the over-the-counter market.

OVERLAPPING DEBT. For a municipal bond issuer, the debt of other issuers payable in whole or in part by taxpayers of the subject issuer.

OVERNIGHT POSITION. The inventory of securities a firm or trader holds at the end of the trading day.

OVERTRADING. A practice in violation of NASD rules in which a broker/dealer overpays a customer for a security to enable the customer to subscribe to another security offered at a higher markup than the loss to be sustained when the buying firm sells the customer's first security at prevailing market prices.

OVERVALUED. A security whose market price is higher than it should be, in the opinion of security analysts studying such fundamental factors as revenue strength and yields on similar securities.

PAPER. Relatively short-term debt securities.

PAR VALUE. The principal amount of a bond that must be paid at maturity.

PARITY BONDS. Two or more issues having the same priority of claim or lien against pledged revenues.

PARKING. (1) Placing assets in a safe investment temporarily. (2) Selling inventory to a customer with an informal understanding that the customer will resell back to the firm later at a previously agreed-upon price.

PARTIAL DELIVERY. A delivery of fewer securities than the amount contracted for in the sales transaction.

PASS-THROUGH SECURITY. A debt security representing an interest in a pool of mortgages that require monthly payments consisting of partial payments of principal and interest on unpaid principal. These payments are passed through from debtor to investor.

PAYING AGENT. Representative designated to pay principal and interest for the issuer.

PAY-AS-YOU-GO-BASIS. A policy of a municipality to pay for capital expenditures from current revenues instead of borrowing.

PAY-AS-YOU-USE-BASIS. A policy of a municipality to borrow to finance capital outlays, a practice that allocates cost over time.

PAYMENT DATE. The day on which interest or principal is due.

PEGGING.　Keeping the offered price of a security at a certain level by means of a bid at or slightly below the price. Pegging is legal only during an underwriting.

PENALTY SYNDICATE BID.　Restrictive financial measures written into agreements among underwriters to discourage resale of securities requiring stabilization.

PER CAPITA DEBT.　A municipality's outstanding debt divided by its population.

PERPETUAL BOND.　A bond with no maturity date. Very rare in the U.S. The British Consols have no final maturity date.

PHILADELPHIA PLAN.　The issuance of equipment trust certificates to finance transportation equipment such as airplanes or railroad cars. Title to the leased equipment remains with a trustee until all outstanding serial maturities of the issue are retired, and it then passes to the issuer.

PLACEMENT RATIO.　The percentage of bonds from new issues sold to investors during the week the securities came to market.

PLEDGED REVENUES.　Money promised to be put aside for the payment of debt service and other deposits required by a bond indenture.

POINT.　A shorthand reference for 1 percentage point. In the bond market, a point equals $10 per $1,000 bond. Prices are expressed as a percent of par.

POLLING THE ACCOUNT.　Canvassing the syndicate members of an underwriting syndicate to determine what to do with unsold bonds.

POLLUTION-CONTROL BONDS.　Debt securities issued by states or authorities to finance construction of air or water pollution-control facilities. The bonds are backed by the credit of the beneficiary of the financing rather than by the credit of the issuer. New issues of such bonds are prohibited under the 1986 Tax Reform Act.

POOL.　A package of mortgages combined into a single security.

POOL INSURANCE.　Guarantees that payments of interest and principal of mortgages contained in a mortgage pool will be paid.

PORTFOLIO.　The set of bonds, stocks, and other securities held by an investor or mutual fund.

POSITION. (1) The status of securities in an investment account—long or short. (2) To buy a block of securities.

POT. The portion of securities in a new offering that is set aside for discretionary sale to institutional investors by the managers of the group. When "the pot is clean," this portion of the issue has been completely sold.

PRELIMINARY OFFICIAL STATEMENT (POS). For corporates, known as the preliminary prospectus or "red herring." An early version of an offering statement, it contains information about the issuer, but it does not contain final pricing, yield, or maturity information. Orders for securities may not be accepted on the basis of this document, and a statement to that effect is printed vertically in red on the front page of preliminary prospectuses. Hence their nickname, "red herring."

PREMIUM. The amount by which the price of, or offering for, a security exceeds its par value.

PREMIUM BOND. A bond whose price is above par.

PREMIUM CALL. A provision in a bond indenture that permits an issuer to call securities at a price above par.

PREPAYMENT PROVISION. A specification stating that repayment of principal may be made by an issuer prior to maturity and on what terms.

PRESALE ORDER. An order to purchase bonds, given to a manager of a syndicate preparing to bid on municipal bonds to be sold competitively.

PRESENT VALUE. The value today of a future payment, or stream of payments, at an assumed interest rate. A method used to calculate how much money should be invested now to produce a certain sum in the future, and to compute bond prices from a yield.

PRESOLD ISSUE. An issue of securities sold out prior to the announcement of price and interest rate. The practice is illegal with registered corporate securities but not with municipal or U.S. Treasury issues.

PRICE. Value or cost of a bond, generally stated as a percent of par value or in terms of annual yield.

PRIMARY MARKET. The market for new issues of securities. Once outstanding, these securities trade in the *secondary market*.

PRIME RATE. The interest rate that commercial banks charge on corporate loans to their most creditworthy customers; the lowest rate banks charge on such loans.

PRINCIPAL. The par value or face value of a bond that the issuer promised to repay at maturity.

PRINCIPAL TRADE. A transaction in which a dealer purchases and owns a security or sells from his or her own security inventory.

PRIOR ISSUE. (1) Term applied to an outstanding bond issue when it is to be refinanced with a refunding. (2) Bond issues that possess a first, or senior, lien on pledged revenues.

PRIOR LIEN BOND. A bond that takes precedence over all other bonds of an issuer because it holds a higher-priority claim. Such bonds are usually issued as a result of reorganizations arising from bankruptcy proceedings.

PRIVATE PLACEMENT. The sale of a new issue of securities directly to an investor or small group of investors without any public offering.

PROCEEDS. The money received by a bond issuer upon the delivery of bonds at a closing.

PROSPECTUS. A document containing most of the information included in the registration statement used by underwriters to solicit orders to buy.

PROTECTIVE COVENANTS. Bond agreements that impose obligations on the issuer, guarding bondholders by requiring segregation of funds, adequate debt service coverage, etc.

PROVISIONAL RATING. An estimate of credit quality of an issuer by a rating agency. Provisional upon receipt by the agency of additional information.

PRUDENT-MAN RULE. A standard of conduct to guide fiduciaries responsible for investing money for others. The rule holds that a fiduciary should invest as a prudent man or woman would, with care and intelligence, seeking to preserve capital and avoid speculation.

PUBLIC HOUSING AUTHORITY BONDS. Tax-exempt bonds, guaranteed by the federal government, issued by local housing authorities to finance public housing. There have been no new issues of these bonds since 1974. Sometimes called *New Housing Authority (NHA) bonds.*

PUBLIC OFFERING. Sale of securities to a large number of investors. Corporate securities are registered with the Securities and Exchange Commission, and municipal securities almost always file official statements with the Municipal Securities Rulemaking Board.

PUT BOND. A bond that a holder may redeem at his option or upon the occurrence of certain circumstances. U.S. Savings Bonds have a put feature.

QUALIFIED LEGAL OPINION. Conditional affirmation of the legality of an issue of securities.

RANGE. A set of prices consisting of the opening sale, high sale, low sale, and latest sale of the day for a given security.

RATE COVENANT. A pledge in financing proceedings requiring the charging of rates or fees for the user of specified facilities at least sufficient to attain a stated minimum coverage.

RATE OF RETURN. Current yield, or yield to maturity.

RATING. A credit-quality evaluation made by independent agencies.

RATING AGENCIES. Corporations that issue credit evaluations. The leading agencies are Moody's Investors Service, Standard & Poor's Corporation, and Fitch.

REALIZED YIELD. Return on bonds based on purchase price and reinvestment of coupon payments at a stated reinvestment rate.

RECEIVER'S CERTIFICATES. Short-term debt issued by a receiver for a bankrupt corporation to supply working capital during the receiver's inquiry. These obligations take precedence over the claims of all other creditors.

RECIPROCAL IMMUNITY DOCTRINE. The theory that neither the federal government nor the states can tax income received from securities issued by the other. The theory, long used to defend tax exemption for municipal bonds, was specifically rejected by the Supreme Court in the 1987 case *South Carolina* v. *U.S.* Since then, tax exemption for municipal bonds is based on federal law and can be withdrawn by Congress.

RED HERRING. A preliminary official statement or preliminary prospectus.

REDEMPTION. Retirement of securities by repayment of their face value or call price to their holders.

REDISCOUNT. Borrowing by a commercial bank from a Federal Reserve Bank using eligible collateral that came, in turn, from the bank's borrowers.

REFUNDING. Issuance of new debt to raise money to redeem either older bonds at maturity or outstanding bonds issued with less favorable terms. The purpose of refunding may be to reduce interest cost, extend the maturity of debt, eliminate existing restrictive covenants, or other contractual changes.

REGISTERED BOND. A bond whose owner's name is printed on the certificate and recorded on the books of the issuer. Legal title may be transferred only when the bond is endorsed by the registered owner.

REGISTRAR. The party responsible for maintaining records on behalf of a bond issuer.

REGISTRATION STATEMENT. A document required by the Securities and Exchange Commission by an issuer of securities before a public offering may be made. The Securities Act of 1933 requires that the document contain all material facts and accurate information. The SEC examines the statement for a twenty-day period, seeking omissions or misrepresentations. If none is found, the statement becomes effective, and the securities may be offered for sale.

REGULAR-WAY TRADE. A bond transaction where delivery and payment are made on the third business day after the trade date, except U.S. Treasury securities, which settle on the next business day.

REGULATION G. A Federal Reserve rule requiring any person, other than a bank or broker/dealer, who extends credit secured by securities to register and be subject to Federal Reserve jurisdiction.

REGULATION T. Federal Reserve guidelines covering use and supervision of credit at broker/dealer firms. The regulation sets margin requirements.

REGULATION U. Federal Reserve rules governing the extension of credit by banks when securities are used as collateral.

REGULATION W. Federal Reserve rules governing installment loans.

REGULATION X. Federal Reserve rules that place equal burdens of responsibility for compliance with Regulations G, T, and U on the borrower and on the lender.

REINVESTMENT RISK. The exposure of a bondholder when investing coupon payments.

REMARKETING. A formal reunderwriting of a bond for which the form or structure is being changed. Most commonly used in connection with changing variable-rate to fixed-rate financings, typically because the construction phase of a project has been completed, because rates are at a level the issuer feels comfortable with, or because of indenture requirements.

REOFFERING. The yield or price scale at which a new issue of bonds is offered for sale.

REOPENING. The offering by the Treasury of additional securities in an issue that has already been offered and sold. The new securities carry the same terms as the outstanding ones, but they are offered for sale at yields prevailing in the Treasury market.

REPURCHASE AGREEMENT (REPO). (1) A Federal Open Market Committee arrangement with a dealer in which it contracts to sell a Treasury or federal agency security at a fixed price, with provision for its repurchase at the same price at a rate of interest determined competitively. These arrangements are used by Treasury and municipal securities dealers to reduce the cost of carrying inventories of securities. (2) A method of financing inventories of securities through sale to a nonbank institution with an agreement to buy back the position. (3) The sale of a security (usually a bond) combined with an agreement to buy it back again on a certain date at a certain price.

RESERVE. An account, described in a bond indenture, restricted for a specific purpose and not available for general appropriation and spending.

RESERVE CITY BANK. A commercial bank with demand deposits over $400 million and its main office in a city where a Federal Reserve Bank or Federal Reserve Bank branch is located.

RESERVE REQUIREMENT. Federal Reserve stipulation that commercial banks set aside a percentage of their deposits in the form of cash and other liquid assets in reserves at the Fed.

RETAIL. Individual investors, as opposed to institutional investors.

RETENTION. The portion of an underwriting firm's allocation of securities from a new issue that it may sell to its customers. The remainder of its allocation is held for group sales to institutional investors and for sale to underwriting firms, not members of the offering group.

RETIREMENT OF DEBT SECURITIES. Repayment of principal and accrue interest due bondholders.

REVENUE ANTICIPATION NOTES (RANS). Short-term municipal debt instruments usually offered on a discount basis, with future nontax revenues pledged to repay the securities at maturity.

REVENUE BONDS. Municipal bonds whose principal and interest are payable from income generated by publicly owned enterprises such as toll roads or airports.

REVERSE REPURCHASE AGREEMENT (REVERSE REPO). (1) A repurchase agreement from the point of view of the buyer of the security. (2) A transaction in which a broker/dealer provides funds to customers by purchasing securities from them with a contract to sell them back at the same price plus interest.

RISK ARBITRAGE. A purchase and short sale of potentially equal securities at prices that may yield a profit. *See* Bona Fide Arbitrage.

ROUND LOT. A unit of trading or a multiple thereof. Increasingly, $100,000 is considered the measure of round lots of bonds.

RULES OF FAIR PRACTICE. A set of regulations of the National Association of Securities Dealers governing the conduct of members.

RUN. (1) In a new-issue sale of serial bonds, the amount of bonds remaining unsold in each maturity. (2) A market maker's list of bond offerings with par values and prices.

RUNNING THROUGH THE POT. In a new-issue offering of bonds, a syndicate manager may take back securities from syndicate members and put them in the "pot" for sale to institutions. This is done if sales to institutional investors are going better than sales to individual investors.

SAVINGS BOND. A bond especially designed for individual investors and issued by the U.S. Government in face values ranging from $50 to $10,000. Interest is exempt from state and local income taxes. See Series EE Bonds and Series HH Bonds.

SCALE. The coupon rates, offering prices, and yields for each maturity of a serial bond issue.

SEASONED ISSUE. An issue of securities that, once distributed, trades actively and has great liquidity.

SECONDARY MARKET. The market for trading securities other than new issues.

SECURED OBLIGATION. Debt whose repayment of principal and interest is backed by a pledge of assets.

SECURITIES ACT OF 1933. Federal legislation designed to protect the public in the issuance and distribution of securities by requiring full disclosure of accurate information about an issue.

SECURITIES AND EXCHANGE COMMISSION (SEC). A federal agency created by the Securities Exchange Act of 1934 to administer the Securities Act of 1933, consisting of five commissioners appointed by the President on a rotating basis for five-year terms. The chairperson is designated by the President and no more than three commissioners may be of the same political party.

SECURITIES INDUSTRY ASSOCIATION (SIA). A national trade group of corporate securities dealers and traders.

SECURITIES INDUSTRY AUTOMATION CORPORATION (SIAC). A company owned two-thirds by the New York Stock Exchange and one-third by the American Stock Exchange to assist in the settlement of securities trades done on the exchanges.

SECURITIES INVESTOR PROTECTION CORPORATION (SIPC). A government-sponsored, private, nonprofit corporation formed under the Securities Investors Protection Act of 1970 to guarantee repayment of money and securities up to $500,000 per customer in the event of a broker/dealer bankruptcy.

SECURITY. An instrument that signifies ownership (stock), rights to ownership (options), or evidence of debt (notes or bonds).

SECURITY DISTRICTS. Thirteen administrative districts of the National Association of Securities Dealers.

SELLING GROUP. Dealers who have been asked to join a syndicate offering new issues of securities but who are not liable for any unsold syndicate balance. Selling group firms do not share in the profits of the overall syndicate.

SENIOR LIEN BONDS. Bonds having a prior claim or a first claim on pledged revenues.

SERIAL BONDS. A bond issue with stated maturities spread over consecutive years.

SERIES EE BONDS. Nontransferable U.S. Government savings bonds issued at discounts with face amounts ranging from $50 to $10,000.

SERIES HH BONDS. Nontransferable U.S. Government savings bonds that pay interest semiannually. Since 1982, Series HH bonds have been available only in exchange for Series EE bonds.

SETTLEMENT DATE. The date, usually three business days after the trade date, on which payment is made and bonds are delivered.

SHORT POSITION. An inventory position that reflects the sale of bonds not owned at the time of the sale.

SHORT SALE. The sale of securities not owned by the seller at the time of the transaction, a maneuver necessitating the purchase of the securities some time in the future to "cover" the trade. A short sale is usually made with the expectation that securities prices will decline.

SHORT-TERM DEBT. Debt with a maturity under one year.

SIMPLE INTEREST. Interest calculated only on the original principal.

SIMULTANEOUS (RISKLESS) TRANSACTION. An exchange in which a dealer takes a position in a security only after receipt of an order from a customer and only for the purpose of acting as principal in order to disguise any remuneration from the sale.

SINKING FUND. (1) An annual reserve required to be set aside from current revenues to provide for the retirement of an outstanding bond issue. (2) A separate account used to redeem securities by open-market purchase, by request for tenders, or by calling, in accordance with the redemption schedule in the bond indenture. The term derives from the concept of "floating" a bond issue; accumulated funds "sink" bonds after they are outstanding.

SLGS. State and Local Government Series of U.S. Government securities sold by the Treasury to municipalities that use them to comply with arbitrage restrictions. Referred to as slugs.

SOFT MARKET. A market for securities with low demand.

SPECIAL ASSESSMENT BOND. A municipal bond payable from special taxes or charges imposed on properties that have benefited from public improvements.

SPECIAL BOND ACCOUNT. An account in which a customer may favorably finance the purchase of exempted securities or nonconvertible bonds traded on stock exchanges.

SPECIAL DISTRICTS. A single purpose or local taxing district organized for a special purpose such as a road, sewer, irrigation, or fire district.

SPECIAL LIEN BONDS. Bonds that carry liens against particular property.

SPECIAL OBLIGATION BONDS. Bonds secured by a specific source of revenues.

SPECIAL TAX BOND. A municipal bond whose payment of interest and/or principal is contingent upon collection of a distinct levy, such as a liquor tax.

SPLIT OFFERING. (1) A sale of securities consisting partly of new securities and partly of already outstanding securities. (2) A municipal bond offering partly of serial bonds and partly of term bonds.

SPLIT RATING. A case where an issuer has been given different ratings by different rating agencies.

SPREAD. (1) The difference between bid and asked prices. (2) Gross profit in an underwriting.

STAGFLATION. A combination of sluggish economic growth, high unemployment, and high inflation. The term was widely used in the late 1970s.

STANDARD & POOR'S CORP. (S&P). A well-known rating agency, which also publishes widely used indexes of price moves of common stocks, including the S&P 500-stock index, and a variety of other financial information. Part of McGraw-Hill.

STICKERING. Changing an official statement of a new issue of securities. A seal, or "sticker," is placed on the document to change it and to draw attention to the changes.

STOP-OUT PRICE. The lowest dollar price at which Treasury bills are sold in an auction.

STRAIGHT SERIAL BONDS. Bonds maturing in installments, with each annual repayment of principal about equal.

"STREET" NAME. Registration of securities in the name of a dealer or other nominee, usually for custodial purposes.

STRIP CALL. Redemption of serial bonds by calling a portion of each maturity.

SUBORDINATED DEBT. Debt junior in claim on assets to other debt.

SUITABILITY. Appropriateness of a security or investment strategy for an investor, taking into account the investor's means, objectives, and knowledge.

SUPER SINKER. A maturity of term bonds, usually in single-family mortgage bond issues, that will be called before any other term maturity. Funds to pay off the called bonds come from prepayments on the underlying mortgages.

SWAP. Exchange of one security for another, usually to carry out some change in investment objective. Swaps are often, but not always, done for tax purposes.

SYNDICATE. A short-term partnership of investment banking firms formed to underwrite an offering of securities.

TAKE DELIVERY. Accepting receipt of securities certificates after they have been purchased and transferred between accounts.

TAKE-OR-PAY CONTRACTS. Agreements that guarantee payments backing new project financing, used most notably by the Washington Public Power Supply System. The covenants obligate power distributors to pay power producers regardless of whether or not the latter actually generate electricity.

TAKE A POSITION. To hold bonds.

TAKEDOWN. (1) In a municipal bond underwriting, the reduction in price that syndicate members pay when they buy bonds from the group for sale to investors. The discount from list price for an account member. (2) In other bond underwriting, the face value of securities that a syndicate member agrees to sell.

TAX ANTICIPATION NOTES (TANS). Short-term state or municipal debt sold on a discount basis and repaid from forthcoming tax receipts.

TAX AND REVENUE ANTICIPATION NOTES (TRANS). Short-term state or municipal debt, usually sold on a discount basis and repaid from taxes or other government receipts collected at a later date.

TAX-EXEMPT BONDS. Obligations issued by states, cities, counties, and local governments and their authorities and agencies that pay interest free from federal income taxes and usually state and local income taxes in the state of issue.

TAX-EXEMPT COMMERCIAL PAPER. Short-term promissory notes issued by states or local governments or their agencies for periods up to 270 days instead of bond anticipation notes, revenue anticipation notes, or tax anticipation notes. Issuers sell paper instead of BANs, RANs, or TANs because maturity dates are more flexible. Now mostly replaced by a variable rate demand obligation (VRDO) or a VRDO/commercial paper hybrid.

TECHNICAL DEFAULT. A failure to meet bond indenture terms, other than payment of principal and interest. An example of technical default is failure to maintain required reserves.

TEN-PERCENT GUIDELINE. A formula used in municipal bond analysis comparing total bonded debt to real estate market value. Debt in excess of 10% of real estate market value is considered excessive.

TERM BOND. A large municipal bond issue with all the bonds maturing on the same date, usually with a mandatory sinking fund.

TERM REPURCHASE AGREEMENT. A repurchase agreement or "repo" with a life extending beyond the normal overnight arrangement.

THIN MARKET. A condition in the secondary market with inactive trading and wide spreads between bid and asked prices.

THIRTY-DAY VISIBLE SUPPLY. The volume of municipal bonds scheduled for sale over the next thirty days as calculated daily by *The Bond Buyer*, a financial newspaper serving the state and local government securities market.

TIGHT MARKET. A condition in the secondary market with active trading and narrow spreads between bid and asked prices.

TOMBSTONE. A newspaper advertisement displaying the most significant terms of a securities offering and the names of the underwriting firms ranked according to their participation in the deal.

TOTAL BONDED DEBT. Amount of debt outstanding for a state or municipality regardless of purpose.

TOTAL RETURN. The sum of current interest income, capital gains (or minus capital losses), and reinvestment income from coupon reinvestment earned on an investment over a specified period of time. Usually expressed as an annual return, compounded semiannually.

TRADE DATE. The date when a bond transaction is made.

TRADER. A person or firm engaged in the business of buying and selling securities for a profit. Traders usually hold securities only for a short period of time, unlike investors who hold securities for longer periods.

TREASURY BILL. Short-term U.S. Government obligations sold in weekly auctions in book-entry form only and on a discount basis to be paid at face value at maturity. Minimum denomination is $1,000, with multiples of $1,000 over the minimum.

TREASURY BONDS. Long-term U.S. Government debt securities. Since April 1986, new issues of Treasury bonds have been noncallable with a maturity of twenty or thirty years, available in book-entry form only, with a minimum denomination of $1,000.

TREASURY NOTES. Intermediate-maturity U.S. Government debt securities, coming due in not less than two years nor more than ten years at time of issue. They are sold in book-entry form only. Notes are sold in minimum denominations of $1,000 and are available in multiples of $1,000 over the minimum amount.

TRUE INTEREST COST (TIC). A method of computing the borrowing cost of a new issue of municipal bonds that takes into account the time value of money as well as the interest paid and premium or discount paid at issuance. It is the nominal annual rate, compounded semiannually, which discounts the future flow of payments to the price paid for the issue.

TRUST AGREEMENT. Agreement between a bond issuer and a trustee (1) authorizing and securing the bonds; (2) containing the issuer's covenants and obligations with respect to the project and payment of debt service; (3) specifying the events of default; and (4) outlining the trustee's fiduciary responsibilities and bondholders' rights.

TRUSTEE. A firm, usually a bank, designated to act in a fiduciary capacity for the benefit of bondholders in enforcing the terms of the bond contract.

TWENTY-FIVE PERCENT CUSHION RULE. In the analysis of municipal revenue bonds, a rule of thumb that revenue from a facility financed by bonds should exceed cost of operation, maintenance, and debt service by 25%.s

TWENTY-FIVE PERCENT RULE. In municipal bond analysis, a rule of thumb that an issuer's bonded debt should not exceed 25% of its annual budget.

UNDERLYING DEBT. The debt of smaller local government units within a larger jurisdiction.

UNDERWRITER. A middleman between securities issuers and investors.

UNDERWRITING AGREEMENT. A contract between an underwriter or syndicate of underwriters and an issuer of securities. The contract contains final terms and price of the securities, and it is signed shortly before the effective date of the offering.

UNDERWRITING COMPENSATION (SPREAD). The gross profit realized by the underwriters, equal to the difference between the price paid to the issuer and the initial offering price charged investors.

UNDIVIDED ACCOUNT. An arrangement in underwriting agreements for sharing liability. In such a structure, each member of the syndicate is liable for any unsold portion of an issue. The degree of liability is based on each member's percentage of participation.

UNEXPENDED PROCEEDS CALL. An extraordinary redemption of municipal bonds, most frequently used with single-family mortgage bonds. If demand for mortgages is not sufficient to utilize all the proceeds of a housing bond issue within a stated amount of time, bonds are called with the unused funds. In other cases, funds not expended on the project financed by the bonds may be used to redeem bonds, at par.

UNIT INVESTMENT TRUST. A fixed portfolio of bonds, sold in fractional, undivided interest, usually $1,000.

UNLIMITED TAX BOND. A bond secured by the pledge of taxes not limited by rate or amount.

UNQUALIFIED LEGAL OPINION.   An unconditional affirmation of a security's legality.

UPGRADE.   An improved credit evaluation by a rating agency.

VARIABLE-RATE DEMAND OBLIGATION (VRDO).   A bond that bears interest at a changeable or floating rate established at specified intervals, e.g., daily, weekly, or monthly, and that contains a put option enabling the holder to tender the bond for purchase on the date a new interest rate is set. Usually a VRDO also has a credit backup, such as a letter of credit, to guarantee the put feature.

VISIBLE SUPPLY.   *See* Thirty-Day Visible Supply.

WARRANT.   A certificate giving its holder the right to purchase a bond at a specific price for a certain period of time.

WHEN ISSUED (WI).   An offering or trade of bonds when, as, and if issued with date of delivery set some time in the future. If the bonds are not issued, the trade is canceled.

YANKEE BOND.   A dollar-denominated bond issued by a foreign government or corporation and registered for sale in the U.S.

YIELD. Rate of return.   The annual return on an investment expressed as a percentage. In the U.S., this is a nominal annual rate compounded semiannually for bonds.

YIELD TO AVERAGE LIFE.   The rate of return on a bond issue when its average life is substituted for the maturity date of the issue.

YIELD TO CALL.   The rate of return on a bond issue calculated using the call date instead of the maturity date and the call price instead of face value.

YIELD CURVE.   The relationship between time to maturity and yield to maturity. Frequently shown on a graph depicting interest rates on securities of similar credit characteristics plotted by maturity. A positive yield curve shows ascending yields, i.e., yields are higher on longer maturities than they are on shorter maturities. Yield curves normally are positive because investors demand higher rates of return in compensation for giving up use of their money for longer periods of time. A *negative yield curve* shows descending yields, i.e., yields are lower on longer maturities than they are on shorter maturities. A *flat* *yield curve* results when short-term and long-term bonds do not differ greatly. A *hump-backed yield curve* occurs when intermediate maturities yield more than either long- or short-term securities.

YIELD TO MATURITY.   Rate of return on a bond issue, taking into account its coupon, time to maturity, and dollar price. It is based on the assumption that all interest received over the life of the issue is reinvested at the coupon rate of interest.

ZERO COUPON BOND.   A debt security that is issued at a deep discount and that pays no annual interest, only payment of full amount at maturity. U.S. savings bonds are zero coupon bond.

INDEX